M

DATE DUE

APR 0 5 2004	
APR 2 7 2004	
JUN 2 9 2004	
DEC 3 0 2004	
APR 2 3 2005	
AUG 1 5 2006	

D1159969

Kafka and the Yiddish Theater

Evelyn Torton Beck

Kafka and the Yiddish Theater

Its impact on his work

The University of
Wisconsin Press

*Madison,
Milwaukee, and
London*

Published 1971
The University of Wisconsin Press
Box 1379, Madison, Wisconsin 53701

The University of Wisconsin Press, Ltd.
27–29 Whitfield Street, London, W. 1

First printing

Printed in the United States of America
George Banta Company, Inc.
Menasha, Wisconsin

ISBN 0–299–05881–6; LC 75–143763

To my husband Anatole
and my children
Nina and Micah

who made this book possible

Contents

Preface   ix

Acknowledgments   xv

Key to Abbreviations   xvii

Note on Texts   xxi

one
Introduction   3

two
Kafka and the Yiddish Theater   12

three
The Change in Kafka's Style: "Wedding
Preparations in the Country" and
"A Commentary" ("Give It Up!")   31

four
Style and Structure in Kafka's Work
Before 1912   49

five
First Impact of the Yiddish Theater:
"The Judgment" (1912)   70

six
The Dramatic in Kafka's Work to 1914   122

seven
The Remaining Work   172

appendix one
Table of Equivalent Spellings   213

appendix two
Plays and Operettas Seen or Read by Kafka   214

appendix three
Djak Levi   218

appendix four
Reviews and Announcements of Yiddish
  Performances in Prague, 1910–1912   224

Bibliography   228

Index   238

Preface

In examining Kafka's life and works, one is struck by the coincidence of two important events. In 1911/12, after years of dormancy, Kafka's interest in Judaism was suddenly reawakened by an encounter with a visiting troupe of Eastern European actors who performed Yiddish plays in Prague. In September 1912, directly following this theater experience, he wrote "The Judgment," the first story to show his characteristic "dramatic style."

From the first, Kafka was deeply impressed by the Yiddish theater and strongly attracted to its players. For months he regularly attended the performances of Yiddish plays and wrote enthusiastically about them in his letters and diaries. In the light of his previously cool attitude toward all forms of Judaism, religious as well as nationalistic, this sudden, intense interest in a form of Jewish culture totally alien to the Westernized Jews of Prague (and regarded by most with hostility) represents a radical shift in feeling and is particularly striking.[1]

1. In the "Letter to His Father" Kafka describes the evolution of his attitude toward Judaism (*Dearest Father: Stories and Other Writings*, trans. Ernst Kaiser and Eithne Wilkins [New York, 1954], pp. 171–76; *Hochzeitsvorbereitungen auf dem Lande und andere Prosa aus dem Nachlass*, ed. Max Brod [New York, 1953], pp. 197–202). Kafka's Jewishness is also discussed in some detail by Max Brod, *Franz Kafka: A Biography*, trans. G. Humphreys Roberts and Richard Winston (New York, 1963); Klaus Wagenbach, *Franz Kafka: Eine Biographie seiner Jugend, 1883–1912* (Bern, 1948) (hereafter cited as *Biographie*); Harry Zohn, "The Jewishness of Franz Kafka," *Jewish Heritage* (Summer 1964), 44–50; Felix Weltsch, "The Rise and Fall of the Jewish-German Symbiosis: The Case of Franz Kafka," *Publications of the Leo Baeck Institute: Yearbook* (hereafter cited as *Leo Baeck Yearbook*) 1 (1956): 255–76; Michel Carrouges, *Kafka versus Kafka*, trans. Emmett Parker (University, Ala., 1968), pp. 77–87; and Gustav Janouch, *Conversations with Kafka: Notes and Reminiscences*, trans. Goronwy Rees (London, 1953).

Although Kafka also frequented both German and Czech theater with some regularity—references to such visits are scattered throughout the diaries[2]—at no other time in his life was
he so deeply involved in a single repertoire, in so concentrated
a period, as with the Polish-Yiddish theater troupe in 1911/12.
Had the involvement been less intense, had it not been followed by his sudden literary breakthrough in 1912 (which
came only after years of artistic failure),[3] one would place less
emphasis on the encounter with the Yiddish theater. But given
the sequence of events, one might well conjecture that the Yiddish plays represented an important factor in Kafka's literary
development and merit close attention by Kafka scholars.

In this study I examine twelve of the fourteen Yiddish plays
Kafka lists by name in the diaries.[4] I also document and analyze the extent of his involvement with the Yiddish theater,
and explore the connections between this theater and his fiction. Not surprisingly, I find that in matters of style, theme,
structure, and characterization, Kafka's imaginative prose was
substantially influenced by the Yiddish plays brought to
Prague by the wandering Jewish actors.

In Kafka's letters and diaries one finds not only the record of
his interest in the Yiddish theater, but also a reflection of the
peculiar sense of isolation experienced by the German-speaking Jews of Czechoslovakia, a group which included Kafka as
well as all the Jewish intellectuals in Prague. Alienated from
the local Czech population by virtue of their ties to German
culture, separated by religion from the other German-speaking
Czechs, these Jews represented a minority within a minority
and felt themselves to be neither Czech nor German.[5] None-

2. A list of all plays mentioned by Kafka can be found in Appendix 2.

3. Kafka's earliest effort in our possession ("Description of a Struggle")
dates from 1904/5.

4. These plays are fully described in Chapter 2, "Kafka and the Yiddish
Theater." The twelve are held by the library of the YIVO Institute for
Jewish Research in New York City; the remaining two could not be found
in any of the Jewish archives in New York City, London, or Jerusalem.

5. They even spoke their own peculiarly "antiseptic" form of German;
see Harry Zohn, "Participation in German Literature," in *The Jews of
Czechoslovakia* (Philadelphia, 1968), pp. 469–70. The position of these

theless, from the turn of the century until 1939, disproportion-
ately many of these German-speaking Jews were active in the
cultural life of Prague, particularly in the field of letters. Thus,
Kafka must be seen as part of a large circle of Jewish writers,
many of whom had known each other since childhood.[6] The
group included prominent dramatists, novelists, poets, essay-
ists, journalists, and scholars—among them, Max Brod (Kafka's
closest friend and literary executor), Oskar Baum, Felix
Weltsch,[7] Franz Werfel, Willy Haas, Hugo Bergmann, Ernst
Weiss, Oskar Pollak, Egon Erwin Kisch, Paul Kisch, Otto Pick,
Emil Utitz, and Johannes Urzidil.[8] In spite of their common
Jewish background, these writers represented no single view of
Judaism: only a few were observant, some substituted Zionism
for religion, but most were "emancipated" Jews who showed
little or no interest in anything Jewish.

Until 1911 Kafka reckoned himself among the latter. Although his forebears had been Orthodox (on his mother's
side he stemmed from learned rabbis), his parents were assimilated, and like most German-speaking Jews in Prague, adhered
only to the superficial forms of the religion. In the "Letter to

Jews is described more fully by Pavel Eisner, *Franz Kafka and Prague*,
trans. Lowry Nelson and René Wellek (New York, 1950); Heinz Politzer,
"Prague and the Origins of Rainer Maria Rilke, Franz Kafka, and Franz
Werfel," *Modern Language Quarterly* 16 (March 1955): 49–62; Hans
Tramer, "Prague: City of Three Peoples," *Leo Baeck Yearbook* 9 (1964):
305–39; and Ruth Kestenberg-Gladstein, "The Jews between Czechs and
Germans in the Historic Lands," in *The Jews of Czechoslovakia*, 1: 21–71.
Zohn, in "Participation in German Literature," p. 469, distinguishes the
"*Bildungsdeutsche* (Germans by education)" from the "*Volksdeutsche*
(ethnic Germans), later known as Sudeten Germans."

6. See Max Brod, *Der Prager Kreis* (Stuttgart, 1966).

7. Kafka, Brod, Baum, and Weltsch were particularly close and constituted a narrower circle within the larger group. After Kafka's death,
the writer Ludwig Winder took Kafka's place, so to speak (Brod, *Der
Prager Kreis*, p. 35).

8. Though born to a Jewish mother, Johannes Urzidil is of the Christian
faith (Zohn, "Participation in German Literature," p. 490). A full study
of the contributions made by the German-speaking Jewish writers of
Czechoslovakia may be found in this article by Zohn, and in Tramer,
"Prague."

His Father," Kafka berates his parent for the "few flimsy gestures you performed in the name of Judaism" (*Dearest Father,* p. 174).[9] As a child Kafka had often accompanied his father to the synagogue and at thirteen had been *Bar Mitsvah,*[10] but in the last years of gymnasium he became an atheist and severed all ties with Judaism. Only years later, after his encounter with the Yiddish theater, did he voice a profound and lasting interest in his Jewishness. While no explicit reference to Jews or Judaism occurs anywhere in his fiction,[11] the letters and diaries contain the record of Kafka's continuing interest in such diverse aspects of Judaism as Jewish ritual, education, and history, anti-Semitism, Zionism, Hasidism, Hebrew studies,[12] Yiddish theater and literature, the Jewish colonies in Palestine, and the conflict between Eastern European and Western Jewry.[13]

9. "Die paar Nichtigkeiten, die Du im Namen des Judentums . . . ausführtest" (*Hochzeitsvorbereitungen,* p. 200).

10. In keeping with the practice of assimilated Jews, Kafka's father referred to the Bar Mitsvah as a "confirmation." See Wagenbach, *Biographie,* p. 59.

11. The one exception is the fragment beginning "In our synagogue there lives an animal about the size of a marten" ("In unserer Synagoge lebt ein Tier in der Grösse etwa eines Marders" [*Dearest Father,* p. 358; *Hochzeitsvorbereitungen,* p. 398]). (Kafka also recorded several alternate openings for the story.) Even here, however, "synagogue" is the only explicitly Jewish reference; the word "Jew" does not appear anywhere in the story.

12. Although Yiddish and Hebrew use the same alphabet and are both written from right to left, the two languages should not be confused. Hebrew is an ancient Semitic tongue (now the official language of the state of Israel), while Yiddish is an Indo-European language which developed from medieval German. In the ghettos of Eastern Europe, Yiddish was the vernacular; Hebrew, "the holy tongue," was reserved for prayer and study. Yiddish, however, contains many Hebrew words (about 10 percent). Kafka clearly understood Yiddish though it was not spoken in his home. See Chapter 2, pp. 28–29, and Chapter 3, p. 43, especially n. 21.

13. Hartmut Binder documents and analyzes Kafka's attitude toward Jewish affairs on the evidence of Kafka's increasing interest in the German-Jewish Prague weekly, *Selbstwehr* ("the name means self-defence, as of Jews, in times of persecution"). See Hartmut Binder, "Franz Kafka

In spite of his genuine concern with Judaism, Kafka never became either a practicing Jew or a political Zionist, though some of his contemporaries (most notably Max Brod) insist that in his last years he contemplated emigration to Palestine. It is impossible to tell whether Kafka was serious in this plan, for by 1924 he was far too ill to travel in Europe, let alone make the arduous trip to Palestine. It seems clear, however, that for some years Kafka hoped to find in Judaism the peace of mind he sought in vain. His personal documents show that he regarded his Jewishness seriously, as a vital part of his being, once it came to his consciousness that he *was* a Jew. And while one would never limit the interpretation of Kafka's work to a single approach, one can say with some assurance that, at least on one level, Kafka abstracts the specific concerns of Judaism (which first came to his attention through the Yiddish plays) and translates them into universal themes which describe the condition of Man, as well as Jew.

and the Weekly Paper *Selbstwehr*," *Leo Baeck Yearbook* 12 (1967): 134–48; and idem, "Franz Kafka und die Wochenschrift *Selbstwehr*," *Deutsche Vierteljahrsschrift für Literaturwissenschaft und Geistesgeschichte* 41 (1967): 283–304. The German is an expanded version of the English.

Acknowledgments

A book is the work of many hands. Although as author, it is I who will receive the credit for this work, there are many others who helped to make it possible. First and foremost, I wish to thank Professor Cyrena Norman Pondrom of the University of Wisconsin (Madison), who first suggested this area of investigation to me and thereafter gave generously of her time. Her help and encouragement were truly indispensable; her imaginative and careful scholarship served as my inspiration and model.

For reading the manuscript with great care and for helpful suggestions and references I wish to thank Professor Jost Hermand (University of Wisconsin, Madison). Professor Jürgen Born of the University of Massachusetts (Amherst), Professor Peter Boerner of the University of Wisconsin (Madison), Dr. Hartmut Binder (Stuttgart), and Professor Harry Zohn of Brandeis University directed me to texts which proved useful. Special thanks go to Zalmen Zylbercweig, Max Brod, Hugo Bergmann, and Isaac Bashevis Singer for information based on personal recollection that was not available elsewhere.

For making available to me fragile and irreplaceable texts I thank Miss Dina Abramowicz, Librarian of the YIVO Institute for Jewish Research in New York City. The librarians at the University of Wisconsin helped me obtain these and other volumes. I am also indebted to the Hebrew University, which granted me access to Kafka's unpublished letters held by the Martin Buber Archive of the Jewish National and University Library in Jerusalem.

I wish to thank those responsible for creating and funding the E. B. Fred Fellowship at the University of Wisconsin and those who administered it, especially Dr. Kathryn Clarenbach.

xv

But for the generous financial support of this fellowship, this book might have been delayed for many years.

For the many hours they spent in the libraries of New York City tracking down bibliographical references when I was unable to do so for myself, and for providing an additional well of information on Yiddish usage and Jewish customs, I thank my parents, Max and Irma Torton. My appreciation also goes to Rabbi and Mrs. Richard Winograd for information concerning Jewish religious thought and practice. I am especially indebted to that patient, kind teacher, Khaverte Novick, who first taught me Yiddish many years ago and whose love and respect for the language have remained with me.

For his generous and valuable help in clearing up the fine points in my translations from the German, I thank my friend Wolfgang Wasow. My gratitude to my typist, Rosemary Bohannan, not only for her excellent typing, but also for the patience, care, and good humor with which she waded through the complexities of this manuscript. Heidi Haeberli provided valuable assistance in proofreading.

For their love and understanding, I thank my children, Nina and Micah. Last, but certainly not least, I thank my husband, Anatole. This book could not have been written without his continued patience, encouragement, and support during these difficult years, or without his unfailingly intelligent advice.

E. T. B.

Madison, Wisconsin
October 1970

Key to abbreviations

Kafka

The following abbreviations have been used for books by or about Kafka.

ENGLISH TRANSLATIONS

Am	Amerika
C	The Castle
CwK	Gustav Janouch, Conversations with Kafka
DI,	
DII	The Diaries of Franz Kafka (in two volumes)
DF	Dearest Father
DS	Description of a Struggle
FK	Max Brod, Franz Kafka: A Biography
GWC	The Great Wall of China
LM	Letters to Milena
PC	The Penal Colony
Tr	The Trial

GERMAN TEXTS

A	Amerika
B	Beschreibung eines Kampfes
Bg	Max Brod, Franz Kafka: Eine Biographie
Br	Briefe
E	Erzählungen
Fe	Briefe an Felice
H	Hochzeitsvorbereitungen auf dem Lande
J	Gustav Janouch, Gespräche mit Kafka
Mi	Briefe an Milena
P	Der Prozess

xvii

S   *Das Schloss*
T   *Tagebücher*

Details of publication for all volumes can be found in the bibliography. Page citations to English editions are included in the text, following the quotations to which they refer; those to the German editions follow the original of the quoted passage in the footnotes. In the case of Brod and Janouch, I quote only from the English editions but provide page references to both the English and German texts.

Whenever possible, I have used existing translations, but in some instances I judged it necessary to substitute my own; where no English translation was available, I have also supplied my own. Therefore, if no English edition is cited, the translation is mine.

The Yiddish theater

All quotations from the Yiddish plays appear in the text in my own translation; page citations occur in the footnotes, following the original of the quoted passage. The following abbreviations, grouped below by author, identify the Yiddish plays discussed in this study.

Zigmund Faynman
   VK   *Der Vitse-Kenig* (The Vice-King)
Avraham Goldfaden
   BK   *Bar Kokhba* (Son of the Star)
   Su   *Shulamit* (a girl's name)
Yakov Gordin
   DSh   *Di Shekhite* (The Slaughtering)
   DVM   *Der Vilder Mentsh* (The Savage One)
   EbA   *Elishe ben Avuya* (Elishe, son of Avuya)
   GMT   *Got, Mentsh, un Tayvel* (God, Man, and Devil)
Yosef Latayner
   Bl   *Blimele* (Little Flower)
   DF   *Davids Fidele* (David's Violin)

Moyshe Rikhter
>   *HM*   *Reb Hertsele Miyukhes* (Mr. Harry the Aristocrat)
>   *MK*   *Moyshe Khayit als Gemaynderat* (Moyshe the
>   Tailor as Councillor)

Avraham Sharkanski
>   *KN*   *Kol Nidre* (the opening prayer of the Yom Kippur
>   service)

Secondary works

To designate titles of journals I have used the abbreviations
set up by *PMLA*.

AUMLA *Journal of the Australasian Universities Language
          and Literature Association*
> *BB* *Bulletin of Bibliography*
> *DVLG* *Deutsche Vierteljahrsschrift für Literaturwissen-
          schaft und Geistesgeschichte*
> *FAZ* *Frankfurter Allgemeine Zeitung*
> *FMLS* *Forum for Modern Language Studies* (University
          of St. Andrews, Scotland)
> *GQ* *German Quarterly*
> *GR* *Germanic Review*
> *GRM* *Germanisch-romanische Monatsschrift*
> *JDSG* *Jahrbuch der Deutschen Schiller-gesellschaft*
> *MFS* *Modern Fiction Studies*
> *MLQ* *Modern Language Quarterly*
> *MLR* *Modern Language Review*
> *NRs* *Neue Rundschau*
> *SGG* *Studia Germanica Gandensia*
> *SSF* *Studies in Short Fiction*
> *WW* *Wirkendes Wort*
> *YFS* *Yale French Studies*
> *ZDP* *Zeitschrift für Deutsche Philologie*

Note on texts

Working with the texts of the early Yiddish theater
(1880–1910) presents special problems. First editions have generally been lost, and one must make use of whatever copies have been preserved. Until the era of Gordin the
Yiddish actors were rather free with dialogue, and it is no
longer possible to determine to what degree the existing texts
are corrupt.

Transliteration from the Yiddish has only recently been stan-
dardized, and as a result, the names of the Yiddish authors and
actors can be found in a variety of Latin spellings. I have con-
sistently followed the "Transcription Key for Yiddish into
Latin Letters" circulated by YIVO Institute for Jewish Research in New York City. In most cases this means that my
transliteration differs from Kafka's; a table of equivalent spellings is provided in Appendix 1. The most common Latin spellings of the names of Yiddish dramatists and critics are listed in
brackets in the bibliography.

In translating passages from German and Yiddish, I have retained ellipsis points wherever they occur in the original. They
seem to have been used in much the same way as a dash is
used in English, rather than to show omission. These ellipsis
points are indicated by close spacing; my own omissions from
quotations are indicated by spaced ellipsis points.

The translations of Levi's article in Appendix 3 and of the
reviews and announcements in Appendix 4 are mine.

Kafka and
the Yiddish
Theater

chapter one

Introduction

Kafka's most familiar writing is taut, sparse, filled with echoing tableaux and significant gestures. The figure of the writer himself, despite the intense connections between biography and fiction, is pared away; the characters of the narratives and parables act with a life of their own, with their own necessities, unconnected by discursive or interpretive prose to any world more real than their own.

> "But look at me!" cried his father, and Georg, almost distracted, ran towards the bed to take everything in, yet came to a stop halfway.
>
> "Because she lifted up her skirts," his father began to flute, "because she lifted her skirts like this, the nasty creature," and mimicking her he lifted his shirt so high that one could see the scar on his thigh from his war wound, "because she lifted her skirts like this and this. . . ."
>
> And he stood up quite unsupported and kicked his legs out. His insight made him radiant. (PC 59–60)[1]

Here we see, in a passage from so early in the corpus as "The Judgment" (September 1912), the starkness and clarity of visual detail, the intensity of emotion, the building tension, and the degree of immediacy which Kafka creates by focusing

---

1. "'Aber schau mich an!' rief der Vater, und Georg lief, fast zerstreut, zum Bett, um alles zu fassen, stockte aber in der Mitte des Weges. 'Weil sie die Röcke gehoben hat', fing der Vater zu flöten an, 'weil sie die Röcke so gehoben hat, die widerliche Gans', und er hob, um das darzustellen, sein Hemd so hoch, dass man auf seinem Oberschenkel die Narbe aus seinen Kriegsjahren sah, 'weil sie die Röcke so und so und so gehoben hat. . . .' Und er stand vollkommen frei und warf die Beine. Er strahlte vor Einsicht" (E 64).

I have changed Muir's translation "But attend to me" to the more literal "But look at me."

closely on the words and actions of the characters in language
that is deceptively simple. Such diction has been called unpre-
tentious, modest, concise, sober, economical, polished.² Yet
perhaps the best word to describe this prose is "dramatic."³
The term has been applied to Kafka before.
Walter Benjamin was among the first to call attention to the
dramatic aspect of Kafka's writing. In an essay in 1934 he observed that "a good number of Kafka's shorter studies and stories are seen in their full light only when they are, so to speak,
put on as acts in the 'Nature Theater of Oklahoma.' Only then
will one recognize with certainty that Kafka's entire work constitutes a code of gestures.... The theater is the logical
place for such [experimental] groupings." Michel Carrouges
makes a similar point in *Kafka versus Kafka:* "Many of the
scenes in his stories, especially *A Fratricide,* are in fact described as though seen by a spectator in the theater." In a recent study of Kafka, Walter Sokel highlights another element
of the dramatic in Kafka's work when he notes that the most
successful of Kafka's stories "are all constructed with drama
and tension.... [They] have a beginning and end....
[Others] also have a middle and accordingly conform completely to Aristotle's classical definition of dramatic...
plot."⁴
     But it is Heinz Politzer who most consistently brings out the
dramatic quality of Kafka's work. Although he never makes
this point specific, it seems to be one of the underlying assumptions of Politzer's *Parable and Paradox.* He describes the short
piece "Give It Up!" as a "dramatic dialogue which is resolved

2. Norbert Miller, "Erlebte und verschleierte Rede: Der Held des
Romans und die Erzählform," *Akzente* 5 (1958): 226; Hans S. Reiss,
Franz Kafka: Eine Betrachtung seines Werkes (Heidelberg, 1952), p. 130.
     3. Note, for example, the incantatory quality of the father's thrice-
repeated "Because she lifted her skirts" ("Weil sie die Röcke gehoben
hat") in the passage quoted above.
     4. Walter Benjamin, *Illuminations,* trans. Harry Zohn (New York,
1968), p. 120; Michel Carrouges, *Kafka versus Kafka,* trans. Emmett
Parker (University, Ala., 1968), p. 83; Walter Sokel, *Franz Kafka:
Tragik und Ironie—Zur Struktur seiner Kunst* (Munich and Vienna, 1964),
p. 43 (hereafter cited as *Tragik und Ironie*).

at the end into one decisive silent gesture"; he speaks of a "turning point" in the narrative and refers to the characters as "figures acting on a stage." In a chapter on "The Judgment" he views the central conflict as a "highly unrealistic ritual" and describes one character's gestures as a "theatrical trick to produce the illusion of superhuman physical size." In connection with *The Trial* he refers to Josef K.'s execution as "melodramatic" and suggests that Kafka is forced to resort to masks and costumes, to borrow "actors and props from the alien world of the theater."[5] Politzer, like Benjamin, emphasizes Kafka's use of gesture, and he repeatedly refers to Kafka's characters as puppets, marionettes, or dolls. In essence, Politzer suggests that Kafka employs stage techniques in place of the usual methods for creating effects in the novel.

These critics do not go on to develop the full sense of their usages of the term "dramatic," nor do many of them go on to link this quality of the diction to one of the most important experiences of Kafka's life, his encounter with the Yiddish theater during 1910, 1911, and 1912.

Many scholars have pointed out that 1912 was a year of literary breakthrough for Kafka. Brod noted it in his Kafka biography in 1937, in which he wrote: "So the power ... of his production grew, until with the writing of 'The Judgment' in a single stroke during the night of September 22/23, 1912, the final breakthrough ensued."[6] This observation is supported by Klaus Wagenbach's biography of Kafka's youth, which ends with 1912 and thus includes the twenty-ninth year of Kafka's life. Heinz Politzer refers to all of Kafka's work before 1912 as "juvenilia" and entitles a section of *Parable and Paradox* "The Breakthrough: 1912." Speaking of "The Judgment," Politzer writes: "He succeeded in breaking through the disjointed style of his early works and created for the first time a coherent tale distinguished by concentrated imagery."[7] Some scholars have

---

5. Heinz Politzer, *Franz Kafka: Parable and Paradox*, rev. ed. (Ithaca, 1966), pp. 2, 61, 212–13 (hereafter cited as *Parable and Paradox*).

6. In this instance I have substituted my own translation, which is based on a different edition of Brod than that cited in the bibliography.

7. Politzer, *Parable and Paradox*, p. 52.

attributed this literary breakthrough to Kafka's relationship
with Felice Bauer, the woman who later became his fiancée
and to whom "The Judgment," the first piece marking his mature style, was dedicated.[8] Heinz Politzer (in a chapter on
"The Judgment") and Kate Flores go even further and link
both the theme and the writing of "The Judgment" to Kafka's
developing relationship with this woman.[9] While these critics
are undoubtedly correct in pointing to the great significance of
the encounter with Felice Bauer, it is less clear exactly what
effect the experience had on Kafka's technique. What fewer
critics have noticed is that the change in style coincided as
well with Kafka's involvement in the Yiddish theater in 1910,
1911, and 1912.

Max Brod called attention to Kafka's interest in the Yiddish
theater in his Kafka biography in 1937, and he again emphasized its significance in an article in 1964.[10] Following Brod,
who views Kafka's novels chiefly as religious allegories emphasizing the position of the Jew in the Diaspora, many commentators have equated Kafka's interest in the Yiddish theater with
his interest in his Jewish heritage.[11] Others have traced partic-

8. Although Kafka was twice engaged to Felice Bauer (1914 and
1917), he never married her. A third engagement, to Julie Wohryzek in
1919, was also broken off. In 1923 Kafka fell in love with Dora Diamant,
the daughter of an Orthodox Polish Jew. Allegedly because her father
did not approve the match, they never married, although Kafka lived with
her until his death in 1924.

9. Kates Flores, "The Judgment," in Franz Kafka Today, ed. Angel
Flores and Homer Swander (Madison, Wis., 1964), pp. 5–24.

10. Max Brod, "The Jewishness of Franz Kafka," Jewish Frontier 13
(May 1964): 27. See also idem, Franz Kafkas Glauben und Lehre
(Munich, 1948), and Verzweiflung und Erlösung im Werk Franz Kafkas
(Frankfurt am Main, 1959).

11. Among these are Hermann L. Goldschmidt, "The Key to Kafka,"
Commentary (August 1949), pp. 129–38; Wladimir Rabi, "Kafka et la
néo-Kabbale," La Table Ronde (1958), pp. 116–28; E. R. Steinberg,
"Kafka and the God of Israel," Judaism 12 (1963): 142–49; Fritz Strich,
Kunst und Leben (Bern, 1960), pp. 139–51.

In the last few years Yiddish newspapers and journals in several
countries have emphasized Kafka's interest in the Yiddish theater. See,
for example, Zalmen Zilbertsvayg [Zylbercweig], "Frants Kafka un dos
Yidishe Teater," Yidishe Kultur 30 (January 1968): 38–43, 56; Mark

ular elements or symbols in Kafka's work to their origins in the Yiddish theater. Clemens Heselhaus, for example, connects the themes of Kafka's stories to the motifs of the Yiddish theater, specifically citing one of the plays as a possible source, while Heinz Politzer links the symbolism of the short tale "Jackals and Arabs" to another of the Yiddish plays.[12] Max Brod, André Nemeth, and Hildegard Platzer Collins argue that the two assistants in *The Castle* are modelled on the two Jews in caftans who appeared on the Yiddish stage and fascinated Kafka.[13] Similarly, Walter Sokel suggests that Kafka's use of theater as a symbol (as in the novel *Amerika*) grew out of his experience with the Yiddish theater. Recently, Hartmut Binder has interpreted Kafka's late story "Investigations of a Dog" in biographical terms which give prominence to the Yiddish theater.[14]

Turkov, "Frants Kafkas Prag," *Der Veg* (Mexico City), January 24, 1967; S. Dorfson [or Horendorf], "Korrespondents," *Di Yidishe Tsaytung* (Buenos Aires), August 21 and 24, 1966. In "Korrespondents" Dorfson repeats the suggestion made by Czech opera director Ludek Mandaus that a Yiddish play published in Prague in 1966 is the work of Kafka, an assertion that has been completely disproven by Kafka scholars. See Ruediger Engerth et al., *"Ein Flug um die Lampe herum: Ein unbekanntes Werk von Kafka?" Literatur und Kritik* 1, no. 6 (1966): 48–55; Dieter Hasselblatt, "Echtheitsgefechte in der Nachhut Kafkas: Ein 'neues' und umstrittenes Schauspiel von... Kafka?" *FAZ*, September 8, 1966, pp. 20–21; and an unsigned news item, "Kein Kafka-Stück: Goldstücker äussert sich zu *Flug um die Lampe*," *FAZ*, September 23, 1966.

For the sake of completeness, I must mention an unsigned article which bears the suggestive title "Kafka and the Yiddish Theater" (*Drama Critique* 10 [Winter 1967]: 6–12), but consists of nothing more than excerpts from Kafka's diaries, reprinted without comment.

12. Heselhaus mentions Yosef Latayner's *Davids Fidele*, referring to the play by its German title, *Davids Geige*. Politzer connects Kafka's jackals to a "red-eyed desert cat" which is prominent in Avraham Goldfaden's operetta *Shulamit*. See Clemens Heselhaus, "Kafkas Erzählformen," *DVLG* 26 (1952): 353–76; and Politzer, *Parable and Paradox*, p. 90.

13. Kafka describes the "two in caftan" in detail (*D*1 79–80; *T* 79–81). See Max Brod, ed., *D*1 328, n. 18; André Nemeth, *Kafka ou le mystère juif*, trans. Victor Hintz (Paris, 1947), p. 46; and H[ildegard] Platzer Collins, "Kafka's 'Double-Figure' as a Literary Device," *Monatshefte* 55 (1963): 7–12.

14. Sokel, *Tragik und Ironie*, p. 507; Hartmut Binder, *Motiv und Gestaltung bei Franz Kafka* (Bonn, 1966), p. 13.

These critics all show some awareness of the importance of the encounter with the Yiddish theater, and their work strongly suggests a connection between the development of Kafka's mature prose style and his experience of the Yiddish theater. One would never claim, of course, that the theater experience was solely responsible for the change in Kafka's style. What one can assert, however, after a close examination of the Yiddish theater of the visiting Polish troupe and a comparison of Kafka's earlier and later writing style, is this: while Kafka's prose before 1912 is marked by loose structure, rambling sentences, overly-detailed descriptions, diffuse effects, slow pace, and indefinite characterizations closely tied to the author's own psychology, the work after 1912, beginning with "The Judgment," is marked by tight construction, direct, limited focus, well-defined characters who take on a life of their own, sparing use of modifiers, reliance on exaggerated gesture and tableau, heightened suspense, and an intensity which builds up to a climax and falls. This change in style, with its emphasis on the visual and the histrionic, bears the imprint of the techniques of the Yiddish theater and can in large measure be traced to Kafka's experience of this theater.[15]

One scholar has begun the analysis that can help to substantiate such assertions. Though talking primarily about the techniques of the cinema, Wolfgang Jahn leads us to an inquiry about the dramatic elements in Kafka's prose. He emphasizes the visual quality of Kafka's work and stresses Kafka's use of gesture, costume, and comic pantomime. He also notes Kafka's "dramaturgical method of working," and analyzes the structure of Kafka's work near 1912 in terms that suggest a relationship to drama.[16]

15. Kafka, of course, did not write *in vacuo*. Other examples of "dramatic" prose can be found in German literature, both in the work of earlier writers such as Kleist and E. T. A. Hoffmann and in the work of some of Kafka's contemporaries, such as Gustav Meyrink. But it is significant that such general influence did not manifest itself in Kafka's work until after the Yiddish theater experience.

16. Wolfgang Jahn, "Kafka und die Anfänge des Kinos," *JDSG* 6 (1962): 353–68; idem, *Kafkas Roman "Der Verschollene" (Amerika)* (Stuttgart, 1965).

When we apply the word "dramatic" to prose narrative, we are automatically using the word in a rather special sense. Wayne Booth, for example, uses the term to describe novels or prose passages in which the author does not speak in his own voice or from which the narrative voice seems to disappear.[17] The action of such works is thus presented to the reader directly, like action on a stage. Brooks and Warren emphasize this same quality of unmediated representation in their discussion of what constitutes dramatic prose: "Fictional method is said to be dramatic when the author gives a purely objective rendering of his material without indulging either in editorial comment and generalization of his own or in the analysis of the feelings and thoughts of his characters.... Where a dramatic method is used the reader must infer the inner situation from the external action and dialogue."[18]

Long passages of uninterrupted dialogue and interior monologue are also often spoken of as being dramatic elements in a novel, for the drama can most readily be distinguished from narrative prose by its form. Scholes and Kellogg suggest that "'interior monologue' is a literary term, synonymous with unspoken soliloquy.... It is, in narrative literature, a direct, immediate presentation of the unspoken thoughts of a character without any intervening narrator. Like direct discourse or dialogue it is a dramatic element in narrative literature."[19]

These definitions, which represent a fair summary of current critical usage, are based on two basic conditions of drama—its unmediated quality and its form. No doubt these are central to the genre, but they are not its only distinguishing characteristics. Taken by themselves, they are not enough to indicate the full significance of the application of the word "dramatic" to Kafka. A work of narrative prose may be largely without au-

---

17. Wayne Booth, *The Rhetoric of Fiction* (Chicago, 1961), p. 162. While Booth does not advocate using the term, he discusses its application to narrative prose.

18. Cleanth Brooks and Robert Penn Warren, *Understanding Fiction*, 2nd ed. (New York, 1959), p. 683.

19. Robert Scholes and Robert Kellogg, *The Nature of Narrative* (New York, 1966), p. 177.

thorial comment, and may include long sections of dialogue as
well, without bearing any resemblance to drama as *theater,*
as, for example, the novels of Henry James. In order for the
concept of the dramatic to become more than a theoretical abstraction in its application to narrative prose, we must extend
our definition to include the connection with the theater and
with the techniques of the stage that the word implies.

The physical reality of the stage is instrumental in distinguishing the methods of the drama from those of narrative
prose, for the basic elements (character, action, dialogue, and
setting) are the same for the two genres. Drama more explicitly presumes an audience, and to a great degree, relies on ar-
tifice and convention. For each scene (or act) of a play, setting
must be specified and remain fixed; characters placed and
identified; costume, gesture, word, and tone set down; lighting
and sound effects made explicit. Action in drama is limited to
what the characters can actually be made to say and do on the
stage. Dialogue in drama carries greater weight, for it must be
theatrically effective as well as functional. The sense of the
spoken word can be altered by appropriate use of rhythm and
timing. Unspoken thoughts can be presented on the stage only
with difficulty, by means of the conventions of monologue and
aside. Where not verbalized, inner feeling cannot be communi-
cated directly (as in narrative), but must be inferred from external signals, such as gesture and tone of voice. Visual effects
and stage properties can be used to manipulate audience reaction and to reveal by symbol what cannot adequately be expressed in words. Suspense, tension, urgency, surprise, ani-
mated action, sharp conflicts, grand scenes, and electrifying
effects are associated with the stage and are related integrally
to the structure of the drama.[20]

While the events of a novel are generally assumed to have

20. "Dramatic structure" may be defined as "the arrangement of plot
materials in a unified, effective form, including exposition, complication,
climax, denouement" (Walter Parker Bowman and Robert Hamilton Ball,
*Theater Language: A Dictionary of Terms in English of the Drama and
Stage from Medieval to Modern Times* [New York, 1961], p. 112). Some
critics also include Aristotle's concepts of *anagnorisis* and *peripeteia* as
integral elements of the dramatic form.

occurred before the time of narration, in drama the time of telling and time of occurring always seem to coincide. The physical immediacy of the performed play creates the illusion that the drama exists in the perpetual present.[21] The form of the drama demands greater economy than the novel; typically, its parts are more closely related, its focus more limited, its time sequences more compressed, its characters developed in less detail. The major issues of a play must be presented with a clarity, speed, and directness not demanded by the narrative form.[22]

When a writer of narrative prose, like Kafka, creates in the novel the apparent self-sufficiency and immediacy of the performed play, we call his work "dramatic." Our application of the term to Kafka need not be based solely on this narrow usage, however, for Kafka not only adapts some of the basic techniques and conventions of the drama to the form of narrative prose, he accepts its limitations and borrows its structure as well. For example, in the separate sections of *The Trial* (which are as self-enclosed as the scenes and acts of a play), the characters are made to behave as if they were confined to a fixed space for the duration of each scene, the setting is treated as if it literally existed on a stage, and the actions of the characters resemble the motions of actors performing on a stage. As one might expect, these qualities of the dramatic are most clearly evident in the works directly following the theater experience, but they are present to some degree in all of Kafka's mature work.

21. In connection with the immediacy of the drama, especially of the staged play, it is important to consider the psychology of the experience. Whereas the events of a novel are narrated, a play unfolds directly before us. We are told the events of a novel; we seem to witness the action of a play. Throughout history, censorship restrictions have been more severe for drama than for any other form of literature. This attests to the belief that the dramatic experience represents a greater "reality."

22. Some exceptions to these necessarily general observations can be found in plays from every period, but they are especially abundant in the last years of the nineteenth century and throughout the twentieth, when the traditional limitations and conventions of dramatic form have been and continue to be deliberately broken apart. Brecht's epic theater, for example, represents a major attempt to bring narrative elements into the dramatic form.

chapter two

Kafka and the Yiddish theater

It is not difficult to document Kafka's intense interest in the Yiddish theater. The *Diaries* for 1911–12 and the *Letters to Felice* for 1912–13 abound with references to Kafka's experience with this theater during these formative years of his life.[1] The following entry of October 10, 1911, is typical:

> Day before yesterday among the Jews in Café Savoy. *Die Sedernacht* [The First Evening of Passover] by Feimann. At times (at the moment the consciousness of this pierced me) we did not interfere in the plot only because we were too moved, not because we were mere spectators. (*D1* 91)[2]

Thus we see that Kafka reacted to the performances of these Yiddish plays with strong emotion. Kafka's preoccupation is further reflected by the detail in which he discusses the plays. For example, on October 14, 1911, Kafka records the story of Goldfaden's *Shulamit*, notes which actors took various roles, and includes a number of Yiddish quotations from the play (*D1* 95–97; *T* 97–99). On occasion, Kafka even takes the trouble to comment on what is essentially a bad play, as in this entry for December 13, 1911: "*Der Schneider als Gemeinderat* [The Tailor as Councillor] at the Jews. Without the Tschissiks but with two new, terrible people, the Liebgold couple. Bad play

1. More than one hundred pages of the *Diaries* (thirty separate entries) concern the Yiddish theater; thirteen of the *Letters to Felice* contain significant references to the Yiddish theater troupe and to the actor Yitskhok Levi.

2. "Vorgestern bei den Juden im Café Savoy. Die 'Sejdernacht' von Feimann. Zuzeiten griffen wir (im Augenblick durchflog mich das Bewusstsein dessen) nur deshalb in die Handlung nicht ein, weil wir zu erregt, nicht deshalb, weil wir bloss Zuschauer waren" (*T* 93).

by Richter" (*D1* 176).[3] A long passage from January 1912 attests to Kafka's continuing involvement with the Yiddish theater and its actors, and reveals the frequency with which he attended the Yiddish plays:

> January 24. Wednesday. For the following reasons have not written for so long . . . ; finally I spent a lot of time with the Jewish actors, wrote letters for them, prevailed on the Zionist society to inquire . . . whether they would like to have guest appearances of the troupe . . . ; saw *Sulamith* once more and Richter's *Herzele Mejiches* for the first time. (*D1* 223)[4]

Kafka first mentions the Yiddish theater in a diary entry for October 5, 1911: "Last night Café Savoy. Yiddish troupe. Mrs. K. 'male impersonator' " (*D1* 79).[5] Max Brod, however, dates Kafka's experience with the Yiddish theater more than a year earlier, in May of 1910. Drawing on his own notebooks for this period, Brod writes: "For May 1 of this year I find this entry in my diary: 'Café Savoy. Theatrical company from Lemberg. . . .' For May 4: 'Went with Kafka to the Savoy this evening. Marvelous!' " (*FK* 110; *Bg* 135). Although it was Brod who introduced him to the Yiddish theater, it was Kafka who became actively enthusiastic about the performances. According to Brod, "I, for example, was a frequent member of the audience at the performances in the Café Savoy. . . . But Franz, after the first time I took him there, entered into the atmosphere completely" (*FK* 110; *Bg* 135). A postcard Kafka sent to Brod in Prague on December 12, 1911, reflects this enthusiasm:

3. " 'Der Schneider als Gemeinderat' bei den Juden. Ohne die Tschissiks, aber mit zwei neuen, dem Ehepaar Liebgold, fürchterlichen Menschen. Schlechtes Stück von Richter" (*T* 189).
The Tshisiks [Tschissiks] were actors (husband and wife) in the Yiddish theater troupe.
4. "24. Januar. Mittwoch. Aus folgenden Gründen so lange nicht geschrieben: . . . endlich hatte ich mit den jüdischen Schauspielern viel zu tun, schrieb für sie Briefe, habe beim zionistischen Verein durchgesetzt . . . , ob sie Gastspiele der Truppe haben wollen . . . ; habe noch einmal 'Sulamith' gesehn und einmal 'Herzele Mejiches' von Richter" (*T* 242–43).
5. "Gestern abend Café Savoy. Jüdische Gesellschaft.—Frau K. 'Herrenimitatorin' " (*T* 79).

Dear Max

We are in luck! They are doing *Sulamith* by Goldfaden. With pleasure I am wasting a card to write you what you have read already. I only hope you have written it to me too. (*FK* 111–12)[6]

Neither Brod's biography nor Kafka's diaries makes clear whether one or two theater companies were involved. In his biography of Kafka's early years Wagenbach assumes that the troupe of 1910 returned to Prague in 1911,[7] but in the notes to the *Diaries*, Brod speaks of two different troupes.[8] Although Brod seems to change his mind in a recent letter to the author,[9] a careful reading of the Prague German-Jewish weekly, *Selbstwehr*, for 1910–12 proves that Brod's earlier assertion was correct and that two different theater troupes visited Prague in 1910 and 1911.[10]

6. "Lieber Max; das haben wir aber getroffen! Sulamit von Goldfaden wird gespielt! Mit Freude verschwende ich eine Karte, um Dir zu sagen, was Du schon gelesen hast. Ich hoffe nur, dass Du mir auch geschrieben hast. Franz" (*Br* 92).

7. Wagenbach writes: "The guest performances of the Yiddish drama company in the Prague Café Savoy in May 1910 constituted [Kafka's] first meeting with a form of Judaism that was still attached to its traditions. . . . in October 1911 this same group returned to Prague and in the next months Kafka visited these performances regularly" (*Franz Kafka: Eine Biographie seiner Jugend, 1883–1912* [Bern, 1958], pp. 176, 179 [hereafter cited as *Biographie*]). Carrouges makes the same assumption (*Kafka versus Kafka*, p. 83).

8. "We had both seen similar performances by another troupe in the same café as early as 1910 (in May)" (*T* 698).

9. Brod writes: "I can only answer this *one* of your questions. The episode concerns only *one* Yiddish theater troupe which visited Prague. . . . We never got to know another troupe" (May 10, 1967). The discrepancy in Brod's assertions may be explained by the fact that although Kafka and Brod visited the Yiddish theater in 1910, they never became personally acquainted with the actors of the first troupe, which remained in Prague for only twelve days. It is quite possible that by 1967 Brod had forgotten the earlier troupe. Binder also asserts that two troupes were involved ("Franz Kafka and the Weekly Paper *Selbstwehr*," *Publications of the Leo Baeck Institute: Yearbook* [hereafter cited as *Leo Baeck Yearbook*] 12 [1967]: 143).

10. The troupe of 1910 was directed by Fr. Spiewakow and included

In the Kafka notebooks and letters which have been made public thus far, we find only one oblique reference to the theater troupe of 1910, when Kafka compares the performances of two actresses in the role of male impersonator. Continuing the entry of October 5, 1911, Kafka writes on October 6 or 8:[11]

> Resemblance between Mrs. K. and last year's Mrs. W. Mrs. K. has a personality perhaps a trifle weaker and more monotonous, to make up for it she is prettier and more respectable. Mrs. W.'s standing joke was to bump her fellow players with her large behind. Besides, she had a worse singer with her and was quite new to us. (*Di* 86)[12]

Thus, from the evidence of Brod's notebooks and of Kafka's diary, it appears that Kafka visited the Café Savoy with Brod at least once in May of 1910. Whether any other visits occurred in 1910 we do not know; it is possible that this was the only one.

According to the evidence of the *Diaries* Kafka visited the Savoy in 1911 on at least fourteen separate occasions. But there is good reason to believe that he visited the Yiddish theater more often than his diaries indicate. In a letter to Felice Bauer on March 11, 1912, he writes: "The entire Yiddish theater [*Jargontheater*] is beautiful; last year I went to these performances about 20 times and to the German theater perhaps not at all."[13]

S. Podzamcze, Pepi, Moritz, and Salcia Weinberg (see "Eine jüdisch-deutsche Theatergesellschaft in Prag," *Selbstwehr*, May 13, 1910, p. 4). The troupe of 1911 was comprised of Yitskhok Levi, Pipes, Mr. and Mrs. Klug, and the Tshisiks.

11. The date of this entry varies in the English and German editions.

12. "Ähnlichkeit zwischen der Frau K. und der vorjährigen Frau W. Frau K. hat vielleicht ein um eine Kleinigkeit schwächeres und einförmigeres Temperament, dafür ist sie hübscher und anständiger. Die W. hatte den ständigen Witz, ihre Mitspieler mit ihrem grossen Hintern anzustossen. Überdies hatte sie eine schlechtere Sängerin neben sich und war uns ganz neu" (*T* 88).

Kafka is comparing the performances of Mrs. Klug and Mrs. Weinberg.

13. "Das ganze Jargontheater ist schön, ich war voriges Jahr wohl 20 mal bei diesen Vorstellungen und im deutschen Theater vielleicht gar nicht" (*Fe* 73).

According to Kafka's diary, he did attend the German theater a few times in 1911, but this was obviously much less than was usual for him.

In accordance with the custom of his time, Kafka uses the word

Brod's recent assertion that he and Kafka visited the Savoy between twenty and thirty times agrees with Kafka's estimate.[14]
Kafka frequently refers to different performances of the same
play, and there are probably plays he does not mention at all.[15]
Furthermore, there are clear gaps in the diaries, and even when
he wrote daily, he often did not bother to report the events
of the day, but recorded only his thoughts and feelings. For
example, on October 22, 1911, he writes with reference to the
Yiddish theater: "For the first time on this fourth evening
. . ." (*Di* 107).[16] Yet the entry for the previous day (October 21) contains no mention of the Yiddish theater, and for the
two days preceding that (October 19 and 20) there are no entries at all. In a newspaper article on Kafka and Brod written
twenty-three years later, Yitskhok Levi, one of the actors of the
1911 troupe and a close friend of Kafka's, recalls: "Max Brod
did not miss a single one of our theater performances."[17] Even
allowing for a good deal of hyperbole, it seems likely, since
Brod and Kafka were almost inseparable in those years, that if
Brod did not miss a single performance, Kafka missed very
few.

The degree to which Kafka's thoughts and emotions were occupied by the Yiddish theater troupe between 1911 and 1913
becomes clear when we examine the diaries and the letters to
Felice of this period. Kafka's comments on the Yiddish theater
fall into several categories. The greatest number of entries con-

---

Jargon here to designate the Yiddish language. He did not, however,
share the distaste for the language expressed by most assimilated Jews
of Prague. In general, this group looked down on Yiddish as a vulgar
dialect of German and did not consider it a language in its own right.
Kafka's interest in the Yiddish theater and his friendship with the actor
Levi constituted a rejection of the values of "establishment Jews" like
his father.

14. Letter to the author, May 10, 1967.

15. While Wagenbach does not set a specific number, he also suggests
that Kafka frequented the Yiddish theater more often than he wrote
about it (*Biographie*, p. 234, n. 708).

16. "Zum erstenmal an diesem vierten Abend . . ." (*T* 111).

17. "Tsvey Prager Dikhter," *Literarishe Bleter* 34 (1934): 558. My
translation of this article appears in Appendix 3.

cern his personal relationship with the actors, particularly Yitskhok Levi, with whom Kafka corresponded for years after Levi left Prague.[18] Few of their letters survive, but we find scattered references to such letters in the *Diaries, Letters,* and *Letters to Felice.*[19] From its beginning the friendship with Levi was intense: "October 16 [1911].... Afternoon to Radotin.... Miss, as a result, the meeting with Levi, of whom I think incessantly" (*Di* 99).[20] When the actor left Prague, Kafka continued to show interest in and concern for him. Shortly after meeting his future fiancée, Felice Bauer, in only the second month of their

18. An unpublished letter from Kafka to Martin Buber reveals that Kafka saw Levi again in Budapest in 1917. In this letter Kafka asked Buber if he would be interested in publishing an article by Levi concerning the plight of the Yiddish actors. Those who knew Levi in Warsaw, years after Kafka's death, report that Levi was obsessed by Kafka and talked about him at every opportunity. Levi apparently carried Kafka's letters with him and offered to read them to any willing listener. (Zalmen Zilbertsvayg, letters to the author, March 18 and April 24, 1967; Isaac Bashevis Singer, private interview, February 7, 1968, Madison, Wisconsin.)

In Prague Levi was known as Yitskhok [Jizchak] or Isak Löwy, and in the *Diaries* Kafka always refers to him simply as Löwy. Sometime after the actor left Prague, he began to use the name Djak Levi. I am using "Levi," which is the standard YIVO transliteration for the Yiddish spelling of the actor's name. For the sake of clarity I am substituting this spelling in the English translations of the diary entries and letters.

Levi is admirably portrayed (under the name of Jacques Kohn) in Isaac Bashevis Singer's story, "A Friend of Kafka," *The New Yorker,* November 23, 1968, pp. 59–63 (reprinted in Singer's *A Friend of Kafka and Other Stories* [New York, 1970], pp. 3–16). Further information about Levi may be found in Appendix 3.

19. Kafka's letters to Levi must have been destroyed when Levi was arrested by the Gestapo in 1942; he did not survive the war. Brod found a copy of one of Kafka's letters to Levi among Kafka's papers; it is included in the *Briefe* (p. 129). A fragment of a letter to Levi is included in the *Diaries* (*Di* 237; *T* 254). Kafka says he "hoped to do something" with these letters to Levi. Brod quotes from one of Levi's letters to Kafka in *FK* 114; *Bg* 140.

20. "16. Oktober [1911]. . . . Nachmittag nach Radotin. . . . Komme dadurch um das Zusammensein mit Löwy [Levi], an den ich fortwährend denke" (*T* 102).

correspondence, Kafka urged her to visit Levi's theater:

> I believe that just now a similar troupe is playing in Berlin, and
> in it, my good friend, a certain I. Levi.... He actually writes
> to me very often and also sends me pictures, posters, newspaper
> clippings, etc.... And for this reason I wonder ... if, sometime,
> you wouldn't want to see these actors about whom, by the way,
> I could talk to you endlessly. (November 3, 1912)[21]

A month later Kafka asked Felice to locate Levi's address for
him and referred again to Levi's letters ("Once again he wrote
to me full of complaints").[22] Kafka seemed eager to include
Felice in his relationship with Levi, or at least to give her some
understanding of his friend: "Today I received a letter from
Levi, which I include, so you [can] see how he writes. I have
his address ... in the meantime [I] also received several letters from him" (December 28/29, 1912).[23] Kafka kept close
track of Levi and received frequent reports of his activities
from friends in Berlin:

> Were you really able to read Levi's letter which I sent you for
> Sunday? He performed in Berlin on Sunday, at least I thought
> I could infer that from his letter.... According to what Werfel,
> who also met Levi, told me, this troupe appealed so to the Leip-
> zig correspondent of the *Berliner Tageblatt* [a daily newspaper]
> that he plans to write about them in a feuilleton of the B. T.
> Please send it to me, if you find it; I still think about the actors
> with pleasure. (February 1/2, 1913)[24]

21. "Nun spielt, glaube ich, gerade jetzt in Berlin eine solche Truppe
und bei ihr mein guter Freund, ein gewisser I. Löwy. . . . Er schreibt
mir nämlich sehr oft und schickt mir auch sonst Bilder, Plakate, Zeitungs-
ausschnitte und dgl. . . . Und darum denke ich . . . ob Sie nicht einmal
diese Schauspieler, von denen ich Ihnen übrigens endlos erzählen könnte, ansehen wollten" (*Fe* 72).

22. "Er hat mir nun wieder geschrieben voll Klage" (*Fe* 148).

23. "Heute habe ich einen Brief von dem Löwy bekommen, den ich
beilege, damit Du siehst, wie er schreibt. Seine Addresse habe ich . . .
habe auch schon einige Briefe in der Zwischenzeit von ihm bekommen"
(*Fe* 213).

24. "Hast Du eigentlich den Brief des Löwy, den ich Dir für Sonntag
schickte, lesen können? Er spielte Sonntag in Berlin, wenigstens glaubte
ich es aus dem Brief herauslesen zu können. . . . Wie mir Werfel, der

Levi's name haunts the *Letters to Felice*, even showing up in passages concerning Kafka's problematic relationship with her: "What is to become of us, my poor beloved? Do you know, that if Levi were not here, if I did not have to arrange a recital for the poor man ... and if, finally, this unquenchable fire of his did not affect me, ... I don't know how these few days would have passed" (June 1, 1913).[25] Kafka's feelings for the Yiddish actors bring out his doubts about his writing and his tendency toward introspection: "October 23 [1911]. The actors by their presence always convince me to my horror that most of what I've written about them until now is false. It is false because I write about them with steadfast love ... but varying ability" (*Di* 108).[26] Kafka was even willing to risk chiding Felice in an effort to make clear to her the sincerity of his affection for the theater troupe. "I certainly did not speak sarcastically about the Yiddish theater," he says; "perhaps [I] laughed, but that is part of love" (November 6, 1912).[27] His attachment to one of the actresses is appar-

---

auch mit Löwy zusammengekommen ist, erzählte, hat die Truppe dem Leipziger Korrespondenten des Berliner Tageblatt . . . so gefallen, dass er in einem Feuilleton des B. T. über sie schreiben wird. Schicke es mir, bitte, wenn Du es findest, ich denke an die Schauspieler immer noch sehr gern" (*Fe* 281).

25. "Was wird aus uns werden, meine arme Liebste? Weisst Du, wenn nicht der Löwy hier wäre, ich nicht einen Vortrag für den armen Menschen veranstalten müsste . . . und schliesslich dieses nicht nieder-zudrückende Feuer des Löwy auf mich wirkte . . . ich wüsste nicht, wie die paar Tage vorübergegangen wären" (*Fe* 392).

Levi almost certainly served as model for the friend in Russia in "The Judgment"; see Chapter 5, pp. 87–89. The correspondence between biography and fiction is, in this case, extremely close. Kafka wrote "The Judgment" only two days after he sent his first letter to Felice. At this time, he had been close to Levi for almost a year.

26. "23. Oktober [1911]. Die Schauspieler überzeugen mich durch ihre Gegenwart immer wieder zu meinem Schrecken, dass das meiste, was ich bisher über sie aufgeschrieben habe, falsch ist. Es ist falsch, weil ich mit gleichbleibender Liebe . . . aber wechselnder Kraft über sie schreibe" (*T* 113).

27. "Über das Jargontheater habe ich gewiss nicht ironisch gesprochen, vielleicht gelacht, aber das gehört zur Liebe" (*Fe* 77).

ent in this self-conscious description of himself at the Café Savoy:

> November 7 [1911].... But really I could not look at [Mrs. Tshisik] seriously either. For that would have meant that I loved her.... And that would have been really unheard of. A young man whom everyone takes to be eighteen years old declares in the presence of the evening's guests at the Café Savoy, amidst the surrounding waiters, in the presence of the table full of actors ... declares to this woman his love to which he has completely fallen victim. (Di 139)[28]

Such entries give us a clue as to what drew Kafka to the theater beyond the interest of the plays themselves.

Other diary entries reflect Kafka's developing interest in Yiddish literature in general. On January 24, 1912, Kafka wrote that he had "read, and indeed greedily, Pines' L'histoire de la Littérature Judéo-Allemande [History of Yiddish Literature], 500 pages, with such thoroughness, haste and joy as I have never yet shown in the case of similar books" (Di 223).[29] He took copious notes on this reading, as the entry made two days later illustrates:

> January 26 [1912].... Jewish theater. Frankfort Purim play, 1708. Ein schön neu Achashverosh-spiel [A beautiful new Akhashverosh play], Abraham Goldfaden, 1876–7 Russo-Turkish War, ... Goldfaden ... heard the crowds in the stores singing

28. "7. November [1911]. . . . Aber ich konnte [Frau Tshisik] eigentlich auch nicht ernst ansehn. Denn das hätte geheissen, dass ich sie liebe. . . . Und das wäre wirklich unerhört gewesen. Ich, ein junger Mensch, dem man allgemein für achtzehn Jahre alt hält, erklärt vor den Abendgästen des Café Savoy, im Kreis der herumstehenden Kellner, vor der Tischrunde der Schauspieler, . . . erklärt dieser Frau seine Liebe, der er ganz verfallen ist" (T 148).
Although Mrs. Tshisik was married, Kafka fancied himself in love with her and admired her acting greatly. Her name appears frequently in the Diaries. She is also mentioned briefly in Isaac Bashevis Singer's story, "A Friend of Kafka."
29. "Las Pines 'L'histoire de la Littérature Judéo-Allemande' [Paris, 1911], fünfhundert Seiten, und zwar gierig, wie ich es mit solcher Gründlichkeit, Eile und Freude bei ähnlichen Büchern noch niemals getan habe" (T 242).

Yiddish songs and was encouraged to found a theater. He was not yet able to put women on the stage. Yiddish performances were forbidden in Russia 1883. They began in London and New York 1884. (DI 226–27)[30]

A number of entries are purely factual records of performances seen, as, for example, "Yesterday evening at the Savoy. *Sulamith* by A. Goldfaden" (DI 95) and "Yesterday *Davids Geige* by Lateiner" (DI 183).[31] These entries suggest how many different plays Kafka saw and which were performed most frequently. Goldfaden's *Shulamit* and *Bar Kokhba* seem to have been particularly favored by the audience at the Savoy. Often these factual statements are followed by plot synopses, character analyses, descriptions of stage technique or tableau, quotations from the plays, and evaluations of the acting, the play, or the playwright. On October 6 and 8, 1911, Kafka details the plot of Latayner's *The Apostate* (*Der Meshumed*); on October 14, Goldfaden's *Shulamit*; on October 26, *The Savage One* (*Der Vilder Mentsh*) by Gordin. On October 22 he criticizes Sharkanski's *Kol Nidre*; on October 26 he notes that the plays of Gordin are superior to those of the other Yiddish dramatists; and on November 5 of the same year he observes: "Performance of Goldfaden's *Bar Kokhba*. False judgment of the play throughout the hall and on the stage" (DI 134).[32] These passages not only show how carefully Kafka observed the plays, but they also give us a clue as to which elements in the Yiddish theater most strongly impressed him: the intensity of the action and its seeming inevitability, the passion of the actors, and the sense of tradition and community which the plays evoked and upon which they depended.[33]

30. The 1949 German edition of the *Diaries* does not include these entries. The editor, Max Brod, notes but does not explain the omission: "The next seven and a half pages contain notes from Pines' book" (*T* 702).

31. "Gestern abend im Savoy 'Sulamith' von A. Goldfaden" (*T* 97); "Gestern 'Davids Geige' von Lateiner" (*T* 196).

32. "Aufführung von 'Bar Kochba' von Goldfaden. Falsche Beurteilung des Stückes im ganzen Saal und auf der Bühne" (*T* 142).

33. The conviction that Yiddish theater was intimately bound to

Although Kafka's letters and diaries unquestionably reveal the extent and seriousness of Kafka's interest in the Yiddish theater, one cannot rely solely on their evidence to determine questions of literary influence. Such proof can be obtained only from close comparison of the plays with Kafka's work.

The plays performed in Prague by the travelling Yiddish theater group were written in the relatively brief period between 1880 and 1910, at a time when the traditions of European drama were being challenged in Sweden, Germany, and France. Nevertheless, the plays performed by the Yiddish actors at the Café Savoy were highly traditional and remained generally untouched by late nineteenth-century "modernism." Because itinerant theater companies kept poor records and most of the few documents that did exist were destroyed during World War II, many facts pertaining to the Yiddish theater in Europe have been lost. Kafka's diaries constitute the only available record of the repertoire of the visiting theater troupe in Prague, and even this listing is probably not complete. The plays are about evenly divided between the classics of the Yiddish theater (by Gordin and Goldfaden) and *shund* —trashy plays with sensational effects and exceedingly complicated plots. Far from representing a single kind of theater, these eclectic and derivative plays reflect the themes, forms, and techniques of several types of drama.

Avraham Goldfaden's *Shulamit* (1880) and *Bar Kokhba* (1882), the earliest plays in the repertoire, are historical verse dramas based on Biblical and Talmudic themes.[34] *Shulamit* is

---

Jewish life, culture, and the Yiddish language was still alive in Kafka ten years later; in discussing Rudolph Schildkraut's performance in a German version of a Yiddish play, Kafka once remarked to Gustav Janouch: "Since [Schildkraut] does not act exclusively in [Yiddish] for Jews, . . . he is not an expressly Jewish actor. He is . . . an intermediary, who gives people an insight into the intimacy of Jewish life. He enlarges the horizons of non-Jews, without illuminating the existence of the Jews themselves. This is only done by the poor Jewish actors who act for Jews in [Yiddish]. By their art they sweep away the deposits of an alien world from the life of the Jews, display in the bright light of day the hidden Jewish face which is sinking into oblivion, and so give them an anchor in the troubles of our time" (*CwK* 42; J 35).

34. In the following listing the year refers to the probable date of

best described as a pageant play designed to prove a point, while *Bar Kokhba* combines the intrigue and revenge motifs of romantic melodrama with a serious moral conflict. Although both plays are deeply religious and didactic in intent, they include elements of operetta: choral odes, pastoral scenes, and interludes of song and dance. Characterization in these early works is broad and generally not based on subtleties of psychology; the characters tend to embody a single trait from which they do not deviate. Although naïve in plot construction and motivation of characters, Goldfaden's plays are more serious and have greater charm than those of his successor, Yosef Latayner.

Latayner learned his craft from Goldfaden, but he vulgarized the themes and borrowed extremely freely from Goldfaden as well as from all of Western drama. Latayner makes liberal use of sensationalism in his domestic comedies *David's Violin* (*Davids Fidele*, 1887) and *The Apostate*[35] and in the romantic melodrama *Blimele* (1894). He is particularly fond of false accusations and of trumped-up witnesses who give themselves away at the crucial moment. Brod and other commentators have already noted the similarity between Latayner's comic figures and the two assistants in *The Castle*.

The plays of Yakov Gordin—*The Slaughtering* (*Di Shekhite*, 1900), *God, Man, and Devil* (*Got, Mentsh, un Tayvel*, 1900), *The Savage One* (1896), and *Elishe ben Avuya* (1906)[36]— show some of the influence of naturalism and realism but are

---

composition; in most cases the actual date is not known, and historians have substituted the year of the first known performance or first published version. Historians offer contradictory dates, and there is no way of establishing complete accuracy. I have followed the dating of Zalmen Zilbertsvayg, *Leksikon fun Yidishn Teater*.

35. Thus far, all efforts to locate this text have failed. Although Kafka describes *The Apostate* in great detail (*D*1 81–86; *T* 80–88), he may have erred in recording either its author or its title. No such play by Latayner is listed in Zilbertsvayg's *Leksikon*, the standard reference work for Yiddish drama.

36. Kafka lists this last play as *Elieser ben Schevia*, but no record of such a play by Gordin exists. Since the details of the play which Kafka describes (and attributes to Gordin) correspond to Gordin's play

mainly domestic dramas dealing with significant moral and social problems.[37] Although not all of his characters are fully developed, Gordin usually shows genuine understanding of the
complexities of human psychology and deals with people in situations that resemble real life.

The plays of the other dramatists included in the repertoire
and mentioned by Kafka—Avraham Sharkanski's *Kol Nidre*
(1896), Zigmund Faynman's *The Vice-King* (*Der Vitse-Kenig*,
1898) and *The First Evening of Passover* (*Di Seydernakht*),
and Moyshe Rikhter's *Mr. Harry the Aristocrat* (*Reb Hertsele Miyukhes*, 1899) and *Moyshe the Tailor as Councillor*
(*Moyshe Khayit als Gemaynderat*, 1903)—are inferior to the
work of the three discussed above, although Latayner's plays
are of greater interest to the historian of the theater than to the
student of literature.[38] Sharkanski and Faynman particularly

---

Elishe ben Avuya, however, it seems reasonable to assume that Kafka
erred in transliterating from the Yiddish.

37. Gordin also borrowed the themes of the classics and translated a
number of classics into Yiddish, but because he infused his work with
a spirit that was essentially Jewish, he created something new out of the
borrowed material. His most successful translation-adaptations are *The
Jewish King Lear* (*Der Yidisher Kenig Lear*) and a similar variation on
the theme (with a feminine heroine), *Mirele Efros*. The Vilna Yiddish-
Polish theater troupe performed *Mirele Efros* in New York in 1968,
with Ida Kaminska in the lead role.

38. Identifying these plays posed some problems. Kafka lists the author
of *The Vice-King* as "Feimann." Since no record of a Feimann exists in
any of the standard encyclopedias or histories of the Yiddish theater, and
since these sources list a Zigmund Faynman as the author of *The Vice-
King*, the problem is no doubt again one of transliteration: Kafka must
have dropped the *n* from Faynman's name. I have been unable to find
the text of Faynman's *First Evening of Passover*.

In addition, the plays were often listed under a variety of titles. The
play Kafka lists as *The Tailor as Councillor* (*Der Schneider als Gemeinderat*) has as its main character Moyshe Khayit, a master tailor who is
alderman of the town. Since the details of Kafka's account of this
play, as well as the author's name, match those of *Moyshe the Tailor as
Councillor*, we may conclude that these plays are identical.

In *The Detroit Yiddish Theater* (Detroit, 1967), pp. 14–15, James
Albert Miller describes the difficulties of locating plays and identifying
playwrights.

favor themes concerning the Spanish Inquisition and the "hidden Jews" who continued to practice their faith despite threats and torture. A favorite figure in these plays is the converted Jew who hates the Jews far more than the Christian does. These plays also often contain comic servants who mimic the actions of hero and heroine.

Although the Yiddish theater in New York was fairly advanced in stagecraft, scenery, and acting by the era of Gordin, the small troupes that wandered through Eastern Europe in the first two decades of the twentieth century were by no means so sophisticated.[39] These actors travelled on minimal budgets and usually did not rent halls or theaters, but played where they could, in small, out-of-the-way cafés. In his study of the Yiddish theater in America, Lifson describes the staging of early Yiddish plays in Europe. He notes that sets were traditional, stage props and furnishings primitive. Lighting was poor, and even where electric lights were available, they were often used without discrimination. Because props were limited, the actors wore extravagant costumes and relied on sensational effects. The dialogue was delivered in heavy accents, at times to outshout the noisy audience. Lifson writes: "Basically [the

39. See the following histories of the Yiddish theater: Samuel S. Citron, "Yiddish and Hebrew Drama," in *A History of Modern Drama*, ed. Barrett H. Clark and George Freedley (New York, 1947), pp. 601–38; Isaak Goido [pseud. Bernard Gorin], *Geshikhte fun Yidishn Teater biz 1920*, 3rd ed., 2 vols. (New York, 1923); E. Harris, "Jewish Drama," in *The Oxford Companion to the Theater*, ed. Phyllis Hartnoll, 3rd ed. (London, 1967), pp. 515–20; David S. Lifson, *The Yiddish Theater in America* (New York, 1965); Solomon Liptzin, *The Flowering of Yiddish Literature* (New York, 1963); Ignats Shiper [Schipper], "Drama-Jiddisches," *Encyclopaedia Judaica*, ed. Jacob Klatzkin et al., 6 (Berlin, 1930): 18–26; Hershel Zohn, "A Survey of the Yiddish Theater" (M.A. thesis, University of Denver, 1949). Additional histories of Yiddish theater are included among the secondary works listed in the bibliography.

Articles concerning individual dramatists can be found in Zalmen Zilbertsvayg, *Leksikon fun Yidishn Teater*, 5 vols. (Warsaw, New York, and Mexico [City], 1931–67); and Shmul Niger [pseud. Samuel Charney] et al., eds., *Leksikon fun der Nayer Yidisher Literatur*, 6 vols. (New York, 1956–).

actor's] gesture was his speech and after that his significant
glaring was his expression."⁴⁰

When we compare Lifson's account of the early Yiddish theater with contemporary descriptions of the Café Savoy, we see
how little the conditions of the Yiddish theater had changed
and how closely the stage of the Savoy resembled the primitive stage of the earlier period. Kafka transmits the smallness
and dinginess of the Savoy; Brod speaks of it as a "small, not
very inviting café" (*FK* 112; *Bg* 138). In a letter to Felice,
Kafka warns of the "probable shabbiness of the...theater
hall" of the Yiddish actors in Berlin (*Fe* 73). Otto Pick refers
to the "primitive stage" of the "Prague Yiddish Theater,"⁴¹ and
Yitskhok Levi describes the circumstances of their performances:

> The "temple of culture" was hidden in a faraway corner of old
> Prague. We performed in a restaurant with set tables. The stage
> was in a corner. We, the actors, had a [place] underground and
> on the right side. And the audience we had on two sides: op-
> posite us and to the left of the stage. The curtain fell in front,
> and at the same time, on the left. . . . We needed no decorations.
> Furniture on the stage: a table, several chairs and that's all. In
> this way we played theater. . . . We also had an orchestra, which
> consisted of... one pianist.⁴²

The tiny stage of the shabby Café Savoy, its simple sets and
extravagant costumes, the exaggerated acting style, the repeated themes of the plays, the "grand scenes" upon which
they depended, their fusion of the comic with the tragic, and
their use of such stage devices as visions and tableaux are

40. Lifson, *Yiddish Theater in America*, p. 138.

41. Otto Pick, "Notiz aus dem *Prager Tagblatt*," June 1, 1913, in
appendix to *Fe* 763.

42. "Tsvey Prager Dikhter," p. 557. Levi's description of the stage
at the Savoy agrees with other contemporary accounts. A review of the
1910 troupe reads in part: "The company had to make do with the
most modest, most circumscribed stage sets: a small podium, behind it,
a green curtain—that was the whole stage. Naturally . . . the actor's freedom of motion . . . became illusory" ("Eine jüdisch–deutsche Theatergesellschaft in Prag," p. 4; this review and others are translated in
Appendix 4).

among the most salient features of the Yiddish theater. It is in
terms of these characteristics that we must see Kafka's theater
experience. The simple settings of many of his narratives, particularly those directly following the theater experience ("The
Judgment" and "The Metamorphosis"), bear a close resemblance to the atmosphere and setting of the Yiddish theater.
Many of the actions described in the narratives give the effect
of being staged. For example, in "The Judgment":

> Georg stood close beside his father, who had let his head . . .
> sink on his chest.
> "Georg," said his father in a low voice, without moving.
> Georg knelt down at once beside his father, in the old man's
> weary face he saw the pupils . . . fixedly looking at him from the
> corners of the eyes. (*PC* 57)[43]

In this sequence the tension between Georg and his father is
created by visual means: the characters are carefully placed
with respect to each other, gesture is given prominence over
word, and the silence is made pregnant. Georg's kneeling in
response to his father's hushed speaking of his name forcefully
reveals Georg's sense of inadequacy and dependence on the
older man.

Kneeling, though not peculiar to the Yiddish theater, occurs
frequently in the Yiddish plays, both for comic effect, as in *Bar
Kokhba* when the emperor is tricked into kneeling while he is
drunk, and for serious purpose, as in *Kol Nidre* when the Span-
iards fall to their knees in fear before the Angel of God. Although the themes of the plays were mostly tragic, the acting
frequently approached melodrama, and tragic effects were often unintentionally undermined and given a comic cast because of clumsy acting, technical difficulties with props, and
awkward texts.[44] Kafka's reliance on gesture, exaggerated ac-

43. "Georg stand knapp neben seinem Vater, der den Kopf . . . auf die
Brust hatte sinken lassen.
" 'Georg', sagte der Vater leise, ohne Bewegung.
"Georg kniete sofort neben dem Vater nieder, er sah die Pupillen in
dem müden Gesicht des Vaters . . . auf sich gerichtet" (*E* 61).
44. Kafka describes such an unintentionally ludicrous scene in *D*1
135–36; *T* 144–45.

tion, and "significant glaring" may well be a reflection of the style of acting at the Savoy. Furthermore, the dark humor of Kafka's narratives brings to mind the tragicomic effects characteristic of the Yiddish theater.

In addition to the standard devices of comedy, there runs through the Yiddish plays a vein of humor more peculiarly Jewish, characterized by paradox. Although heavily ironic, self-mocking, and often tinged with sadness, this humor nonetheless remains basically optimistic.[45] One authority perceives Jewish humor as a "mellowing" agent which takes the bite out of the tragic situation of the Jew in history; another suggests that this humor developed as a main line of defense for the Jew who was powerless economically, politically, and socially.[46] The essential situation of the Jews as "the Chosen People," chosen by God for the grimmest persecution as well as the greatest glory, is related to this humor. (Was it perhaps in this ironic sense that Josef K. was "chosen" for his trial?)

The humor of the Yiddish plays is manifest above all in the very language in which they are written. Especially rich in idiom and nuance, the Yiddish language is characterized by warmth and intimacy, a fact which Kafka himself observed when he wrote that to call the Jewish mother by the German *Mutter* is to create a false image, since the German language is colder and more formal than the Yiddish (*Di* 111; *T* 115–16).[47] Because Yiddish is laced with Hebrew, the "holy" tongue, the language can create layers of meaning and suggest "a world that exists beneath the words."[48] This sort of double ref-

---

45. The frequently repeated Yiddish phrase "It's tough to be a Jew!" ("'S'iz shver tsu zayn a yid!") expresses the pain and bitterness as well as the pride involved in being a Jew: he bemoans his fate while celebrating it.

46. Nathan Ausubel, *A Treasury of Jewish Folklore* (New York, 1948), p. xx; Irving Howe and Eliezer Greenberg, eds., *A Treasury of Yiddish Stories* (New York, 1954), p. 26.

47. See also Kafka's analysis of the Yiddish language in his "An Introductory Talk on the Yiddish Language" (*DF* 381–86; *H* 421–26), delivered as an introduction to one of Levi's recitation evenings. The manuscript for this speech was lost, and this text is based on a copy made by Elsa Brod (see *DF* 408, n. 55; *H* 454, n. to p. 421, l. 26).

48. Howe and Greenberg, *Yiddish Stories*, p. 47.

erence is found not only in individual words and phrases derived from the Hebrew, but also in the casual application of references to ritual and religious matters to everyday secular situations. Kafka recognized the highly connotative nature of Yiddish; and his vocabulary, which often suggests several layers of meaning behind each word, may be a reflection of the "background" the sacred Hebrew element gives to the secular Yiddish. Many of the Yiddish proverbs which critics have applied to Kafka's narratives—for example, "Who has no wife is not a person" (with reference to the Kafka bachelor) and "When a scholar goes to take a wife, he should bring with him a simpleton" (with reference to the parable "Before the Law") —are found in the Yiddish plays as part of their natural expression of Yiddish culture.[49]

Jewish humor is apparent in the attitudes of the characters of the Yiddish plays and determines their reactions. Typically, the Jew sees himself in an ironic light, recognizing the essential absurdity of his situation even in the most dangerous or tragic circumstances. In several plays laughter is provoked at the expense of a character who refuses to see his real situation and is not aware of the foolish figure he cuts. Something of this humor survives in the work of Kafka, whose attitude toward the tragedy of his heroes' situation is heavily ironic.[50] (It is only in this perspective, for example, that Gregor's situation in "The Metamorphosis" can be seen as comic.) By making clear his own awareness of the absurdity of his hero, Kafka forces the reader to view his hero with a sense of irony that the character himself lacks.

49. "Ver es hot kayn vayb nit, der iz kayn mensh nit" (*DSh* 11); "Ven a Talmid khokhom geyt mikadesh zayn a vayb, zol er firen mit zikh am amkhorets [am ha'arets]" (*DSh* 19). Politzer discusses Josef K. as *amkhorets* in *Parable and Paradox*, pp. 173–77.

50. For further discussion of humor in the work of Kafka, see Jean Collignon, "Kafka's Humor," *YFS*, no. 16 (1955/56), pp. 53–62; Michel Dentan, *Humour et création littéraire dans l'oeuvre de Kafka* (Geneva, 1961); Hans S. Reiss, "Franz Kafka's Conception of Humour," *MLR* 44 (1949): 534–42; Marthe Robert, "L'Humor de Franz Kafka," *Revue de la Pensée Juive* 6 (1951): 61–72; Felix Weltsch, "Franz Kafkas Humor," *Der Monat* 6 (1954): 520–26; idem, *Religion und Humor im Leben und Werk Franz Kafkas* (Berlin-Grünewald, 1957).

To what degree Kafka picked up this way of looking at the world from the Yiddish plays and to what degree it was present in his home environment is impossible to determine with certainty. Yet the attitude of comic irony which pervades many of Kafka's narratives ("The Metamorphosis," *The Trial, The Castle*) is related at least in part to his experience of the Yiddish theater and to his friendship with the actor Yitskhok Levi. As an Eastern European Jew, Levi typifies the kind of humor that permeates the plays; this is evident from Kafka's description of him. In a letter to Felice, Kafka tells of Levi's misfortunes, which culminated in a serious illness, and he quotes from Levi's letter, "God is great: when he gives, he gives from all sides."[51]

The Yiddish plays, then, must be seen as an essential expression of Yiddish culture, which is reflected in Kafka's narratives by his use of cultural symbols, his choice of themes and characters, his manipulation of language, and his attitude toward his heroes. Moreover, the staged quality of the described actions and the structure of individual scenes within the larger works mirror the plays themselves. Meno Spann perceptively contrasts Kafka's patience with and interest in the Yiddish plays— which, as we have seen, were very often poorly written, unsophisticated, and melodramatic—with his contemptuous attitude toward Czech drama of similar caliber.[52] Clearly, the Yiddish plays touched some deep emotional response in Kafka that dimmed his critical faculties. It is probably for this reason that the impact of these plays was both immediate and long-lasting and effected a major change in his style.

51. Levi writes in a peculiar combination of German and Yiddish: "Gott ist gross, wenn er gebt [*sic*], so gebt er von allen Seiten" (*Fe* 360).

52. Meno Spann, "The Minor Kafka Problem," *GR* 32 (1957): 176.

chapter three

The change in Kafka's style: "Wedding preparations in the country" and "A commentary" ("Give it up!")

In order to demonstrate the change in style following Kafka's theater experience, it is necessary to compare passages from various stages in his career. Kafka used both his early writings and the experiences of his youth as a quarry for his mature works; and in at least two instances, we find in the Kafka corpus two versions of the same passage, the one written early, the other late in his career. Both Emrich and Politzer call attention to Raban's reverie in the unfinished story "Wedding Preparations in the Country," in which Raban imagines himself taking the shape of a huge bug, tucked safely into bed, while his clothed body goes out into the world to perform the unpleasant tasks which Raban wants to avoid.[1] This fantasy clearly provides the central metaphor of "The Metamorphosis."

This same novel fragment contains another passage which Kafka later reworked into an independent sketch. Nowhere is the change in Kafka's style and method more directly evident than in the two formulations of this passage, whose brevity makes it particularly well-suited for close textual analysis. The later version, written in 1922, was found among Kafka's papers by Brod, who published it in the volume *Description of a Struggle* under the title "Give It Up!" (Kafka had left the page

1. Wilhelm Emrich, *Franz Kafka: A Critical Study of his Writings,* trans. Sheema Zeben Buehne (New York, 1968), p. 27; Politzer, *Parable and Paradox,* p. 27. "Wedding Preparations in the Country" will hereafter be abbreviated as "Wedding Preparations."

labeled simply "A Commentary," and I prefer to use this name
in place of Brod's.)² This short piece of prose has attracted some
lively critical attention in recent years. Politzer uses the anecdote to demonstrate his method of explication, devoting the
opening chapter of *Parable and Paradox* to this end. Eric
Standaert has provided some interesting comments on and cor-
rections to Politzer's analysis in an article entitled "Give It Up:
A Commentary on the Methodological Starting-Point of Heinz
Politzer's Kafka Book."³ In their detailed discussions, neither
Politzer nor Standaert make any reference to the brief episode
in "Wedding Preparations" whose basic elements so strongly
resemble those of the later "A Commentary."

The nature of the changes in Kafka's style and method is
made clear by comparison of the two paragraphs, which follow. The first is from "Wedding Preparations" (1907), the second is "A Commentary" (1922).⁴

> Raban was startled. Was it not late already? Because his over-
> coat and jacket were open, he quickly reached for his watch. It
> had stopped. Annoyed, he asked his neighbor, who was standing

2. This decision was not arbitrary. In changing the title to "Give
It Up!" Brod took an unjustified liberty not only in the title, but in the
punctuation of the title (Kafka does not use the exclamation point).
Brod's title severely diminishes the effectiveness of the twice repeated
phrase "Give it up": it is as if one were to refer to a joke by its punch
line, and then proceed to tell the joke. See Booth, *Rhetoric of Fiction*,
p. 198, n. 25, on the rhetoric of titles.

3. "Gibs Auf: Ein Kommentar zu dem Methodologischen Ausgangspunkt in Heinz Politzers Kafka-Buch,' *SGG* 6 (1964): 249–72 (hereafter cited as "Politzers Kafka-Buch"). Standaert also criticizes Brod's
judgment in not using Kafka's original title, "A Commentary."

4. All dating is based on Malcolm Pasley and Klaus Wagenbach,
"Datierung sämtlicher Texte Franz Kafkas," in *Kafka Symposion*, by
Jürgen Born et al. (Berlin, 1965), pp. 55–83. See also Wagenbach,
Biographie, p. 238.

The text of "A Commentary" included in *Collected Writings* (*DS*
201; *B* 117) deviates from the original manuscript in details of text,
punctuation, and capitalization (see Standaert, "Politzers Kafka-Buch").
All citations in German from "A Commentary," therefore, refer to the
facsimile of Kafka's manuscript which appears on the frontispiece of
the revised edition of Politzer's *Parable and Paradox* (Ithaca, 1966).

somewhat farther back in the entrance, for the time. He [the neighbor] was carrying on a conversation, and still engrossed in the laughter that accompanied it, he said, "Certainly, past four o'clock," and turned away.

It was very early in the morning, the streets clean and empty, I was on my way to the train station. As I compared the tower clock with my watch, I saw that it was much later than I had thought, I had to hurry, my shock at this discovery made me uncertain of the way, I didn't know my way around this city very well yet, fortunately there was a policeman nearby, I ran to him and breathlessly asked him for the way. He smiled and said: "From me you wish to learn the way?" "Yes," I said, "as I cannot find it myself." "Give it up, give it up" he said and turned away with a grand gesture, as people do who want to be alone with their laughter.[5]

There are a few obvious differences and many striking similarities in the two paragraphs. The most obvious difference lies

5. "Raban erschrak da. War es nicht schon spät? Da er Überzieher und Rock offen trug, griff er rasch nach seiner Uhr. Sie ging nicht. Verdriesslich fragte er einen Nachbarn, der ein wenig tiefer im Flur stand, nach der Zeit. Der führte ein Gespräch und noch in dem Gelächter, das dazu gehörte, sagte er: 'Bitte, vier Uhr vorüber' und wandte sich ab" (*H* 10).

"Es war sehr früh am Morgen, die Strassen rein und leer, ich ging zum Bahnhof. Als ich eine Turmuhr mit meiner Uhr verglich, sah ich dass schon viel später war als ich geglaubt hatte, ich musste mich sehr beeilen, der Schrecken über diese Entdeckung liess mich im Weg unsicher werden, ich kannte mich in dieser Stadt noch nicht sehr gut aus, glücklicherweise war ein Schutzmann in der Nähe, ich lief zu ihm und fragte ihn atemlos nach dem Weg. Er lächelte und sagte: 'Von mir willst Du den Weg erfahren?' 'Ja' sagte ich 'da ich ihn selbst nicht finden kann.' 'Gibs auf, gibs auf' sagte er und wandte sich mit einem grossen Schwunge ab, so wie Leute, die mit ihrem Lachen allein sein wollen" (*B* 117, corrected to agree with manuscript facsimile in *Parable and Paradox*).

The translations in the text are my own. It was extremely difficult to translate Kafka's "Raban erschrak da," for the German conveys the idea of both fear and startled reaction. The same problem occurs in the second passage in the rendering of "der Schrecken über diese Entdeckung," which I translated as "my shock at this discovery"; in the German, *Schrecken* connotes both fear and shock.

in the fact that the first is embedded in a larger (albeit unfinished) narrative, while the second is complete in itself. Secondly, "Wedding Preparations" is written in the third person, while "A Commentary" is strictly a first-person narration.[6] In each case a man is moved to look at his watch to check the time. In the first paragraph this person is standing in a crowded doorway which opens onto a busy city street; in the second he is alone on an empty street. In the first the man's watch has stopped, while in the second his watch is merely slower than the public clock to which he compares his own. In both cases there is an attendant sense of anxiety concerning the time, but in "Wedding Preparations" this feeling precedes the actual checking of the time, while in "A Commentary" it follows this act. In both paragraphs the man asks a question. In the first the man, irritated because his watch has stopped, asks the time of someone standing near him. In the second the narrator becomes confused as a result of the discrepancy in time and asks the way of a policeman. In each case this response is accompanied by some form of laughter. In both versions the person who answers finally turns away from the questioner, but in neither case are the further feelings of the questioner indicated.

Hence, these two paragraphs present different formulations of the same basic situation. But since the first paragraph is not, like the second, independent, we may not expect to analyze this passage apart from the work in which it exists. Some resemblances in the circumstances of the characters in the two works simply are not evident if we confine ourselves to a study of the paragraph from "Wedding Preparations" by itself. We could not possibly know from this passage alone that Raban, like the narrator of "A Commentary," is on his way to the train station. We also could not know that while the narrator in "A Commentary" is literally alone (at least at first) and a stranger in the city, these details have their parallel in "Wedding Preparations," for Raban feels himself alone and estranged. At the

---

6. This fact is of particular interest, since it represents the reverse of Kafka's usual procedure. Kafka began *The Castle,* for example, as a first person narration and later changed it to the third person.

crucial point, the narrator in "A Commentary" describes himself as "breathless" (*atemlos*); in "Wedding Preparations" just after this incident we are told, "He [Raban] had to breathe more deeply" (*DF* 5; *H* 11).

A close comparison of these two passages shows that in "A Commentary" Kafka was able to expand the meaning of the brief incident in "Wedding Preparations" so that it could stand as an independent piece. The broader, more universal implications of "A Commentary" are the result of Kafka's skillful compression of detail and ordering of elements.

"Wedding Preparations" is the unfinished story of Eduard Raban, a young man employed in an office (*im Amt*), who, when we meet him, is on his way to the train that will take him to the country to visit his fiancée. From the two chapters that exist, certain things about Raban become clear. We know, for instance, that he does not really want to go to the country, that his feelings about his fiancée are ambivalent, and that, in general, he is uneasy about himself. In the long interior monologue that precedes the paragraph cited from "Wedding Preparations," we learn that "Raban felt tired" (*DF* 3; *H* 8). The extent of his exhaustion may be measured by his own words: he is too tired to enjoy his holiday, he is too tired to understand (*alles einzusehn*), he is even too tired to make the short trip to the train station without exhausting himself. By the repetition of "tired," the author indicates that Raban's is clearly a more than physical exhaustion. He seems tired out from the very effort of living. Raban's fatigue also reflects his spiritual confusion and sense of isolation. He thinks, "But even all that work does not give one a claim to be treated lovingly by everyone; on the contrary, one is alone, a total stranger and only an object of curiosity." Raban can hardly bring himself to think about his situation as pertaining to himself; he continues, "And so long as you say 'one' instead of 'I,' there's nothing in it and one; on the contrary, one is alone, a total stranger and only an self that it is you yourself, you feel as though transfixed and are horrified" (*DF* 3).[7] In spite of the fact that Raban is given a

7. "Aber durch alle Arbeit erlangt man noch keinen Anspruch darauf, von allen mit Liebe behandelt zu werden, vielmehr ist man allein,

personal psychology and described in some detail, he nevertheless remains undefined and colorless as a character. This is in
marked contrast to the narrator in "A Commentary," who is not
at all individualized, but whose acts and words are charged.

The first passage cited, which signals Raban's sudden awareness of the time, occurs near the beginning of the story. It is
preceded only by Raban's introspection (part of which is
quoted in the paragraph above) and by several long descriptions of the passing scene. Despite (or perhaps because of)
Kafka's pedantic attention to scenic detail in this passage and
his frequent use of modifiers, there is a static quality to these
descriptions. In fact, it is almost impossible to visualize the
scene; people are described as if they were objects of a scien-
tific inquiry, not as images in a work of art. The separate details of the objects described do not merge to form a whole.
The following example is typical and could easily be multi-
plied: "Two gentlemen were exchanging information. The one
held his hands palm-upward, raising and lowering them in regular motion, as though he were balancing a load" (*DF* 2).[8]
The preponderance of modifiers in the descriptions is particularly striking: "A little girl was holding a tired puppy in her
outstretched hands" (*DF* 2).[9] Although it is clearly Raban who
is viewing the scene ("On the pavement straight in front of
him...[*DF* 2]),[10] his presence as viewer is not felt, and
the description remains impersonal, while Raban himself seems

---

gänzlich fremd und nur Gegenstand der Neugierde. Und solange du
man sagst an Stelle von *ich*, ist es nichts und man kann diese Geschichte aufsagen, sobald du aber dis eingestehst, dass du selbst es
bist, dann wirst du förmlich durchbohrt und bist entsetzt" (*H* 8).

Whereas Raban is permitted to think about his situation in the impersonal form *man*, the narrator of "A Commentary" speaks for himself in the first person. According to Raban's analysis (which probably
corresponds to Kafka's own), the latter is by far the more painful.

8. "Zwei Herren machten einander Mitteilungen. Der eine hielt die
Hände mit der innern Fläche nach oben und bewegte sie gleich-
mässig, als halte er eine Last in Schwebe" (*H* 7).

9. "Ein kleines Mädchen hielt in den vorgestreckten Händen ein
müdes Hündchen" (*H* 7).

10. "Auf dem Trottoir gleich vor ihm . . ."(*H* 7).

to fade out of the picture.[11] Emrich suggests that these overly detailed, yet strangely elusive descriptions serve to reveal the distance that separates Raban from the world around him. Raban refers to himself as a *thing,* an "object of curiosity" (*Gegenstand der Neugierde*). Emrich writes: "To Eduard Raban ... all the observed events appear incomprehensible and strange. He feels it a torture to set forth into this profusion of life as it undulates meaninglessly past."[12] Although Emrich rightly stresses Raban's estrangement from the ordinary activities of life—this is at the heart of the story—he exaggerates the importance of these lengthy descriptions. Raban's tenuous relationship to everyday life is revealed to us far more clearly through his involved thought processes, which also serve to establish his weak, self-pitying nature.

The first chapter of "Wedding Preparations," in which the passage quoted occurs, alternates between brief external descriptions of Raban, long sequences of inner narration (of Raban's thoughts and feelings), and detailed descriptions of the immediate surroundings. The shifts often seem arbitrary, and these passages have a rambling, nondramatic quality; as a result, the passages do not build on one another. The dialogue—for example, the conversation between Raban and his acquaintance Lement—is without tension and moves painfully slowly. Compared to the intensity of "A Commentary," this early narrative seems entirely uncompressed.

The lack of focus and the uncertain structure of "Wedding Preparations" as a whole is mirrored in the smaller segment. In the passage cited, the tension created by the initial statement—"Raban was startled"—is immediately lessened by the explanation of his fear: "Was it not late already?" Raban seeks to remedy the fear by checking the time ("he quickly reached for his watch") but discovers that his watch has stopped. The effect of this discovery upon Raban is not—as one might expect—anxi-

11. It is interesting that Raban is described in words that are suggestive of fading: "His lips were as *pale* as the *faded* red of his . . . tie" ("Seine Lippen waren *blass* wie das *ausgebleichte* Rot seiner . . . Krawatte" [*DF* 3, *H* 8; italics mine]).

12. *Franz Kafka,* p. 27.

ety, but annoyance (*Verdruss*), a feeling less intense than the
fear (*Schrecken*) that had preceded it. The progression from
fear to annoyance results in another diminution of the tension,
which continues to decline as the paragraph progresses. The
focus shifts from Raban to the neighbor, who is described in
rather prosaic terms as "standing somewhat farther back in
the entrance-way.... He was carrying on a conversation."
These details deflect attention from Raban's situation. When,
in answer to his anxious question, the neighbor gives Raban a
perfectly straight reply—"Certainly, past four o'clock"—the episode simply ends, and the tension aroused by the initial statement—"Raban was startled"—dissolves. The rhythm of this passage is the opposite of dramatic, for it moves from a high to a
low point and deflates tension.[13]

Raban's fear, the lateness of the hour, and the speed with
which he reaches for his watch are met only by the silence of
his watch. The neighbor of whom Raban asks the time is so
engrossed in conversation that he answers the question still in
the emotions of that involvement ("still engrossed in the laughter that accompanied it"). Naturally enough, the man returns
to his conversation, but Kafka presents this not as a turning
back to his companion, but as a turning *away* from Raban,
thereby emphasizing Raban's feelings of isolation and uncertainty which define the larger theme of "Wedding Preparations."

However unreal the "real" world may have seemed to Raban
or to Kafka, at this early point in his literary development
Kafka was still concerned with establishing the "reality" of his
fictional world and was unable to present it simply as "given."
In "Wedding Preparations" Kafka attempts to make his fictional world real by justifying its elements in terms of the logic
of the "known," natural world. For example, the speed with
which Raban reaches for his watch is explained by the fact

13. "Dramatic" is not intended here as a general value judgment,
but is meant to be purely descriptive. Although it would be foolish to
deny that Kafka's later dramatic style succeeds while his earlier nondramatic style does not, his success (or lack of it) is in no way inherent
in the method itself, but is the result of Kafka's use of that method.
In another writer this process might be reversed.

that Raban wore his coat and jacket open. The laughter accompanying the answer to Raban's question is explained by the fact that the man was still involved in conversation when he replied. Immediately following this incident, Raban opens his umbrella, picks up his suitcase, and tries to step out into the street, unsuccessfully at first. The narrator explains: "But when he was about to step into the street, his way was blocked by several women in a hurry" (*DF* 5).[14] This explanation puts the "blocking of his way" (*versperren des Weges*) completely into the realm of the literal, in a fashion that severely limits its power to point beyond itself. Similarly, other details in "Wedding Preparations" which might carry some symbolic significance are explained away and swallowed by the narrative line of events.

By 1922 Kafka had given up justifying details in terms of logic, and in "A Commentary" he simply presents his fictional world as given. Because he is at no pains to explain the meaning behind anything, he forces the reader to take a more active part in interpreting his work. The secret of Kafka's method in "A Commentary" lies in its brevity, its deceptive simplicity, and above all, in the compression and ordering of its elements. Its strongly visual quality makes of the reader an observer. Both Politzer and Standaert imply that "A Commentary" follows a dramatic pattern, although they disagree as to where the crisis or turning point occurs.[15] The contrast between the two passages is extreme: whereas "Wedding Preparations" is slack, a strong tension runs through "A Commentary." The lat-

14. "Als er aber auf die Strasse treten wollte, wurde ihm der Weg durch einige eilende Frauen versperrt" (*H* 10).

15. It is impossible to accept Politzer's assertion that the turning point occurs in the second sentence (*Parable and Paradox*, p. 3). Standaert argues persuasively against Politzer on this point and concludes: "For this reason, not the second, but the third sentence marks *the turning point* in this brief report" ("Politzers Kafka-Buch," p. 256). If by turning point Standaert means the highest point in the action, which is followed by the denouement (as he implies), then it is not possible to agree with his analysis either. The policeman's answer, "From me you wish to learn the way?" represents a point of crisis; the climax occurs with the policeman's final reply, "Give it up, give it up."

ter follows the dramatic pattern of rising and falling action, and like the drama, begins from a point of complete rest: "It was very early in the morning." It is not only morning, the beginning of a new day, but very early, a time suspended between night and day, when night life has ceased and day activity not yet begun; it is the stillest moment of the day.

As in drama, setting, mood, and atmosphere are established at once. The empty street suggests a bare stage with only a clock tower in view, and there is a total absence of sounds or of other people. In fact, the opening sentence of "A Commentary" —"It was very early in the morning, the streets clean and empty, I was on my way to the train station"—exactly parallels standard dramatic notation, into which it can be transposed almost intact to read: *Time:* early morning; *Place:* on the street, clean and empty; *Characters:* a man, alone. In a work of drama, convention allows the dramatist to place the characters on the stage before the play begins and to give the situation of the main character as soon as he appears. Thus, the last clause of the first sentence ("I was on my way to the train station") is the equivalent of dramatic exposition, for it provides the necessary information upon which the action builds. Because he is on his way to the train station, the narrator wishes to know the time. Because it is later than he had thought, the narrator becomes confused, and out of his confusion the central action takes shape: it becomes his purpose *to find the way.*[16]

The real complexity of "A Commentary" lies in the levels of meaning hidden in the simple word "way." By resounding through this brief narrative without explicit definition or limitation, the word expands and takes on greater significance.[17] A momentary silence surrounds, and thereby emphasizes, the

16. This analysis of action is based on the work of Francis Fergusson, who suggests that "one must be clear, first of all, that *action (praxis)* does not mean deeds, events, or physical activity: it means, rather, the motivation from which deeds spring" ("Introduction," *Aristotle's Poetics* [New York, 1961], p. 8).

17. This is one of the many possibilities by which a word or phrase may be given emphasis in drama: it may be repeated, it may be accompanied by special sound or action, it may provoke a peculiar answer, or it may be followed by a prolonged silence.

word "way": the narrator is breathless when he asks the way, the policeman smiles, then laughs. The narrator's breathlessness and the policeman's smile resemble the accents of the theater. The word is further emphasized by the strangeness of the answer it elicits, a question in response to a question.

On the basis of the ordering of the clauses in the first sentence, Politzer assumes that the narrator of "A Commentary" is shy.[18] This interpretation seems inappropriate and is, in fact, contradicted by the narrator's subsequent forthright approach to the policeman. If we recognize that in this sketch Kafka is adapting the methods of the drama to prose, then it follows quite naturally that the narrator is introduced last, only after time and place have been established. Furthermore, the entire dialogue between narrator and policeman is highly theatrical. The policeman does not merely turn away (as did the neighbor in "Wedding Preparations"); he turns away with an exaggerated gesture that gives emphasis to his words and calls attention to his act. The inclusion of a simile ("as people do who want to be alone with their laughter") in so terse a narrative is itself remarkable and has the effect of an elaborate stage direction. There is in the simile the suggestion that by turning away the policeman is trying to hide his laughter. The action—"and turned away with a grand gesture"—is too grandiose for the ordinary world; this is a stage gesture that makes sense only if we visualize it, as the structure and language of "A Commentary" invite us to do.[19]

In contrast to the mass of detail surrounding Raban, we know almost nothing about the narrator of "A Commentary,"

18. Politzer writes: "He seems to be shy, for it strikes us as a personal trait that he mentions himself after having described the time and place of the sketch" (*Parable and Paradox*, p. 2).

19. On this point I am indebted to Walter Benjamin's essay on Kafka, in which Benjamin writes: "In an unpublished article on 'A Fratricide,' Werner Kraft perceptively identified the events in this little story as scenic events. . . . 'Just as this bell, which is too loud for a doorbell, rings out toward heaven, the gestures of Kafka's figures are too powerful for our accustomed surroundings and break out into wider areas'" (*Illuminations*, pp. 120–21). Werner Kraft's analysis of "A Fratricide" applies equally well to the method of "A Commentary."

not even his name, age, appearance, or occupation. For this
reason he is reminiscent of the stripped character typical of
certain allegorical plays, such as *Everyman.* The policeman
may be likened to the secondary characters of the medieval
morality plays, who symbolize a single, immediately recogniz-
able trait. As a public figure the policeman represents law and
order, in the light of which the narrator's appeal for help is
quite natural and entirely in keeping with our expectations. At
first the policeman's presence offers the possibility of relief
from the tension which has been created by the turn of events
and which has been heightened by the staccato rhythms of the
long second sentence. "Breathless" reflects not only the
narrator's effort of running but also his eagerness to find help.
But the policeman's response—"From me you wish to learn the
way?"—creates a new complication that increases the tension,
and in addition introduces an element of humor. A man becomes lost and asks a policeman to help him find the way; in
response, instead of an answer, he receives another question.
When the man insistently explains his need, he receives only
cryptic advice that leaves him entirely in the dark.

In Eastern European folk humor (on which the comic perceptions of the Yiddish plays are based), it is proverbial that a
Jew will always answer a question with another question. In
part, this habit grows out of Talmudic debate, in which no
question is ever considered simple. The wise man and the
scholar know that even the simplest question carries with it
myriad assumptions and complications which must be clarified
before the original question can even begin to be answered.[20]
By framing his question so broadly ("asked him...the
way"), the narrator makes a simple answer impossible. The policeman's response may be meant to indicate to the narrator
that only a fool would expect a direct answer to such a broad
question.

Although Kafka came from an assimilated home in which

20. There is an old Jewish proverb that says, "A fool can ask more
questions in an hour than a wise man can answer in a year" ("In a
shu kon a nar mer kashes shteln eyder a khokhem ken entfern in a gants
yor").

German was spoken, his whole environment was intimately connected with Eastern European Jewish folk mannerisms. His letters and diaries show that his parents' speech retained not only the flavor of the Yiddish language, but also much of its vocabulary (particularly idioms) and patterns of thought.[21] Furthermore, his "Introductory Talk on the Yiddish Language" (*DF* 381–86; *H* 421–26) shows that Kafka was informed about the history of the Yiddish language (though the language is older than he suggests) and that he appreciated its subtleties and its humor. If we recognize the humor inherent in the narrator's situation in "A Commentary," then the ominous associations of the policeman's reply become secondary to its more broadly comic implications.

It is easy to see the interview between policeman and narrator in terms of the comic routines that were part of the entertainment on the Yiddish stage. Kafka seems to have borrowed the tone and attitude for "A Commentary" from Jewish culture, which, like the Yiddish variety act, relies heavily on wordplay, intonation, and gesture to give significance to or alter the meaning of the spoken word. In this context, the intonation of the policeman's reply—"From me you wish to learn the way?"—seems peculiarly Jewish.[22] If the question were framed in Yid-

21. There is some disagreement among scholars as to how well Kafka knew Yiddish. While Wagenbach asserts that he "hardly understood Yiddish" (*Biographie*, p. 179), Yonas Turkov claims that Levi taught Kafka to read and write the language ("Frants Kafka un Djak Levi," *Di Goldene Keyt* [1967], p. 151). The evidence contradicts both arguments. Kafka once admitted to Janouch, "I also had difficulties with the language. Then I discovered that I understood more Yiddish than I had imagined" (*CwK* 43; J 36).

Kafka himself frequently uses Yiddish expressions in the *Diaries;* see *D*i 79–81, 86, 95–96, 111, 125, 129, 142, 166, 170, 190, 215, 217, 223–26, 239, *D*ii 98; *T* 80–82, 87, 97–99, 115, 132, 136, 151, 177, 182, 204–5, 234, 236, 243, 256, 444. He is obviously at ease with Yiddish idioms and appreciates their humor. One often has the feeling that in his narratives Kafka does not so much invent the stances and gestures of his characters as choose them instinctively from among those typical of Eastern European Jews.

22. "Von mir willst Du den Weg erfahren?" This is in no way to suggest that the policeman is actually Jewish.

dish, the emphasis would fall on *mir* and the tone would rise sharply at the end of the sentence. This inflection would call further attention to the narrator's foolishness in expecting a meaningful reply to his question. In Yiddish, the policeman's half-mocking, half-ironic reply would, at the same time, point to his own insignificance. (The Jew, particularly in the Yiddish drama, usually sees himself as a "little man" [*a kleyn mentshele*], especially before the greatness of God.) The policeman's reply does not seem so inappropriate if we think of it in the context of the Jewish attitudes reflected in the Yiddish plays; and in this context it is possible to reconstruct the logic that could lead him to his peculiar response. He might, for example, be pondering the possible meaning of the word "way" and be thinking, "What do you want from *me*? I am only a little person! From *me* you want to know the way?" His tone would reflect both resignation and surprise. The Jew is resigned to the fact that he can never find definite answers, although he is deeply committed to the search.[23] The policeman's tone of surprise may be taken as evidence of his intuition that the questioner does expect a conclusive answer.

Politzer makes much of the policeman's rudeness in using the familiar form of address (*du*).[24] If we assume that Jewish attitudes are to some degree reflected in this anecdote, then the policeman's use of the familiar becomes less crucial. In Yiddish the use of *du* does not indicate the degree of disrespect that it does in German, although two distinct forms exist. In comparison to German, Yiddish is a far less formal language, and its rules have not always been rigorously observed.[25]

23. One might well ask, if the Jew is so committed to the search, and if the policeman's attitude reflects a Jewish point of view, how do we account for the resignation of the policeman's final advice, "Give it up, give it up"? The perceptions behind this anecdote are Kafka's, however, and although Kafka may have been influenced by Jewish thought, his ambivalent attitudes toward life and truth are entirely his own.

24. He writes: "The 'I' of the official towers so forcefully above the 'Thou' of the man that we do not realize right away the presumption underlying his words. He actually addresses the man with a 'Thou' (*du*), instead of the formal 'you' (*Sie*)" (*Parable and Paradox*, p. 6).

25. The informality of the language reflects a general informality

But regardless of what meaning we assign to the answering of a question with a question, we must acknowledge that the policeman's final words, "Give it up, give it up," are even less satisfying and more surprising than his previous response had been. This peculiar advice represents the high point of the action, after which the narrative takes a sharp downward turn and ends in an attenuated rest. The preponderance of *w* and *l* sounds in the last sentence, especially after "sagte er" ("he said") and culminating in "allein sein wollen" ("to want to be alone"), with its interior rhyme, effectively signals the end of the action.

It is possible to see in the action of this anecdote an Aristotelian "recognition" and "reversal." The narrator's immediate perception of the policeman as a potential source of help represents a kind of recognition. When the policeman responds to the narrator's quest for help with another question, he reverses and confuses their roles; and his final answer, "Give it up," is a reversal of fortune for the questioner, who is left to rely entirely on his own meager resources. (He is, after all, a stranger in town.) What is he to give up? And what is he to do? The narrative offers no solution, and the reader is left in the position of the observer in the theater, who, when the curtain falls, must interpret for himself the meaning of what he has seen. Kafka leaves the questions raised by this sketch entirely open, and, perhaps, we have no right to demand more.[26] In order to make sense of the action of "A Commentary" we must focus on what Kafka does present. If the action is *to find the way*, then the advice "give it up" acts as a commentary on this action. It suggests that for this narrator, at least, there is no answer and no way out.

Politzer has noted that the policeman and the narrator are not operating on the same levels of meaning in "A Commen-

in the relationships of the people who spoke it; the familial quality of Jewish life has often been commented upon. The attempt to standardize Yiddish grammar and spelling was not effective until the late 1930's.

26. This kind of open ending is typical of the drama; for example, when Nora slams the door in *A Doll's House*, Ibsen has taken the action as far as he wants it to go. The unresolved nature of the action is part of the plot.

tary," a technique which is the basis of comic irony, particularly in Yiddish drama. Whereas Raban's question about real time had elicited an answer in kind, the narrator's question about the way does not. The narrator *seems* to ask about a real way (we cannot be certain of his meaning), but he is answered with what can only be a reference to another, more symbolic way. It is not clear who shifts the meaning of the word first; what is important is that no direct answer is forthcoming, nor, does it seem likely, will be forthcoming, no matter how many persons the narrator might approach. While the characters of "A Commentary" remain oblivious of the deeper significance of their own words, the reader (like the theater audience) is expected to be aware of their dilemma and to comprehend its symbolic significance. From this perspective, the policeman functions like a chorus of one and represents the many possible helpers who populate the real world and who are all equally unable to provide any help or any answers.[27]

The implications of "A Commentary" are already present in its first formulation in "Wedding Preparations," although they are not in any way developed there. Raban's brief conversation with his neighbor is buried among the many particulars of an ordinary day in Raban's life. In "A Commentary" the incident calls greater attention to itself because it stands alone; it takes on the quality of a recorded improvisation not limited to a specific time or place.

Heinz Politzer has already called attention to a diary entry of January 16, 1922, which illuminates the significance of clock time for Kafka. Describing his own condition, Kafka writes: "The clocks are not in unison; the inner one runs crazily on ... the outer one limps along at its usual speed. What else can happen but that the two worlds split apart" (*D*II 202).[28]

27. Kafka's heroes often try to rely on helpers, but despite their efforts, no real help is ever forthcoming. Some, such as the assistants in *The Castle*, are more of a hindrance than a help.

28. "Die Uhren stimmen nicht überein, die innere jagt . . . die äussere geht stockend ihren gewöhnlichen Gang. Was kann anderes geschehen, als dass sich die zwei verschiedenen Welten trennen" (*T* 552).

While it is true that the characters' sense of time, both in "Wedding Preparations" and "A Commentary," is slower, not faster than ordinary time, we must not take Kafka too literally. The significance of the diary entry lies not in the unnatural speed of Kafka's inner clock, but in his revealing, by means of the clock image, that his private, inner world was irrevocably separated from the external, real world. Raban's stopped watch acts as a signal to the reader that Raban is not in step with the world in which he lives. Since the reader has already perceived this from Raban's thoughts about himself ("one is alone, a total stranger" [DF 3]), this detail serves only to reinforce what he already knows.

That Kafka looked upon ordinary, "correct" clock time as a symbol of the "other world" (*die äussere*), the world from which he felt locked out, is made clear by another diary entry, one that stands much closer in time to the writing of "Wedding Preparations" and which illuminates the early as well as the later work. On January 24, 1915, Kafka describes a painful meeting with his fiancée, Felice Bauer, and sums up the hopelessness of their relationship:

> I think it is impossible for us ever to unite. . . . I yield not a particle of my demand for a fantastic life arranged solely in the interest of my work; she, indifferent to every mute request, wants the average: a comfortable home, an interest on my part in the factory, good food, bed at eleven, central heating; sets my watch—which for the past three months has been an hour and a half fast—right to the minute. (D_{II} 111)[29]

These words make plain Kafka's wistful admiration for Felice's faith in "the real minute" (*die wirkliche Minute*), which he

29. "Ich glaube, es ist unmöglich, dass wir uns jemals vereinigen. . . . Ich lasse nichts nach von meiner Forderung nach einem phantastischen, nur für meine Arbeit berechneten Leben, sie will, stumpf gegen alle stummen Bitten, das Mittelmass, die behagliche Wohnung, Interesse für die Fabrik, reichliches Essen, Schlaf von elf Uhr abends an, geheiztes Zimmer, stellt meine Uhr, die seit einem viertel Jahr um eineinhalb Stunden vorausgeht, auf die wirkliche Minute ein" (T 459).

The sense of the German is "sets my watch . . . to correspond to real time."

ironically contrasts with his own "fantastic life." A similar separation between the real and the imagined occurs in "A Commentary" (as well as in "Wedding Preparations," where the split takes the more literal form of a fantasy).

By isolating this incident, by divesting it of all specific detail, by shifting the emphasis from time (which is specific) to way (which is ambiguous), Kafka infused this minor incident with a sense of mystery and drama. And by successfully adapting the techniques of drama to narrative prose in "A Commentary," Kafka was able to transform Raban's ordinary "Weg zum Bahnhof" into a symbol of the universal "way" travelled by all men.

chapter four

Style and structure in Kafka's work before 1912

"Description of a Struggle," "Wedding Preparations in the Country," *Meditation,* and a few fragments in the *Diaries* constitute Kafka's imaginative writing before 1912.[1] These differ markedly from "The Judgment," the work that begins Kafka's mature period. In these early works Kafka seems as yet unsure of the direction of his art and fails to create a fully realized fictional universe.

"Description of a Struggle" (1904/5), the earliest of these works, is a long narrative composed of several loosely connected episodes. A midnight walk through the streets of Prague taken by two acquaintances engaged in a peculiar struggle for ascendency provides the frame for the encounters that make up the central portion of the story. The rambling

1. "The First Long Train Ride," *Herderblätter,* May 1912, the first chapter of a projected novel (never completed) with Max Brod, is not properly included in an analysis of the early work. According to Brod's biography, this fragment is based on the actual travel diaries which Brod and Kafka kept on a trip in 1911, and the two main characters, Richard and Samuel, represent slightly altered portraits of the authors themselves. Kafka's other youthful efforts—"The Aeroplanes at Brescia," *Bohemia,* September 28, 1909; and the three reviews "A Novel about Youth," *Bohemia,* January 16, 1910; "On Kleist's 'Ancedotes,'" fall 1911 (not published); and "Hyperion," *Bohemia,* March 20, 1911— are all works of nonfiction and not relevant to this discussion. Begun in early 1912 and substantially revised after the breakthrough in November 1912, the unfinished novel *Amerika* combines the panoramic sweep of Kafka's early work with the dramatic qualities of his mature work and will be discussed with the later work. For details concerning the development of this novel, see Pasley and Wagenbach, "Datierung sämtlicher Texte," in *Kafka Symposion,* by Born et al., pp. 62–63.

structure of the whole is mirrored in the individual episodes, whose slow pace and diffuse effects create an essentially undramatic text. These episodes do not follow one another in a coherent pattern, but represent abrupt shifts in character, setting, and situation. Leaving his companion, who falls down and disappears until the final frame episode, the narrator communes with himself in an "unfinished" landscape. He meets a fat man being carried through the forest on a litter. The fat man relates an encounter with a praying man, who in turn describes a few significant fragments from his own life. The apparently unmotivated struggle between the narrator and his acquaintance is reflected in these dreamlike, fragmentary encounters, which seem to question the meaning of all human relationships and cast doubt on the very solidity of the material world.

In contrast to the limited focus and staged quality of Kafka's mature fiction, "Description of a Struggle" is highly subjective. Setting does not remain fixed, but shifts according to the will of the narrator: "I walked on, unperturbed. But since, as a pedestrian, I dreaded the effort of climbing the mountainous road, I let it become gradually flatter, let it slope down into a valley in the distance. The stones vanished at my will and the wind disappeared" (DS 37).[2] Time and space are given the fluidity of dreams; except in the frame story, time does not exist and space is flexible: "Meanwhile the banks of the river stretched beyond all bounds" (DS 86).[3] The narrator swims in the air, rides on the back of his companion, and beats him harshly to make him run. The narrator appears to change shape: "After all I was small, almost smaller than usual. . . . Nevertheless I was mistaken, for my arms were as huge as the clouds of a steady country rain" (DS 86).[4] These patently un-

2. "Unbesorgt ging ich weiter. Weil ich aber als Fussgänger die Anstrengung der bergigen Strasse fürchtete, liess ich den Weg immer flacher werden und sich in der Entfernung endlich zu einem Tale senken. Die Steine verschwanden nach meinem Willen und der Wind verlor sich" (B 28).

3. "Dabei dehnten sich die Ufer dieses Flusses ohne Mass" (B 59).

4. "Ich war doch klein, fast kleiner als gewöhnlich. . . . Aber trotzdem hatte ich mich geirrt, denn meine Arme waren so gross, wie die Wolken eines Landregens" (B 59–60).

real elements may be meant to signal to the reader that he is
entering the narrator's private world of fantasy, or they may
simply reflect the author's view that what we accept as real
and certain is often no less fantastic than what we dismiss as
unreal. In either case, these elements injected into the realistic
setting destroy the illusion of an independent fictional world
which the author has begun to create in the frame episode.

The shifts in the narrative voice are made without corresponding changes in the language, tone, or imagery. Descriptive passages narrated by the three main characters (narrator,
fat man, praying man) in diverse situations reveal a striking
similarity in detail, sentence structure, word choice, rhythm,
and tone. For example, the narrator's distance from events is
manifest by his dispassionate tone and by the details with
which he records his own experience: "In the vestibule stood a
housemaid, whom we hadn't seen before. She helped us into
our coats and then took a small lantern to light us down the
stairs. Her neck was bare save for a black velvet ribbon round
her throat; her loosely clothed body was stooped and kept
stretching as she went down the stairs before us, holding the
lantern low" (DS 14).[5] Although the episodes recalled by the
fat man and the praying man are said to be of special significance to them, the same attitude of passive detachment informs their words. The fat man records his first meeting with
the praying man: "In the church there were only a few old
women who kept turning their shawled heads sideways to
glance at the praying man. This attention seemed to please
him, for before each of his pious outbursts he let his eyes rove
about to see how many people were watching him" (DS 52).[6]

5. "Im Vorzimmer stand ein Stubenmädchen, wir sahen sie jetzt zum
erstenmal. Sie half uns in die Überröcke und nahm dann eine kleine
Handlampe, um uns über die Treppe zu leuchten. Ihr Hals war nackt
und nur unter dem Kinn von einem schwarzen Samtband umbunden
und ihr lose bekleideter Körper war gebeugt und dehnte sich immer
wieder, als sie vor uns die Treppe hinunterstieg, die Lampe nieder-
haltend" (B 13).

6. "In der Kirche waren nur einige alte Weiber, die hie und da ihr
eingewickeltes Köpfchen mit seitlicher Neigung drehten, um nach dem
Betenden hinzusehen. Diese Aufmerksamkeit schien ihn glücklich zu

The praying man describes a social gathering: "Then I noticed that the girl was no longer sitting beside me. She must have left soon after her last words, for now she was standing far away from me by a window, surrounded by three young men who were talking and laughing out of high white collars" (*DS* 70).[7]

Several of the longer sections of "Description of a Struggle" are in the form of dialogue (which should help to focus the conflict and define the characters), yet neither the individual characters nor the work as a whole takes on independent life. The dialogue does not so much represent communication between two people as it resembles a monologue, in which the same person is providing both questions and answers.[8] The conflict inherent in the following exchange between narrator and praying man is quickly deflated by the introspection of the former and the apathy of the latter, and the conflict fails to develop. The narrator begins:

> My lips were dry and disobedient as I said: "Ought it not to be possible to live differently?"
>
> "No," he said, questioning, smiling.
>
> "But why do you pray in church every evening?" I asked then, while everything between him and me, which until then I had been holding together as though in my sleep, collapsed.
>
> "Oh, why should we talk about it? People who live alone have no responsibility in the evenings. One fears a number of things." (*DS* 82–83)[9]

---

machen, denn vor jedem seiner frommen Ausbrüche liess er seine Augen umgehn, ob die zuschauenden Leute zahlreich wären" (*B* 37).

7. "Da bemerkte ich, dass das Mädchen nicht mehr neben mir sass. Sie musste bald nach ihren letzten Worten weggegangen sein, denn sie stand jetzt weit von mir an einem Fenster, umstellt von drei jungen Leuten, die aus hohen weissen Krägen lachend redeten" (*B* 49).

8. Sokel interprets the entire Kafka *oeuvre* in terms of two central struggles: the "I" against itself (the "pure self" against the "facade," here represented by the narrator and the acquaintance), and the struggle of the "I" against the external "powers that be."

9. "Meine Lippen waren trocken und ungehorsam, als ich sagte:
" 'Sollte man nicht anders leben können!'
" 'Nein,' sagte er fragend, lächelnd.

In this dialogue, the rambling, unrhythmic quality of the language tends rather to dissolve the existing tension than to build upon it. Furthermore, language often seems to be used for its own sake, without revealing character or furthering the action.[10] For example, the fat man speaks: "Yes, revenge it is, for how often have we attacked them, I and my friend the supplicant [praying man], amidst the singing of our swords, the flash of cymbals, the great splendor of trumpets, and the leaping blaze of drums!" (DS 51).[11]

In addition to language, the characters share a sense of physical uncertainty. The narrator imagines that he resembles "a stick dangling in the air" (DS 21).[12] He is unsure of his size and pleads, "Please, passers-by, be so kind as to tell me how tall I am—just measure these arms, these legs" (DS 87).[13] Despite his extraordinary obesity, the fat man lacks solidity: without losing speed a mosquito flies through his body. The praying man is thin and insubstantial. It is said of him, "Your whole length you are cut out of tissue paper ..., like a silhouette, and when you walk, one must be able to hear you rustle."[14] He finally confesses that he prays so conspicuously to gain "being" through others.[15] These similarities link the characters and suggest that they are all constructions of a single consciousness,

"'Aber warum beten Sie am Abend in der Kirche,' fragte ich dann, indem alles zwischen mir und ihm zusammenfiel, was ich bis dahin wie schlafend gestützt hatte.
"'Nein, warum sollten wir darüber reden. Am Abend trägt niemand, der allein lebt, Verantwortung. Man fürchtet manches'" (B 57).

10. Herbert Tauber notes this point in Franz Kafka: An Interpretation of His Works (New Haven, 1948), p. 3.

11. "Ja, Rache ist es, denn wie oft haben wir diese Dinge angegriffen, ich und mein Freund der Beter, beim Singen unserer Klinge, unter dem Aufglanz der Cymbeln, der weiten Pracht der Posaunen und dem springenden Leuchten der Pauken" (B 37).

12. "Eine Stange in baumelnder Bewegung" (B 17).

13. "Bitte, vorübergehende Leute, seid so gut, sagt mir, wie gross ich bin, messet nur diese Arme, diese Beine" (B 60).

14. "Sie sind Ihrer ganzen Länge nach aus Seidenpapier herausgeschnitten, . . . so silhuettenartig [sic], und wenn Sie gehen, so muss man Sie knittern hören" (B 48).

15. "Um angeschaut zu werden und Körper zu bekommen" (B 57).

presumably that of the central narrator who is trying to establish a solid relationship with the outside world.[16] The characters' shared physical uncertainty may be symbolic of their common doubt concerning the solidity of the physical universe and the reliability of all human relationships. The literal level of the narration is confused and incoherent, however, and thus hardly capable of supporting extensive symbolic interpretation.

Of all the characters, it is the acquaintance, "der Bekannte" (literally, "he who is known"), who is most closely connected to the narrator. He and the narrator mirror each other's actions, echo each other's words, and are bound to one another in an unstable love-hate relationship. In the last section of the narrative their struggle seems to be brought to a sudden end by the narrator's surprising confession, "I'm engaged, I confess it" (*DS* 93), although the text in no way suggests that a genuine resolution has been reached.[17] It seems far more likely that what we have witnessed is part of an endless, continuing struggle. The narrator, at least, seems reconciled to a permanent impasse.

Although it is possible to find some thematic unity in the insubstantial characters and confusing episodes described in "Description of a Struggle," basically this work is marred by the stylistic confusion and indirection which characterizes all of Kafka's early work. Despite their detailed self-analyses, the motivation of the characters remains vague and the deeper significance of the events unclear. Because of its loose structure, slow pace, uneconomic use of language, and its failure to establish even a single firm conflict between clearly differentiated characters, "Description of a Struggle" cannot be included

16. This is also the opinion of Tauber, *Franz Kafka*, p. 1, and of Politzer, *Parable and Paradox*, p. 27. Sokel is of a somewhat different opinion; he views the fat man "as form raised to the second power and the praying man as the third power of the narrator" (*Tragik und Ironie*, p. 540, n. 1).

17. "Ich bin verlobt, ich gestehe es" (*B* 64).

I cannot agree with Sokel (*Tragik und Ironie*, p. 37) or Tauber (*Franz Kafka*, p. 9), who assume that this confession definitely decides the struggle in favor of the narrator.

among Kafka's successful works. Kafka seems to have concurred in this judgment, for he never permitted this story to be published in its entirety during his lifetime.

With the exception of four episodes from "Description of a Struggle," the pieces included in *Meditation* are the only works written before September 1912 that Kakfa submitted for publication.[18] This collection cannot properly be considered a work of fiction, although it represents Kafka's attempt to cast the personal experiences of his life into the form of imaginative prose. Kafka the man is but thinly disguised behind the amorphous "I" of these vignettes: the attempt fails because the author does not sufficiently divorce himself from the work. Of the eighteen pieces included in the volume, fourteen are first-person narration (ten in the singular, four in the plural); the remaining four use the impersonal "who" (*wer*) or "one" (*man*).[19] Thirteen of the eighteen sketches use the present

18. The pieces from "Description of a Struggle" are "The Trees" and "Clothes," first published in *Hyperion*, no. 1 (January/February 1908); and "Conversation with the Praying Man" and "Conversation with the Drunken Man," first published in *Hyperion*, no. 8 (March/April 1909). "The Trees" and "Clothes" were later included in *Meditation* (1913); the versions here differ somewhat from those in *Hyperion*. Seven other pieces from *Meditation* were first published independently: "Rejection," "The Tradesman," "Absent-minded Window-Gazing," "The Way Home," "Passers-by," and "On the Tram" in *Hyperion* (January/February 1908); and "Reflections for Gentlemen-Jockeys" in *Bohemia*, March 27, 1910. Although *Meditation* was not published until 1913, the pieces included in the volume were written between 1904 and 1912 (Pasley and Wagenbach, "Datierung sämtlicher Texte," in *Kafka Symposion*, by Born et al.). Three of the pieces included in *Meditation* ("Unmasking a Confidence Trickster," "The Sudden Walk," and "Resolutions") were written after Kafka's first, passing encounter with the Yiddish theater (in late 1911 and early 1912), but these are properly included in a study of the early work not merely because they antedate "The Judgment," but because they display the same confessional qualities as the other early works. The other works in this period ("Description of a Struggle," "Wedding Preparations in the Country") were published only years after Kafka's death.

19. The English often substitutes "you" for "one."

tense. None of these divisions, however, is absolutely rigid, for frequent shifts in voice or tense occur within a single episode. For example, "Absent-minded Window-Gazing" shifts from the future ("What will we do on these spring days ...?") to the past ("This morning the sky was gray.") to the present ("so one is surprised"),[20] and from "we" (*wir*) to "one" (*man*). These shifts seem to generalize the purely personal and give some permanence, however slight, to the fleeting moment of experience.

These sketches include a variety of themes: a child's experience of a summer night ("Children on a Country Road," which was to have been part of "Description of a Struggle"); an ironic commentary on the dubious pleasure of winning a horse race ("Reflections for Gentlemen-Jockeys"); the imagined sensation of being an Indian on horseback ("The Wish to Be a Red Indian"); the arrival of a ghost child into a bachelor's apartment ("Unhappiness"). The private, confessional nature of these essays is apparent throughout; most do not even attempt to create character or establish conflict, but instead, focus primarily on the narrator's reaction to his experience. "The Trees," "The Way Home," "Clothes," "Excursion into the Mountains," "Absent-minded Window-Gazing," "Passers-by," and "On the Tram" particularly reflect the detached philosophical attitude of the narrator, who is observing and analyzing himself, the human condition, and the nature of the physical world around him. Such a meditative, subjective point of view is basically undramatic. The loneliness and isolation of the individual (almost always, like the author, a bachelor) are revealed in a number of pieces which give to the whole a note of sadness and longing. "Rejection" presents an imagined rejection by a pretty girl; "The Street Window" describes the lure of the street for one who lives alone; "The Tradesman" portrays the solitary tradesman at the end of his working day. "Bachelor's Ill Luck," a sketch closely related to a diary entry of 1911 (*D*I 150–51; *T* 160–61), describes what Politzer calls

20. "Was werden wir in diesen Frühlingstagen tun?... Heute früh war der Himmel grau....so ist man überrascht" (*E* 37).

the typical Kafka hero, the *Ur*-bachelor,[21] and reveals the close
connection between these sketches and Kafka's private anxie-
ties. Though written in late 1911 and early 1912, "Unmasking a
Confidence Trickster," "The Sudden Walk," and "Resolutions"
are largely in the spirit of the personal meditation and still far
from the objective style of "The Judgment." Of these last three,
only "Unmasking a Confidence Trickster" begins to create a
fictional world; like the other "meditations," it too is characterized by impressionistic description and self-analysis. For example, the narrator's encounter with the swindler is interrupted
by the following wordy intrusion: "At the same time the houses
all around [us] took part in this silence, and the darkness over
them, up to the stars. And the steps of invisible passers-by,
whose ways one didn't feel like guessing, the wind which again
and again pressed itself against the opposite side of the
street."[22] Despite the suspense inherent in the situation described in "Unhappiness" (the appearance of the mysterious
ghost child in the narrator's room), the dialogue in this episode
is slow and plodding:

> "Hush, hush," said the child over her shoulder, "It's all
> right."
> "Then come farther into the room, I'd like to shut the door."
> "I've shut it this very minute. Don't bother. Just be easy in
> your mind."
> "It's no bother. But there's [*sic*] a lot of people living on this
> corridor, and I know them all, of course; most of them are com-
> ing back from work now; if they hear someone talking in a room,

21. Politzer, *Parable and Paradox*, p. 37. Politzer presents an excellent analysis of the relationship of this sketch to the themes of Kafka's
mature work; see ibid., pp. 29–47.

22. "Dabei nahmen an diesem Schweigen gleich die Häuser rings-
herum ihren Anteil, und das Dunkel über ihnen bis zu den Sternen.
Und die Schritte unsichtbarer Spaziergänger, deren Wege zu erraten
man nicht Lust hatte, der Wind, der immer wieder an die gegenüber-
liegende Strassenseite sich drückte" (*E* 30).

Nonetheless, a degree of tension is created in the confrontation between the narrator and the trickster which one might attribute to the
fact that Kafka worked on this story again in August 1912 (see *D*1
265; *T* 281) after a longer period of involvement with Yiddish theater.

they simply think they have a right to open the door and see what's happening." (*PC* 41)[23]

Often we are left only to share the narrator's blurred sense impressions or to follow his private dialectic. In "Children on a Country Road" (*PC* 21–25; *E* 25–29), sound is given prominence over sight: "I heard the wagons rumbling past the garden fence, sometimes I even saw them through gently swaying gaps in the foliage" (*PC* 21).[24] Throughout this little story, the sounds of the night and of the children's voices predominate. The description in "Clothes" (*PC* 36; *E* 40) more closely resembles philosophical speculation than the images of fiction: "Often when I see clothes with an abundance of pleats, frills, and fringes ... I think...."[25] The image of clothing only provides the excuse for the narrator's thoughts, which overpower the images he begins to create. The narrator of *Meditation,* the only character who could give unity to these separate moments, is but minimally developed; we know nothing about him except that he is a bachelor and lives alone. Kafka fails to make the private experience that has provoked the particular meditation concrete or universally meaningful.

In the early period, only in "Wedding Preparations" does Kafka partially succeed in creating a convincing fictional world. But as we have seen in Chapter 2, even in this third-person narration the characters do not fully take shape or come

23. " 'Ruhe, Ruhe!' sagte das Kind über die Schulter weg, 'alles ist schon richtig.'

" 'Dann kommen Sie weiter ins Zimmer herein, ich möchte die Tür schliessen.'

" 'Die Tür habe ich jetzt gerade geschlossen. Machen Sie sich keine Mühe. Beruhigen Sie sich überhaupt.'

" 'Reden Sie nicht von Mühe. Aber auf diesem Gange wohnt eine Menge Leute, alle sind natürlich meine Bekannten; die meisten kommen jetzt aus den Geschäften; wenn sie in einem Zimmer reden hören, glauben sie einfach das Recht zu haben, aufzumachen und nachzuschaun, was los ist' " (*E* 46).

24. "Ich hörte die Wagen an dem Gartengitter vorüberfahren, manchmal sah ich sie auch durch die schwach bewegten Lücken im Laub" (*E* 25).

25. "Oft wenn ich Kleider mit vielfachen Falten, Rüschen und Behängen sehe ... , dann denke ich ..." (*E* 40).

to life. Eduard Raban, the central character, becomes lost among the many details of his surroundings and in the complexities of his own thoughts. Kafka never completed "Wedding Preparations," and it is doubtful that he considered the work successful. It remains of interest primarily because its style contrasts so sharply with the style we have come to associate with Kafka, and because this work contains the kernel for several of the later stories.

Although "The Urban World" belongs to the period of Kafka's earliest writing, and although it was left in the form of an incomplete diary entry (for February 21, 1911 [*D1* 47–54; *T* 45–52]), we can see from this brief sketch that Kafka was beginning to adapt the techniques of drama to prose form even before the writing of "The Judgment" on September 22/23, 1912. "The Urban World" is a work of transition; similarities in structure as well as in details of plot strongly suggest that it represents an early, unfinished version of "The Judgment,"[26] and despite its shortcomings as a work of art, it illuminates the development of Kafka's literary technique. The central situation of the two works is the same: in both a son comes to tell his father of a major decision he has recently made. The father responds with angry accusations and objections. In both stories there is a friend who plays a significant role in the relationship between father and son. "The Judgment" ends with the self-inflicted death of the son; "The Urban World" breaks off with the interview with the friend.

In "The Urban World" Kafka moves away from the self-conscious description and introspection that characterized his earlier works, and begins to create the concrete images and objective point of view which are the hallmarks of his mature style and which were first given complete expression in "The Judgment." This was nine months after his first experience with the Yiddish theater (May 1910) and eight months before his own record of regular attendance at the Yiddish theater began. Since the diaries are extremely fragmentary in 1910 and do not

26. Kafka mentions "The Urban World" in connection with the writing of "The Judgment" (*D1* 276; *T* 294).

really begin to be continuous until 1911, the fact that Kafka himself did not record his first visit (and possibly others that year) is of little significance, and does not preclude the possibility of influence as early as 1911 (see Chapter 1).

"The Urban World" is the story of Oskar M., an older student who has never completed his dissertation or found any vocation for himself. When Oskar comes to tell his father of a new scheme he has devised, he is met with angry accusations and abuse. An argument ensues; Oskar insists that this terrible man cannot be his real father, and he leaves the house with the promise to return. He then goes to the home of his friend, Franz, whom he rudely awakens from a sound sleep with urgent pleas for advice and the request that Franz join his family for dinner. Here the work breaks off.

The story contrasts sharply with "Wedding Preparations," especially in its greater economy of detail. "The Urban World" consists of three scenes which correspond to three different settings: a street, the parental living room, and Franz's apartment. In each sequence the characters are made to behave as if they were within the confines of a stage; the individual scenes are completely divided from each other both in time and space. In its strict limitation of detail, the setting for each scene resembles the sparseness of a simple stage.[27] The street is an empty square; the parental living room contains only a table, a chair, a window, and a stove. In Franz's apartment we see an anteroom, a glass door, a leather sofa, and a chair. Transitions from one scene to another are not shown; rather, such changes occur abruptly, as they would in drama, where the curtain falls on one set and opens onto another. In addition, for each sequence of action within a single setting, time and place are established before the action proper begins. For example, the opening of the story—"Oskar ... stopped short in the middle of a snowstorm on an empty square one winter afternoon" (DI 47)[28]—can be transposed into stage language

27. Cf. Kafka's description of the Yiddish stage at the Café Savoy (DI 87; T 89).

28. "Oskar . . . blieb an einem Winternachmittag mitten im Schneefall auf einem leeren Platze stehn" (T 45).

almost intact to read: "A winter afternoon. An empty square. It is snowing. Oskar, alone."

Kafka adapts dramatic technique in "The Urban World" not only for the purposes of establishing time, place, and setting, but for introducing and developing the characters as well. Each character in the story is identified only by a brief tag which resembles the listing of characters on a playbill: Oskar, *an older student;* his father, *an old man;* Franz, *his friend, engineer.* As in the drama, we find out nothing more about the characters until they become involved in the action.

"The Urban World" also differs markedly from "Wedding Preparations" in the number of characters, their degree of complexity, and the methods by which their problems are conveyed. In the thirty pages which make up "Wedding Preparations" Kafka suggests a series of multiple relationships.[29] In contrast, "The Urban World" introduces only three characters —Oskar, father, friend—all of whom are limited in function and interaction. Although other characters appear, the story confines itself to the two confrontations between Oskar and his father and Oskar and Franz.[30]

In contrast to the rambling interior monologues around which "Wedding Preparations" is built, "The Urban World" follows the structural pattern of drama (which builds from a point of rest, rises, and falls), and like the drama, uses the spoken word as the primary means of developing character and

---

Joseph Kresh anglicizes the spelling of Oskar (Oscar) in the English translation, but for the sake of clarity and uniformity, I am maintaining the German spelling throughout.

29. These are Raban-Betty, Raban-Gilleman, Raban-Lement, Lement-Gillemann, Raban-neighbor, Raban-passenger, Raban-coachman, and behind all of these, Raban-himself.

30. Although the mother is mentioned, she is completely identified with the father, and no independent relationship is suggested. In the quarrel between Oskar and his father, the maid enters to tend the fire, but she serves only to break the action momentarily. In the third sequence Franz's landlady appears but takes no direct part in the action. A confrontation between Oskar, his parents, and Franz is suggested by the text; had the work been completed, it is probable that such a meeting would have been included.

establishing conflict. The difficulties between father and son
must largely be deduced from the dialogue:

> "Finally," said [the father], when Oskar had hardly put his
> foot into the room, "Please stay by the door. I am so furious with
> you that I don't know what I am about to do."
> "But Father," said Oskar. . . .
> "Silence," shouted the father and stood up. . . . "Silence, I
> command. And keep your 'buts' to yourself, do you under-
> stand."[31]

The characters are described by the narrator primarily in
visual terms of costume, as is the case in drama. Oskar is presented "in his winter clothes with his winter coat, over it a
shawl around his neck and a fur cap on his head" (Dι 47–48).[32]
The father is described as "a smooth-shaven man with a
heavy, fleshy face" (Dι 48).[33] Franz is identified by the single
detail, "a goatee" (einen Ziegenbart). This beard is the kind of
visual detail used by the dramatist to set two characters apart
on a stage (although on the Yiddish stage all of the Orthodox
Jews wore beards).

Kafka's reliance on gesture and exaggerated action relates the
technique of this story to dramatic method, in which the emotional condition of a character is not reported from outside, but
is generally revealed through action and gesture. Kafka's notation for such gestures once again resembles stage directions.
Instead of telling the reader that Oskar was tense, Kafka indicates the character's feelings by noting, "He swallowed his
breath."[34] Surprise is indicated by "Oskar was silent for a moment with his mouth open" (Dι 52).[35] The degree of Oskar's

31. " 'Endlich', sagte dieser, kaum dass Oskar den Fuss ins Zimmer
gesetzt hatte, 'bleib, ich bitte dich, bei der Tür, ich habe nämlich eine
solche Wut auf dich, dass ich meiner nicht sicher bin.'
" 'Aber Vater', sagte Oskar. . . .
" 'Ruhe', schrie der Vater und stand auf. . . . 'Ruhe befehle ich. Und
deine "Aber" lass dir, verstehst du' " (T 45).
32. "In seinen Winterkleidern mit dem Winterrock darüber, einem
Shawl um den Hals und einer Fellmütze auf dem Kopf" (T 45).
33. "Einen glattrasierten Mann mit schwerem Fleischgesicht" (T 45).
34. "Er schluckte an seinem Atem" (T 47).
35. "Oskar schwieg einen Augenblick mit offenem Mund" (T 49).

emotion is indicated by his actions: "Oskar grabbed the weak man by the front of his coat and sat him up" (*Di* 52).[36] His aggression is evident in the motion which accompanies the words: " 'What I want of you,' said Oskar softly, and gave the bed a kick with the heel of his foot" (*Di* 53).[37] At the end of the interview with Oskar's father, we read: "Thereupon Oskar pushed with his shoulder against the easily opened door as though he intended to break it down."[38] The act of pressing against the door is a visual representation of Oskar's emotional condition. We recognize that Oskar is trying to break away from his father's influence (although he clearly also wants his approval) not only from the spoken word, but from the violence of the act itself. Such economy is integral to the method of the drama.

Yet despite this effort to make "The Urban World" effective, Kafka's early experiment failed. Several elements, largely nondramatic, intrude into the self-contained world that he had begun to build in this narrative and work against the tension that he tries to create. As a result, the characters are not convincing, and the central conflict between father and son fails to crystallize.

The weakness of "The Urban World" can be traced directly to its inconsistencies of technique. Even from its incomplete form, we can see that Kafka tried to follow what is basically a dramatic pattern in building this story. The opening scene is expository: it sets the stage and mood, it presents the main character at the moment of the decision upon which the rest of the action depends. The next scene introduces the antagonist (the father) and begins to develop the conflict; the third scene introduces Franz, Oskar's helper and adviser. Although Kafka was building the story toward its climax, at this point in his development he was as yet unable to sustain the intensity gen-

36. "Oskar fasste den schwachen Menschen vorn beim Rock und setzte ihn auf" (*T* 50).

37. " 'Was ich von dir will', sagte Oskar leise und gab dem Bett einen Stoss mit dem Fussabsatz" (*T* 51).

38. "Darauf drängte Oskar mit der Schulter gegen die leicht aufgehende Türe, als habe er sich vorgenommen, sie einzudrücken" (*T* 49–50).

erated by the confrontation between father and son. Instead of
building gradually, through a series of crises, Kafka jumps directly from the exposition to the moment of highest tension
(the father's attack) and moves away from that high to a temporary resolution (Oskar's asking permission to go out). The
quarrel between father and son does not build, as in "The
Judgment," to a terrible moment of climax and revelation, but
instead, shifts indecisively from high to low points until the
tension inherent in the struggle flags. The stages of Oskar's reaction (explanation, apology, permission, promise) are inter-
spersed with accusations and confessions, none of which are
given coherent shape.

An even more serious failing in the technique of "The Urban
World," one which is clearly the result of Kafka's inadequate
handling of dramatic method, is his manipulation of the narrative voice. Although it is kept minimal, it nonetheless is not
completely silent. The intrusions of the narrator destroy the illusion of an independent fictional world, deflect attention away
from the characters, and diminish the intensity of the conflict.
For example, the initial description of Oskar is interrupted by
an evaluation which the reader is not in a position to test: "Oskar M., an older student—if one looked at him closely one was
frightened by his eyes" (D1 47).[39] At other times the narrator
explains the gestures, thereby severely limiting the possibilities
of interpretation and greatly minimizing their effectiveness.
For example, "He blinked his eyes [while] in thought," or "He
was so lost in thought that once he took off his cap and stroked
his face with its curly fur" (D1 48).[40] In the following description the explanation of the father's tapping deflects attention
from his impatience: "With this, as was his custom, he called
attention to the passage of time by regularly tapping on the
surface of the table" (D1 49).[41] In the description of Franz's

39. "Oskar M., ein älterer Student—wenn man ihn nahe ansah, erschrak man vor seinen Augen" (T 45).

40. "Er zwinkerte mit den Augen vor Nachdenken"; "So sehr hatte
er sich in Gedanken verlassen, dass er einmal die Mütze abnahm und
mit ihrem krausen Fell sich über das Gesicht strich" (T 45).

41. "Dabei machte er, wie es seine Gewohnheit war, durch regel-
mässiges Beklopfen der Tischplatte darauf aufmerksam, wie die Zeit
verging" (T 46).

landlady ("who because she was displeased by the visit walked aimlessly up and down in the anteroom" [D1 52])[42] the pacing would by itself indicate emotional distress; the explanation is superfluous and minimizes the detail.

Although Kafka relies heavily on dialogue in "The Urban World," the exchanges between the characters are awkward and lack the tension that would make them effective. For example, Oskar argues with Franz:

> "What I want of you. . . . Very little. I already told you what I want while I was still in the ante-room: that you get dressed."
>
> "If you want to point out by that, Oskar, that your news interests me very little, then you are quite right."
>
> "All the better. Then the interest my news will kindle in you will burn entirely on its own account, without our friendship adding to it." (D1 53–54)[43]

Kafka's failure to arouse interest by such wordy discussion contrasts sharply with his ability to create intense conflict in "The Judgment."

Comparison of "The Urban World" with Kafka's first mature prose work, "The Judgment," shows that the essential details of the latter were already present (in more obvious form) in the earlier sketch.[44] At the center of conflict in "The Judgment" is old Bendemann's belief that his son, Georg, wants him out of the way. In context, however, it is not possible to tell with any degree of certainty to what extent the father's belief is valid; the suggestion is presented with an ambiguity that threatens and amuses, albeit in a rather morbid way. In "The Urban

---

42. "Die aus Unzufriedenheit mit dem Besuch nutzlos im Vorzimmer auf und ab ging" (T 50).

43. " 'Was ich von dir will. . . . Sehr wenig. Ich habe es dir doch schon aus dem Vorzimmer gesagt: dass du dich anziehst.'

" 'Wenn du damit, Oskar, andeuten willst, dass mich deine Neuigkeit sehr wenig interessiert, so hast du ganz recht.'

" 'Das ist ja gut, so wird das Feuer, in das sie dich setzen wird, ganz auf ihre eigene Rechnung gehn, ohne dass sich unsere Freundschaft eingemischt hätte' " (T 51).

44. Such comparison is needed to provide proper perspective on "The Urban World." "The Judgment," however, merits the fuller treatment it will be given in Chapter 5 and will be discussed only briefly here.

World" this same theme, the son's wishing or driving his father to the grave is already present, but only on the literal level where it takes the form of a banal reproach, "Shame on such a son, who ... drives his old father to his grave!" (DI 48).[45]

The purely formal nature of the relationship between father and son in "The Judgment" is conveyed by an ironic description: nightly, Georg and his father sit side by side in their common living room, each buried in his own newspaper. In "The Urban World" the alienation between father and son is not merely suggested, but made explicit by the father's remark "At the moment I see nothing, ... for I got out of the habit of looking at you at all."[46]

Although the extreme power old Bendemann holds over his son is central to "The Judgment," it is revealed fully only at the end, when Georg actually carries out his father's command, death by drowning. Throughout the story, there is ample evidence to warn the reader that Georg's self-confidence is being deliberately undermined, but Georg himself remains unaware of the degree of his own vulnerability. In "The Urban World" the same theme, dependency of son on father, occurs; but Oskar, unlike Georg, is to some extent aware of his own weakness. He describes a hypothetical situation which clearly resembles his own and exclaims: "If [in response to Oskar's idea for his dissertation] with your venerable voice you had then thrown into my face the reproaches you did, my idea would simply have been blown away and I should have had to march off at once with some sort of apology or without one" (DI 50).[47] Although Oskar believes—perhaps erroneously—that the danger is past ("Now, just the contrary!"),[48] his awareness acts as a psychological safeguard and minimizes the effectiveness of this detail as a literary device.

45. "Pfui über einen solchen Sohn, der ... seinen alten Vater ins Grab drängt" (T 45–46).

46. "Ich sehe vorläufig nichts, . . . denn ich bin aus der Übung gekommen, dich überhaupt anzusehn" (T 46).

47. "Wenn du daraufhin mit deiner ehrwürdigen Stimme die Vorwürfe von vorhin mir ins Gesicht gesagt hättest, dann wäre mein Einfall einfach weggeblasen gewesen, und ich hätte sofort mit irgendeiner Entschuldigung oder ohne solche abmarschieren müssen" (T 47).

48. "Jetzt dagegen!"

In "The Judgment" the father ominously foreshadows his son's death by the strange directive "and while you're answering me be you still my living son" (*PC* 60).[49] This casual remark suggests hidden danger which reverberates through the remainder of the narrative. This detail was also already present in "The Urban World," where it occurs as a simple statement of fact: "But after all you *are* my son" (*D1* 49; italics mine).[50] Oskar undermines the father's hold over him by calling on his father's moral scruples: 'Leave me alone now.... The bare possibility that you can correctly predict my end should really not induce you to disturb me in my reflections. Perhaps my past gives you the right to do so, but you should not make use of it" (*D1* 50).[51]

In "The Judgment" the father becomes a demonic figure endowed by Georg with the strength of a god and the power of a judge. In "The Urban World" Oskar also distorts his father's image; he announces accusingly: "This is not my father who speaks to me in this way.... Something has happened to you since noon, or you are a stranger whom I now encounter for the first time in my father's room."[52] By admitting openly that he no longer recognizes him, Oskar restores the father to more normal proportions and renders him harmless.

The ambiguous ending of "The Judgment"—Georg's carrying out of his father's judgment while uttering a declaration of innocence, "Dear parents, but I have always loved you"[53]—is essential to the story; Georg *is* both innocent and guilty. Oskar, in "The Urban World," also pleads both guilt and innocence:

49. "Und für den Augenblick der Antwort sei du noch mein lebender Sohn" (*E* 65).

50. "Aber schliesslich bist du mein Sohn" (*T* 46).

51. "Lass mich jetzt. . . . Die blosse Möglichkeit, dass du mein Ende richtig voraussagen kannst, sollte dich wahrhaftig nicht dazu verlocken, mich in meiner guten Überlegung zu stören. Vielleicht gibt dir meine Vergangenheit das Recht dazu, aber du solltest es nicht ausnützen" (*T* 48).

52. "Das ist ja nicht mein Vater, der so mit mir spricht. . . . Es ist seit Mittag etwas mit dir vorgegangen oder du bist ein fremder Mensch, dem ich jetzt zum erstenmal im Zimmer meines Vaters begegne" (*T* 49).

53. "Liebe Eltern, ich habe euch doch immer geliebt" (*E* 68).

"Inwardly I was always a good son, but the fact that I could not show it outwardly embittered me so, that I preferred to vex you if I couldn't make you happy" (*Di* 48–49).[54] But this wordy explanation of Oskar's behavior is not effective enough to carry the force of a confession, and although it occurs early in the story, the author does not build upon it. Instead, he simply lets it drop.

The character of the friend provides another important point of comparison. Franz in "The Urban World" is virtually a sketch for the figure of the friend in "The Judgment." Although in the latter work the friend never appears in person, he is essential to the struggle between father and son.[55] Moreover, the unresolved uncertainty surrounding his existence—"Do you really have this friend in . . . Petersburg?" the father asks (*PC* 56)[56]—is integral to the ambiguity and complexity of "The Judgment." In contrast, in "The Urban World" there is no doubt surrounding the friend: Franz exists on the same level of reality as Oskar and the father. There is nothing in him or in his relationship to Oskar to suggest that he is to take on any symbolic significance. He is therefore less effective as a character and less interesting than Georg's "friend in Russia."

The greater effectiveness of "The Judgment" stems from the hidden quality of its details: what is made explicit in "The Urban World" lies beneath the surface of "The Judgment." Where "The Judgment" suggests a psychology and underlying motivation for each of the characters by hints and indirection, "The Urban World" lays bare and explains; in the latter the conflict is entirely on the surface and the characters are fully aware of their own, as well as of each other's, weaknesses. "The Urban World" completely lacks that sense of mystery and irony which is associated with the dramatic and which forms the basis of Kafka's method in "The Judgment." Thus we may view "The Urban World" as a work of transition, with its dramatic methods still somewhat clumsy and inconsistent, with a

54. "In meinem Innern war ich immer ein guter Sohn, nur dass ich es nach aussen nicht zeigen konnte, verbitterte mich so, dass ich dich lieber ärgerte, wenn ich dich schon nicht erfreuen konnte" (*T* 46).

55. See *Fe* 396–97 and *Di* 278; *T* 296.

56. "Hast du wirklich diesen Freund in Petersburg?" (*E* 60).

degree of self-consciousness in Kafka's use of gesture that distracts and disturbs.

The "breakthrough" came in the time separating "The Judgment" from "The Urban World"; Kafka learned to control his material with greater precision. And, of course, the year and a half between the writing of these two stories is also the period of Kafka's intense involvement with the Yiddish theater. The coming change of style, although discernable to some degree in "The Urban World," is fully reflected in "The Judgment," the work that directly follows the theater experience.

chapter five

First impact of the Yiddish theater: "The judgment" (1912)

"The Judgment," written in a single sitting on the night of September 22/23, 1912, is the first of Kafka's mature prose works because it presents a convincing, self-enclosed fictional world in which fully realized characters engage in conflict. Obvious parallels between the bachelor-hero and the author of the story have caused many critics to connect the theme of "The Judgment" to Kafka's personal life, and there is no doubt some validity in this observation.[1] There are, however, textual reasons to doubt that personal events provide full explanation for the changes in Kafka's style. Moreover, it was precisely in the period 1910–12, in the years just preceding his meeting with Felice Bauer and the writing of "The Judgment," that Kafka was most actively searching for his style.[2] These years of literary experimentation exactly coin-

1. Kafka invited biographical speculation himself by linking "The Judgment" to Felice Bauer in the *Diaries* (*D1* 279; *T* 297) and especially in the *Letters to Felice* (*Fe* 53, 144, 156 f., 162, 298, 394, 396 f., 419, 435), where he repeatedly refers to "The Judgment" as "your little story."

2. The *Diaries* for these years include not only descriptions of the difficulties Kafka experienced in developing his style, but also variant versions of prose pieces which illustrate these difficulties. There are, for example, six versions of the essay beginning "When I think about it, I must say that my education has done me great harm in some respects" ("Wenn ich es bedenke, so muss ich sagen, dass mir meine Erziehung in mancher Richtung sehr geschadet hat" [*D1* 14–22; *T* 14–16]) and three versions of the prose piece " 'You,' I said and gave him a little shove with my knee" (" 'Du', sagte ich und gab ihm einen kleinen Stoss mit dem Knie" [*D1* 22–29, 40; *T* 17–24, 36]). The German edition includes only three versions of "When I think about it" and only two of " 'You,' I said." All versions are included in the English.

70

cide with Kafka's intense interest in the Yiddish theater, and echoes of the Yiddish plays, present in much of Kafka's work, are particularly insistent in "The Judgment," the first work which Kafka himself considered successful.[3] Parallels in theme, details of plot and structure, and devices of characterization strongly suggest that three of the Yiddish plays—Yakov Gordin's *God, Man, and Devil* and *The Savage One* and Avraham Sharkanski's *Kol Nidre*—provided sources for a number of significant elements in "The Judgment."

Since Kafka went frequently to the "theater of the Jews," and since the Yiddish actors performed a small, set number of plays, repeated at intervals, we can assume that Kafka saw each of the plays in the repertoire a number of times. In addition to seeing actual performances, Kafka mentions hearing private readings of these plays by his friend, the actor Yitskhok Levi. On October 16, 1911, Kafka records:

> Thursday. All afternoon yesterday Levi read from *Gott, Mensch, Teufel* by Gordin and then from his own Paris diaries. The day before yesterday I saw the performance of *Der Wilde Mensch* by Gordin. Gordin is better than Lateiner, Scharkansky, Feimann, etc., because he has more detail, more order and more logical sequence in this order. (*Di* 111–12)[4]

The detail, order, and logical sequence within that order which Kafka admired in Gordin's plays are qualities characteristic of Kafka's own work, particularly "The Judgment." It is our perception of inner order in the story that convinces us of the necessity of all its actions.

The plays of Gordin clearly made a strong impression on Kafka, and he rightly judged Gordin superior to the other playwrights of the Yiddish theater. Gordin was by far the best

3. "Only *in this way* can writing be done" ("*Nur so* kann geschrieben werden" [*Di* 276; *T* 294]) he says of the writing of the story.

4. "Donnerstag. Gestern hat Löwy den ganzen Nachmittag 'Gott, Mensch, Teufel' von Gordin und dann aus seinen eigenen Tagebüchern von Paris vorgelesen. Vorgestern war ich bei der Aufführung des 'Wilden Menschen' von Gordin. Gordin ist deshalb besser als Lateiner, Scharkansky, Feimann usw., weil er mehr Details mehr Ordnung und mehr Folgerichtigkeit in dieser Ordnung hat" (*T* 116).

dramatist writing for the Yiddish theater at the turn of the century, and *God, Man, and Devil* is one of his finest works.[5] Like
most of Gordin's plays, it is in the tradition of dramatic realism,
although the plot includes the supernatural.[6] *God, Man, and
Devil* is the story of Hershele Dubrovner, a poor but virtuous
Torah scribe whose essential purity is challenged by the Devil.
In a dispute with God concerning the true nature of man,
Satan convinces God to let him tempt Hershele. In the figure
of Uriel Mazik, Satan comes to Hershele and offers to make
him rich, while seducing him with ideas of freedom. At first
Hershele resists, but at the insistence of family and friends, he
finally accepts Mazik's offer. At this point Mazik slyly suggests
that Hershele divorce his wife (by whom he has had no children) and take in her place his beautiful young niece Freydeniu, whom he has raised as his own child. This idea, at first
shocking to Hershele, takes root, and Hershele accomplishes
the marital change. After the marriage, he begins to indulge in
the worldly pleasures he had previously shunned and to show
increasingly less respect towards his aged father (a retired
jester), who shares his home. When Mazik and Hershele go
into partnership, Mazik literally moves in with Hershele, and
together they prosper. The wealthier Hershele becomes, the
more obsessed he grows with money: isolating himself from
family and friends, he grows ever closer to Mazik. Three years
after the new marriage Hershele has boarded out his father
(whom he once honored excessively), neglected his young
wife, ruined his best friend Khatskel, and forced Khatskel's son
to work the machines in his factory. His obsession with money
culminates in a vicious fight during which he attempts to kill

5. This play has remained popular on the Yiddish stage. It was produced in Yiddish in New York in 1919 and revived in 1958. Translations
exist in Russian, Polish, Hebrew, and Ukranian. Part of the play was
translated anonymously into German under the title *Geld* (Money) and
a synopsis of the plot with a translation of the prologue exists in English.
See Zilbertsvayg, *Leksikon fun Yidishn Teater*, 1 : 419.

6. Gordin borrows the theme of Goethe's *Faust*, transforming Faustus
into Hershele, a pious Jew, and Mephistopheles into Mazik, a "sharp"
operator.

Mazik, but succeeds only in wounding him. Soon after, Hershele is witness to a severe accident in his factory in which his friend Khatskel's son loses an arm. Spattered with blood, Hershele hears the terrible shrieks of pain and begins to be afraid. A direct confrontation between Hershele and Khatskel occurs near the end of the play when Hershele learns of the death of Khatskel's son (who died as a result of the accident) and automatically pronounces the traditional blessing "Blessed be the True Judge" ("Barukh Dayan Emet"). Khatskel is surprised to hear Hershele repeat these words, and he asks whether Hershele really still believes in the True Judge. Whn Hershele answers yes, Khatskel challenges him: does he really believe that he will ever be able to settle his account with him, a mere man, let alone with God? Hershele is taken aback by this attack; but Khatskel shows Hershele how he himself is responsible for the suffering of many innocent people, and especially for the death of Khatskel's son, who was killed in his factory by his machines. The theme of the ultimate judgment of man is now clearly stated, and it remains dominant until the end of the play. Left alone, Hershele broods about his condition. In his despair, God's prayers come back to him, and he fully recognizes and accepts his own guilt. With the blood-soaked prayer shawl of the dead son, he carries out his friend's (and by implication God's) judgment and hangs himself. When his body is discovered, Mazik comments that even the power of money seems limited, for although he had been able to cripple, seduce, and spoil Hershele, he had not been able totally to annihilate the human spirit within him. Mazik admits that he has lost his wager, and the play ends on a note of affirmation: Hershele's death is followed by the blowing of the *shofar*, the ram's horn which signals the presence of God. The choral odes affirm the harmony of the universe. The play, which opens with a picture of an ordered universe, moves through disorder on earth (Mazik's temporary corruption of Hershele) and ends with a reaffirmation of this order (symbolized by Hershele's return to God).

God, Man, and Devil is written in four acts with a prologue. The prologue presents the larger world view in whose context the story of Hershele Dubrovner must be understood—a picture of cosmic order in which even Satan has his proper place. The nature of this order is proclaimed by God and repeated by the choruses of young and old angels, who affirm the continuity of life and the inevitability of death, and link continual striving with living. Because these choruses open and close the play, they provide a literal as well as a moral frame for the action.

Like *God, Man, and Devil,* "The Judgment" depicts the fall of a good man, but unlike the play, the story does not provide an external framework of beliefs to guide us in interpreting the work. "The Judgment" is the story of Georg Bendemann, a young man recently engaged to be married who, after much deliberation, has decided to send word of his engagement to an old friend in Russia. This friend is as yet totally unaware of the many favorable changes of a business and personal nature that have taken place in Georg's circumstances since his last visit home. Georg comes to his father bearing the letter that tells the friend of his engagement. The father responds by insisting that the son is not telling the full truth about himself and by challenging the existence of the friend. At first Georg tries to reason with his father, but as the father becomes more insistent, Georg loses control. The father levels a series of accusations at his son, implying that he has changed since the death of his mother, charging him with not being serious, wanting to get rid of him, disgracing the memory of his mother, giving in to lust, betraying his friend, feeling self-important, and acting only in self-interest. In his tirades the father eventually reverses himself and not only admits to knowing the friend, but insists that he has been writing to him all along, and that, in fact, he represents the friend on the spot. These grotesque accusations culminate in the father's judgment of his son, whom he condemns to death by drowning. The story ends with the son's immediate execution of his father's judgment.

While most critics readily accord "The Judgment" an important place in Kafka's literary development, they dispute its symbolic significance.[7] None of the standard approaches to

7. The most important interpretations of "The Judgment" are the following: Binder, *Motiv und Gestaltung,* pp. 125–35; Edmund Edel, "Franz

Kafka's work—the biographical (Flores, Marson), psychoana-
lytical (Falke, Greenberg, Neider), theological (Tauber,
Steinberg), mythic (Ruhleder, Weinberg), literal (Magny), or
the combination of such approaches (Politzer, Sokel)—yields
a wholly satisfying reading. The recent contextual explications
of White and Pondrom best account for the difficulties of the
story without violating the text: the friend in Russia exists symbolically for both father and son as an objectification of the
withdrawn part of Georg which could never contemplate marriage and with which Georg is trying to come to terms. Not
only is Georg a damaged person, but so is his father, for he
knows his son's weakness and cruelly capitalizes on it. This father is no more ready to accept an adult son than Georg is able
to accept adult responsibility. The story is told through the
eyes of Georg; the judgment represents Georg's judgment of
himself and of how he imagines society and parental authority
would judge him. His suicide may be taken either as Georg's
acceptance of guilt, or as his recognition of the impossibility of
resolving his conflicts within himself or with his father.[8]

Kafka: 'Das Urteil,' " WW 9 (1959): 216–25; Rita Falke, "Biographisch-
Literarische Hintergründe von Kafka's 'Urteil,' " GRM 10 (1960): 164–
80; M[arvin] F[elheim], "The Judgment," in Study Aids for Teachers
for Modern Stories, ed. M. Felheim, F. B. Newman, and W. R. Steinhoff
(New York, 1951), pp. 36–39; Kate Flores, "The Judgment," in Franz
Kafka Today, ed. Flores and Swander, pp. 5–24; Martin Greenberg,
"The Literature of Truth: Kafka's 'Judgment,' " Salmagundi 1 (Fall
1965): 4–22; Claude-Edmonde Magny, "The Objective Depiction of
Absurdity," in The Kafka Problem, ed. Angel Flores (New York, 1946),
pp. 75–96; E. L. Marson, "Franz Kafka's 'Das Urteil,' " AUMLA, no.
16 (1961), pp. 167–78; Charles Neider, "The Shorter Fiction," The Frozen
Sea: A Study of Franz Kafka (New York, 1948), pp. 71–86; Politzer,
Parable and Paradox, pp. 53–65; Cyrena Norman Pondrom, "The Coherence in Kafka's 'Das Urteil': Georg's View of the World," SSF (in
press); Karl H. Ruhleder, "Franz Kafka's 'Das Urteil': An Interpretation," Monatshefte 55 (1963): 13–22; Sokel, Tragik und Ironie, pp.
44–76; Erwin R. Steinberg, "The Judgment in Kafka's 'The Judgment,' "
MFS 8 (1962): 23–30; Tauber, Franz Kafka, pp. 12–17; Kurt Weinberg,
Kafkas Dichtungen: Die Travestien des Mythos (Bern, 1963), pp. 318–
50; John J. White, " 'Das Urteil': An Interpretation," DVLG 38 (1964):
208–29.

8. Substantiation for this interpretation may be found in Pondrom's
essay.

Much of the action of "The Judgment" is sensational and
grossly exaggerated. If we recognize that many of the elements
of this story really are theatrical—that is, that they are literally
taken over from the theater—then we will have a better grasp
of Kafka's technique in the story. The first act of *God, Man,
and Devil* ends in a good-humored disorder which foreshadows the spiritual chaos to come. Mazik's arrival and offer of
money has thrown the little circle into confusion, and one of
the results is that the father, who ordinarily limits his wine sip-
ping, has become tipsy and a little silly. Still showing the
greatest respect and concern for his father, Hershele begs his
father not to disgrace himself in his old age and to retire. The
father, however, has lost self-control and pays his son no heed.
Hershele is terribly embarrassed for his father and feels
obliged to take action. Apologetically, he picks up his father
and carries him off to bed.

> HERSHELE: Dear Father, take care, go to bed, I beg you.
> LEYZER: No! No! (*Sings.*) He's on his way, to get some hay...
> HERSHELE: Don't take it amiss, dear Father, I don't want to be
>   disrespectful. Quite the contrary, heaven forbid you should suf-
>   fer any disgrace. (*Hershele picks him up and carries him.*)
> LEYZER (*kicks his feet and shouts*): No! No! Let me be! He's on
>   his way to get some hay...[9]

This scene has its direct parallel in "The Judgment." From
the beginning Georg's father has acted peculiarly. Instead of
commenting on Georg's decision, he asks Georg to tell him the
truth, to admit that he does not have this friend in Petersburg.
Georg's reaction, like Hershele's, is one of embarrassment:

9. "HERSHELE: Tateniu, zay zikh matrikh, gey tsu zikh, ikh bet dikh.
    "LEYZER: Neyn! Neyn! (*Zingt.*) Iz er gegangen tsu derlangen...
    "HERSHELE: Hob kayn feroybel nit, tateniu, ikh vil dir khulile nit
        puge bekoved zayn. Farkert, du zolst khulile nit laydn kayn
        b'ziunut. (*Nemt im oyf di hent un trogt im.*)
    "LEYZER (*driget mit di fis un shrayt*): Neyn! Neyn! Lo mikh ob!
        Iz er gegangen tsu derlangen..." (*GMT* 34)
My translation of the father's ditty captures the rhythm and flavor but
not the exact meaning of his song. He is singing a trivial song which
translates literally as "He went to give [himself a bit of liquid from the
bottle]."

"Georg rose in embarrassment" (*PC* 56).[10] Twice Georg reasons with his father, twice Hershele asks his father to retire. Twice Georg's father repeats his accusation, twice the old jester sings his ditty. As in *God, Man, and Devil* the exchange in "The Judgment" ends with the son bodily picking up his father and carrying him to bed ("He carried his father to bed in his arms" [*PC* 58]).[11] While Hershele's father kicks his legs and shouts "No! No!" old Bendemann makes it difficult for Georg by clutching Georg's watch chain. The structure of the two scenes and their functions within their respective works are essentially the same: the son takes charge of an awkward situation by literally carrying the father to bed, where the old and foolish belong.

Another theatrical incident occurs in act 2 of *God, Man, and Devil* when, in order to amuse his niece and to relive his days of triumph, the old father jumps onto a chair and begins to declaim in the traditional mock-serious tone of the wedding jester. He describes marriage as the end of carefree youth and warns of the strangers who will take the bride from her loving parents. At first the niece joins in the charade and pretends to cry, but as the old man becomes more convincing, she begins to weep in earnest. What begins as a joke, she takes seriously. A surprisingly similar incident occurs in "The Judgment" when the father jumps onto the bed and begins to declaim to his son. The father's actions are grossly theatrical: he wags his finger and waves his arm over his head, he lifts his nightgown and kicks his legs. His speech is exaggerated and his manner is melodramatic. (It is at this point that Georg calls him "comedian" [*Komödiant*].) The difference in the two scenes is that in *God, Man, and Devil* Hershele's wife enters and breaks the spell. She speaks with the voice of reason and common sense: "Oy, father-in-law dear, what you can think of! (*The old man is frightened and seats himself in the corner.*) Just look, *he* makes jokes and *she* weeps. (*She wipes the niece's tears.*) Foolish child!"[12] In "The Judgment" there is no other character

10. "Georg stand verlegen auf" (*E* 60).
11. "Auf seinen Armen trug er den Vater ins Bett" (*E* 63).
12. "Oy, shver lebn, vos aykh ken aynfaln! (*Leyzer dershrekt zikh un*

to break the spell, and Georg continues to take his father's ti-
rade in deadly earnest. Kafka's narrative presents a self-enclosed world in which the characters are totally absorbed in
their roles, and in which there is no commonsense perspective
by which we can interpret the action.

Although the complex plot of *God, Man, and Devil* may
seem far removed from the stark simplicity of the action of
"The Judgment," many of the more bizarre elements in Kafka's
story correspond strikingly to the details of Gordin's play. Most
basic are the structural similarities. Both *God, Man, and Devil*
and "The Judgment" build up to a scene of accusation and
judgment, followed by the self-inflicted death of the hero,
whose demise marks a return to order. In both works the hero
is a son whose relationship with his father is an important focus of attention; in both the accusation concerns a major
change in the hero which takes the form of self-indulgence and
is associated with sudden financial success.

The specific details of the accusations in the two works are
extremely close: Hershele is accused of abandoning his father,
Georg of wanting to be rid of his. Hershele is condemned for
isolating himself in business affairs, Georg for holding himself
aloof and hiding in business. Hershele is blamed for shaming
his wife (by his obvious sexual interest in his niece), Georg is
charged with disgracing the memory of his mother (presumably by his sexual desire for Frieda). Both are accused of betraying a friend. Finally, in a parallel that is closer in spirit
than in detail, Khatskel holds Hershele responsible for the
death of his son; the father denounces Georg for being a "devilish" person.

While some of these points coincide exactly, others correspond only in essence. The death of Georg's mother functions
as a parallel to Hershele's divorce; both result in the achieve-
ment of sexual satisfaction for the son and lead to his entrange-
ment from father and friend. Before the divorce Hershele
would not have allowed himself even to look at a girl (Ortho-

---

zetst sikh in vinkele.) Ze nor, *der shver* makht khoyzik un *zi* veynt.
(*Visht ir ob di trern.*) Narele!" (*GMT* 37–38; italics in dialogue mine).

dox Jewish law forbids it), let alone indulge in sexual pleasure. There is a parallel suggestion in "The Judgment" (made evident in the association of Georg's success with the death of his mother) that Georg would not have allowed himself to become engaged while his mother was alive.[13] The anticipated match between Hershele's niece and Khatskel's son (which provides an important subsidiary theme in God, Man, and Devil) parallels the theme of engagement in "The Judgment." Hershele, halfway in age between his father and his niece, literally takes the niece away from the younger man, an act which brings to mind old Bendemann's threat to "sweep" Georg's fiancée from his side.

The merging of the innocent with the devilish, central to the father's charge against Georg ("In truth, you were an innocent child, but in greater truth you were a devilish human being"),[14] corresponds to the literal partnership formed between Hershele and Mazik, Torah scribe and Devil. The dark opinion of man inherent in Bendemann's charge parallels Mazik's view of man as essentially corrupt.[15] Like Mazik, Bendemann seems to suggest that to be human is to be demonic.

While it is easy to identify the betrayal in God, Man, and Devil—Hershele deliberately drives Khatskel into bankruptcy— it is more difficult to isolate its source in "The Judgment." Some critics suggest that Georg is betraying the friend's bache-

13. This inability, linked with Georg's fear and hatred of the father, suggests the Oedipal nature of the basic family relationship. Sokel (Tragik und Ironie, p. 75), Falke ("Hintergründe," p. 173), and Pondrom ("Coherence in 'Das Urteil' ") develop this point in greater detail.

14. "Ein unschuldiges Kind warst du ja eigentlich, aber noch eigentlicher warst du ein teuflischer Mensch!" (E 67).

15. Mazik tells God: "Their spirit strives high and still they are sunk in the dirt and mire of their material life. . . . Outwardly they have bettered and beautified themselves, but inwardly they have become even more crippled and spoiled; in the newly-cultured man sits the old wild Adam." ("Zeyr gayst shtrebt hoykh un dokh zaynen zey zer tif ferzunkn inem shmuts un koym fun zeyr materialn lebn. . . . Fun oysvenig hobn zey zikh zeyr fil ferbesert un fershenert, un fun iniveynig zaynen zey nokh mer fardorbn und ferkripelt; in dem nay-gebildetn mentshn zitst der alter vilde Adam" [GMT 7].)

lorhood by becoming engaged, others that he is betraying his purity by becoming involved in business.[16] In either case, the ambiguous suggestion of betrayal in "The Judgment" corresponds to the real situation in *God, Man, and Devil*, although it is possible to guess what Bendemann has in mind: Georg's proposed marriage, his success in business, and his determination to live a normal bourgeois life.

In contrast to *God, Man, and Devil*, which leaves no doubt that the friend was right to recall Hershele to his former self (a norm of decency from which Hershele has grossly deviated), "The Judgment" ends in ambiguity. Neither the biased father, nor the withdrawn friend, nor the egotistical, immature Georg can serve as a valid norm of human behavior. While Hershele is morally and literally in the wrong, Georg is judged wrong for actions that are essentially natural and normal.

Nonetheless, the father in "The Judgment" and the father in Gordin's play share several significant traits, particularly their propensity for comic antics. The comic attributes of Hershele's father may help to explain some of the peculiarities of the father in "The Judgment." In *God, Man, and Devil* the father's age is given as seventy (considered old age in nineteenth-century Europe). His profession is considered so significant a part of his character that it is included in his name, Leyzer Badkhan, for *Badkhan* means "jester" or "fool." In the play his stock-in-trade is whispering foolish secrets into people's ears. He likes wine, and when he drinks, his foolishness increases. Through most of the play he is looking for rhymes, singing foolish little ditties, and telling silly secrets, even on inappropriate occasions. It is difficult to separate his role as jester from the suggestion that he is slightly senile. His decision to hide behind his jesting in order to protect himself is certainly lucid, and in general, the comic aspects of his character seem intended more to reflect the remnants of his profession than to

16. The former suggestion is made by Politzer, *Parable and Paradox*, p. 58, and by Sokel, *Tragik und Ironie*, p. 50. In regard to the latter, White, in " 'Das Urteil,' " relates the friend to the realm of the absolute, Georg to the empirical world.

signify senility. Both are suggested, however, and one cannot always clearly separate the two possibilities. This fusion of Leyzer Badkhan's joking and hiding behind senility, while at the same time speaking the truth, may be reflected in the figure of the father in "The Judgment," who has been variously judged insane, senile,[17] or just playing games.[18] In "The Judgment" it is extremely difficult to tell to what extent the father is playing some vast, diabolical joke, to what extent he is earnest, and to what extent his image is distorted by Georg's perception of him.

Early in the play the old father confesses that he fears his son: "[*Whispering*] ... with me it is not as with all people. (*Aloud.*) With other people a son has respect for his father, but I fear Hershele.... Outwardly I am a hero, but I fear him; with my mouth I jest, but I don't feel just right."[19] He especially fears that Hershele will throw him out. Like Leyzer Badkhan, old Bendemann acts the hero, but it is clear that he feels threatened by his son's success in business and is resentful of his engagement. Leyzer admits to feeling inadequate in Hershele's presence. "I am a small person and he squashes me with his learning.... When he is here, Leyzer Badkhan becomes two inches smaller than he really is.... And now, since he has become a wealthy man, when he looks at me with his cold, hard eyes, I get a funny feeling in my shoulder."[20] Old Bendemann also describes himself as feeling squashed by a son who prides himself in his importance. He plays on the word *unterkriegen* ("to conquer," or "to get the better of"), making the metaphor

17. Magny, "Depiction of Absurdity," in *The Kafka Problem*, ed. Flores, p. 84.

18. Neider, *The Frozen Sea*, p. 75.

19. "[*Shtilerheyt*] ... bay mir iz nit vi bay ale mentshn. (*Loyt.*) Bay laytn hot a zun derkherts far a tatn un ikh hob moyre far Hersheniu.... Klumarsht ikh bin a held, ober ikh shrek zikh far im. Mitn moyl badkhn ikh zikh, ober ikh fil zikh gor nit peysakhdik" (*GMT* 36).

20. "Ikh bin a kleyn mentshele un er tsukvetsht mikh mit zayn lomdes.... Az er iz do, vert Leyzer Badkhan nokh mit tsvey vershkes klener vi er iz.... Un itst, zind er iz gevorn a nagid, ven er git a kuk oyf mir mit zayne kalte [f]ertrakhte oygn, hoybt mir on kitseln in der patilnitse" (*GMT* 36).

almost literal: "And now ... you thought you'd got him down
[conquered him], so far down that you could set your bottom
on him and sit on him and he wouldn't move" (*PC* 59).[21]

In *God, Man, and Devil* the rejection that the old father
fears comes to pass; by the end of the play he is literally
boarded out to strangers. In "The Judgment" such rejection
does not become fact, but there are hints in the text that Bendemann's fears were not totally unfounded.[22] It is the father's

21. "Wie du jetzt geglaubt hast, du hättest ihn untergekriegt, so
untergekriegt, dass du dich mit deinem Hintern auf ihn setzen kannst
und er rührt sich nicht" (*E* 64).

I think Sokel is mistaken in seeing the friend in Russia, rather than
the father, as antecedent of "ihn" in this passage, although the reference
is somewhat ambiguous. *Untergekriegt* is an extension of the verb *zugedeckt* ("covered up") which the father used only ten lines before to
describe himself: "But I'm far from being covered up yet" ("aber
zugedeckt bin ich noch nicht" [*PC* 59; *E* 63]). Thus Bendemann accuses Georg of deciding to marry when he thought his father could not
move. Two paragraphs later, the father repeats his charge, and in this
context there is no ambiguity: "You have . . . betrayed your friend and
stuck your father into bed so that he can't move. But he can move, or
can't he?" ("Hast du . . . den Freund verraten und deinen Vater ins
Bett gesteckt, damit er sich nicht rühren kann. Aber kann er sich rühren
oder nicht?" [*PC* 60; *E* 64]). The repetition of the phrase "can't move"
("sich nicht rühren") further suggests that the father is referring to his own
supposed subjugation, and not the friend's in all three instances.

In trying to make "The Judgment" reflect a general pattern in Kafka's
work, Sokel distorts the nature of the conflict (which is basically an
internal one) and goes so far as to suggest that Georg is using the
fiancée as a weapon in the struggle against the friend and that Georg
does not want to come to terms with the friend. Sokel's statement "The
friend is combined with a suppressed part of Georg's existence" agrees
with my interpretation, however. See Sokel, *Tragik und Ironie*, p. 48.

22. Georg had, in fact, planned to leave his father alone in the apartment when he married and moved to his own house: "He had not yet
explicitly discussed with his bride-to-be what arrangements should be
made for his father in the future, for they had both of them silently
taken it for granted that the old man would go on living alone in the old
house" ("Er hatte mit seiner Braut darüber, wie sie die Zukunft des
Vaters einrichten wollten, noch nicht ausdrücklich gesprochen, denn sie
hatten stillschweigend vorausgesetzt, dass der Vater allein in der alten
Wohnung bleiben würde" [*PC* 58; *E* 62]).

fear of such rejection that accounts, at least in part, for the vehemence of his attack.

The link between father and friend that comes as such a shock to Georg also has its parallel in *God, Man, and Devil*, where father and friend are literally linked.[23] Throughout the play it becomes increasingly clearer that Leyzer is far more comfortable with his son's friend Khatskel (the "simple" person, as he calls himself) than with his own son. Old Leyzer's genuine preference for the friend corresponds to Bendemann's calculatedly stinging words to Georg: "He [the friend] would have been a son after my own heart" (*PC* 59).[24]

The verdict in "The Judgment" resembles the divulging of a great secret, much like the old jester's habit of telling secrets in *God, Man, and Devil*. The jester steps out of his comic role only once, to announce the death of Khatskel's son: "For the first time in my life it falls on me to tell a secret which will not make anyone laugh."[25] In analyzing Georg's behavior, old Bendemann, like the father in the play, reveals a secret (which Georg has hidden even from himself) and which is not in the least funny. In another parallel, both fathers pride themselves on their ability to see through their sons' motives. "The eye of the jester saw that long ago!" is Leyzer's response to Hershele's plan to remarry.[26] "But fortunately no one has to teach a father to see through his son," Bendemann boasts.[27]

In both works some play on time is associated with the old father, whose time is past. Leyzer's favorite jest, repeated on several occasions, consists of calling someone aside and whispering in a serious tone, "What time is it?" In "The Judgment" the father refuses to let go of Georg's watch chain, and he uses an old newspaper (*Zeitung*) as a surprise weapon against his

---

23. The old father, the divorced wife, and Hershele's friend form a little group from which Hershele is excluded.

24. "Er wäre ein Sohn nach meinem Herzen" (*E* 63).

25. "Tsum ershtn mol in mayn lebn kumt es mir oys tsu zogn a sod, fun velkhn me vet nit lakhn" (*GMT* 97).

26. "Dem badkhans oyg hot dos lang gezen!" (*GMT* 55).

27. "Aber den Vater muss glücklicherweise niemand lehren, den Sohn zu durchschauen" (*E* 64).

son.[28] Both works reflect the natural pattern of life dictated by time, the inevitable rise and fall of generations. But, whereas old Leyzer is understandably saddened by the waning of his powers, old Bendemann refuses to accept the reversal of roles; he interprets Georg's success as usurpation of power and fights to maintain a position of superiority over his son. "I am still much the stronger," he boasts (PC 61).[29]

The two central characters, Hershele and Georg, are also represented in similar fashion in these works: each is characterized by two antithetical personalities. In *God, Man, and Devil* there is Hershele the Torah scribe and Hershele the wealthy manufacturer; in "The Judgment" there is the withdrawn Georg (as he was before the death of the mother and again after his collapse in the quarrel with his father) and Georg the man of business. The withdrawn Georg, symbolized by the friend in Russia whose business is stagnating and who remains out of touch with the world around him, parallels the pious, childless, ascetic Hershele of the first act of *God, Man, and Devil*.[30] The second Georg, the successful young merchant about to be married, parallels the business-oriented, worldly Hershele of the second and third acts. The friend in Russia (the withdrawn Georg) and the pious Hershele are characterized as impractical men who have no understanding of busi-

28. The watch chain is mentioned by Flores, "The Judgment," in *Franz Kafka Today*, ed. Flores and Swander, p. 7, and by Politzer, *Parable and Paradox*, pp. 56–57; White, " 'Das Urteil,' " p. 220, connects the watch chain (*Uhrkette*) to the newspaper (*Zeitung*). Watches (*Uhren*) may also be a symbol of pride in bourgeois respectability; Kafka remarks of one of the comic characters in the Yiddish plays, "the purse-proud alderman hung with watches" ("der protzige, mit Uhren behängte Gemeinderat" [*Di* 176; *T* 189]). This character, conspicuously displaying gold watches, also urges his son to put on several watches and chains to impress guests.

29. "Ich bin noch immer der viel Stärkere" (*E* 65).

30. If one accepts the interpretations of White (the friend as "absolute"), Sokel (the friend as "das reine Ich," "the pure self"), and Politzer (the friend as defender of "bachelor's purity"), the friend in Russia bears a striking resemblance to Hershele's better self, the pious Jew he was before Mazik's arrival.

ness affairs and who shun the pleasures of the flesh. Although in *God, Man, and Devil* this aspect of Hershele is praised, the friend in "The Judgment" is neither clearly positive nor negative; he objectifies only a part of Georg's personality and therefore should not be judged independently.

But Georg's friend in Russia corresponds not only to a part of Hershele's personality; he also has a literal counterpart in Hershele's friend Khatskel. The pattern of these friendships is the same. Hershele and Khatskel, like Georg and the friend in Russia, grew up together. Their lives, at first parallel, diverged when they reached adulthood. Hershele became a learned man and Torah scribe, Khatskel took a job as common laborer.[31] Georg remained at home, while the friend, dissatisfied with his possibilities at home, went to Russia. Later, Hershele became wealthy and took a new wife; Khatskel became jobless, fell into extreme poverty, and finally lost his only son. At first Georg and the friend succeeded equally well in business, but later, Georg's flourished while the friend's declined. Finally, Georg became engaged, and the friend turned into a permanent bachelor, ailing and alone. The contrast between the hero and his friend is the same in the two works. In both cases the hero seems to succeed where the friend fails. Yet, in the context of the action, it becomes apparent that this success is only illusory.[32]

In both works the attitude of the hero towards his friend is a mixture of pity and mild contempt. Hershele tells himself that Khatskel is to blame for his condition of poverty: "I took the trouble to learn about and understand life, he remained the

31. According to *shtetl* tradition, success is measured not in terms of money, but of learning. Therefore, from the beginning, Khatskel failed where Hershele succeeded.

32. Sokel speaks of Georg's success as illusory (*Scheinerfolge*) and as a facade (*Tragik und Ironie*, pp. 44, 48). We need to make the following qualification, however: Georg's success is illusory only in that he cannot sustain it; until his collapse, he was genuinely successful. Similarly, Hershele's earlier success as Torah scribe is not to be taken as illusory. In Gordin's universe, only the temptations of the material world are represented as empty illusions. In this, Gordin's world view resembles that of the medieval morality plays.

same plain Khatskel Drakhme."[33] Georg voices similar pride in comparing his own success to the meager accomplishments of the friend in Russia, whom he thinks of as "a big child" (*ein altes Kind*), someone "who had obviously run astray." There is also a strong similarity in the dreamlike condition of the heroes as they think about their repective friends. Hershele "remains seated, lost in thought" (*GMT* 74). Georg closes his letter "with playful slowness."[34] Hershele's thoughts about Khatskel follow an actual interview, during which it has become painfully clear that the two friends can no longer communicate. Khatskel verbalizes the rift: "I am a simple person and when you, Hershele, were a poor man I could still understand you. But now? I can't begin to understand you."[35] Is not this lack of understanding, this inability to communicate, precisely what Georg fears would come about were his friend to return home? "But if he [the friend] did follow their advice [to return home] and then didn't fit in . . . couldn't get on with his friends or without them, felt humiliated, couldn't be said to have either friends or a country of his own any longer . . .?" (*PC* 50).[36] What is offered as a vague, threatening possibility in "The Judgment" is fact in *God, Man, and Devil.*

33. "Ikh hob genumen die miye tsu lernen un tsu farshteyn dos lebn un er iz geblibn der zelber proster Khatskel Drakhme" (*GMT* 74).

34. "In spielerischer Langsamkeit" (*E* 53). I cannot agree with Sokel (*Tragik und Ironie,* p. 73), who interprets the word "playful" (*spielerisch*) in this context as evidence of Georg's lack of seriousness. There is no other textual evidence to make us doubt Georg's intentions toward his fiancée. His inability to carry out his plans for marriage is certainly no reason to question his sincerity. If Georg does not defend his fiancée to his father, it is perhaps because he feels overwhelmed by the old man. Pondrom's suggestion that the word *spielerisch* signals to us that we are about to witness an inner debate seems more consistent with the remainder of the text.

35. "Ikh bin a proster mentsh un ven du Reb Hershele bizt geven a oreman hob ikh dikh nokh gekont farshteyn. Ober itst? Ikh hoyb nit on tsu farshteyn" (*GMT* 73).

36. "Folgte er aber wirklich dem Rat und würde hier . . . niedergedrückt, fände sich nicht in seinen Freunden und nicht ohne sie zurecht, litte an Beschämung, hätte jetzt wirklich keine Heimat und keine Freunde mehr . . . ?" (*E* 54).

In his biography of Kafka, Brod suggested that the friend in
"The Judgment" is modelled on the Yiddish actor, Yitskhok
Levi (*FK* 114; *Bg* 140). This assertion is supported by a letter
to Felice of December 27/28, 1912, in which Kafka describes
Levi in similar tone and with the same words that he had applied to the friend in Russia in "The Judgment" three months
before. In the letter Kafka writes:

> In the meantime I have received several letters from [Levi].
> They are all the same and full of complaints; the poor man cannot
> be helped; now he travels back and forth between Leipzig and
> Berlin to no purpose. His earlier letters were entirely different,
> more lively and full of hope, perhaps the end is really near. You
> took him for a Czech; no, he is Russian.[37]

In "The Judgment" we find Georg thinking of his friend in
these terms:

> Now [the friend] was carrying on a business in Petersburg,
> which, though very promising in the beginning, seemed to have
> been stagnating for a long time already, as the friend . . . com-
> plained. So he was wearing himself out to no purpose in a for-
> eign country . . . , [his] yellow skin color seemed to indicate a
> developing illness. . . . What could one write to such a man, who
> had obviously run astray, whom one could pity, but not help.[38]

A slight tone of superiority, despite genuine concern, is not
quite suppressed in either letter or story. The similarities in de-

37. "Ich habe auch schon einige Briefe in der Zwischenzeit von ihm
bekommen. Sie sind alle einförmig und voll Klagen; dem armen
Menschen ist nicht zu helfen; nun fährt er immerfort nutzlos zwischen
Leipzig und Berlin hin und her. Seine frühern Briefe waren ganz anders,
viel lebhafter und hoffnungsvoller, es geht vielleicht wirklich mit ihm zu
Ende. Du hast ihn für einen Tschechen gehalten, nein, er ist Russe"
(*Fe* 213).

38. "Nun betrieb er ein Geschäft in Petersburg, das anfangs sich
sehr gut angelassen hatte, seit langem aber schon zu stocken schien, wie
der Freund . . . klagte. So arbeitete er sich in der Fremde nutzlos ab, . . .
dessen gelbe Hautfarbe auf eine sich entwickelnde Krankheit hinzudeu-
ten schien. . . . Was wollte man einem solchen Manne schreiben, der
sich offenbar verrant hatte, den man bedauern, dem man aber nicht
helfen konnte" (*E* 53).

tail are quite direct. Both men are bachelors living in foreign
countries. Levi's letters are said to be "full of complaints"; the
friend in Russia "complained." Levi "travels back and forth . . .
to no purpose"; the friend "was wearing himself out to no purpose." Levi's many maladies, which Kafka feared might kill
him, are paralleled by the friend's "yellow skin color" and "developing illness." Kafka's attitude toward Levi ("the poor man
cannot be helped") matches the narrator's feelings about the
friend ("such a man . . . whom one could . . . not help"). The
parallel continues into the sphere of business. In a later letter
to Felice, Kafka speaks of "Levi's childlike way of handling his
business. . . . It is an old story."³⁹ The friend in Russia is "a big
child" whose "business . . . seemed to have been stagnating for
a long time."

Kafka's awareness of Levi's Russian origin ("he is Russian")
may well account for his identifying the friend with Russia.⁴⁰
Levi's association with Russia was further emphasized by his
acting in the Yiddish plays, many of which were set in Russia.⁴¹
Since Levi usually took the lead role, it is likely that it was
he who played the part of the Russian Jew Hershele Dubrovner when *God, Man, and Devil* was staged. Some memory of

39. ". . . Bei der kindlichen Geschäftsführung des Löwy. . . . Es ist
schon eine alte Geschichte" (*Fe* 360).

40. White interprets Russia as symbolic of the infinite or the absolute
("'Das Urteil,'" p. 211). Sokel suggests that Russia signifies isolation,
particularly from family (*Tragik und Ironie*, pp. 51, 66–67). But in the
Diaries Kafka repeatedly connects Russia with Eastern European
Jewry (see *Di* 115, 132, 195–97, 217–20; *T* 121, 140, 210–12, 236–38).
Levi was actually from Warsaw, a city which at that time was under
Russian rule. Since the Poles were not an independent nation, but
themselves a subject people who, as a group, were notoriously anti-
Semitic, it is hardly surprising that Kafka thinks of Levi as Russian,
not Polish. Levi must be seen as an Eastern European Jew whose native
language was Yiddish.

41. Three of Gordin's four plays included in the repertoire (*God,
Man, and Devil, The Savage One*, and *The Slaughtering*) take place in
Russia. There is evidence that Kafka was aware of the geographical
setting of these plays, for he writes of *The Savage One:* "In addition to
this the scene of action is Russia" ("Nun ist überdies der Ort der Handlung Russland" [*Di* 113; *T* 118]).

Levi in the role of Hershele, combined with Kafka's personal memories of Levi, probably helped to shape the figure of the friend in Russia in "The Judgment."[42]

In addition to parallels in characterization, "The Judgment" and *God, Man, and Devil* exhibit similar themes. Repeated references to business dealings—the same word, *Geschäft*, serves in Yiddish and in German—provide thematic unity for story and play: the word is given symbolic as well as literal meaning in both. Old Bendemann's allusion to "certain ugly things" (*gewisse unschöne Dinge*) refers to business dealings that he suspects Georg of keeping from him, as well as to Georg's sexual activities.[43] This detail has a literal counterpart in *God, Man, and Devil,* for under Mazik's influence Hershele secretly engages in shady business practices which gain him greater wealth.

Frequent ironic references to the "plenty" of business provide comic contrast to the extremes of poverty depicted in *God, Man, and Devil.* As Hershele attains wealth, he neglects his "holy business" and acquires an all too serious interest in secular business affairs. In the last act, when Hershele recognizes his error, the word *business* (*Geschäft*) is given a spiritual frame of reference. It is equated with the business of living, "bills of reckoning" become bills to be paid to God, "financial bankruptcy" becomes symbolic of moral failure.[44] In "The Judgment," a story of only fifteen pages, some form of the word *Geschäft* occurs seventeen times. On the literal level it refers to Georg's financial affairs; symbolically it includes the

42. The German-Jewish newspaper *Selbstwehr*, which Kafka began to read at this time, ran weekly reports of pogroms and other anti-Semitic activities taking place in Russia. The impression given is that it was indeed not healthy for a Jew to live in Russia. "The unfamiliar fullbeard" ("der fremdartige Vollbart" [*PC* 49; *E* 53]) associated with the friend in Russia is reminiscent of the beard worn by all Orthodox Jews, including those portrayed on the Yiddish stage.

43. On the psychological level, the two themes merge.

44. The play well illustrates the Yiddish proverb "Toyre iz di beste skhoyre" ("Torah [in the sense of learning or knowledge] is the best merchandise"), which Kafka mentions in connection with a Yiddish operetta (*Di* 170; *T* 182).

"business of getting married."[45] This ambiguous reference
(which parallels the wordplay of God, Man, and Devil) allows
Georg to contemplate his decision to marry with the same distance he could bring to less delicate matters.[46]

The theme of business is curiously connected to drowning in
both God, Man, and Devil and "The Judgment." In a comic
exchange Khatskel teases Hershele's father about his nonexis-
tent business enterprises: "How are you? How's business? Your
ships at sea were not drowned, your walls not burned, your
goods not spoiled?" The surprisingly serious tone of the father's
reply—"God forbid, nothing of mine was drowned, and nothing
ruined"—calls attention to his words and to the lines which follow: "So where is our Reb Hershele Dubrovner, our pious one,
our great scholar, our silken Jew?"[47] This first introduction of
Hershele's name directly following the father's mention of ca-
tastrophe is an ironic foreshadowing of the death of the hero
and the tragic end of the play, when something of the father's
will indeed have become ruined.[48] Although Hershele does not,
like Georg, drown himself, water is as important a symbol in

45. Weinberg, in Kafkas Dichtung, p. 320, relates the word Geschäft
("business") to the idea of Priesterschaft ("priesthood"), an interpretation
not supported by the text.

46. A common Yiddish idiom may be relevant here. In Yiddish one
says "mayne gesheftn!" ("my business!") of something remote from
one's natural inclinations which one has somehow become obliged to do.
The idiom expresses both pride and discomfort, an ambivalence that
corresponds to Georg's feelings about his engagement.

47. "KHATSKEL: Nu, vos makht ir, Reb Leyzer? Vi geyn ayere
    gesheftn? Ayere shifn oyfn yam zaynen nit dertrunkn gevorn,
    ayere moyern nit ferbrent gevorn, ayere podriadn nit kalye
    gevorn?
    "LEYZER (shtil): Khulile, Reb Khatskel, bay mir iz kayn zakh nit
    dertrunkn gevorn, un nit kalye gevorn.
    "KHATSKEL: Nu, vu iz dos epes unzer Reb Hershele Dubrovner?
    Unzer braver frumak, unzer groyser lamdn, unzer zaydener
    yud?" (GMT 18).
The last two lines reveal a somewhat ironic attitude toward Hershele's
extreme piety, which Gordin satirizes lightly.

48. In "The Judgment" the father also foreshadows his son's end:
"And while you're answering me be you still my living son" (PC 60).

God, Man and Devil as in "The Judgment." In the very first scene of the play, the hero is associated with water:

> LEYZER: You know that in copying the Torah, when he comes to the name of God he goes to the *mikve* [ritual bath]....
> PESENIU: Father-in-law, you could say he goes into the water.
> LEYZER: You don't like *mikve*, let it be water, as long as he comes out wet.... He went to immerse himself.[49]

The reference to the ritual bath occurs again in a more serious context at the end of the play, when Khatskel accuses Hershele: "Once, before writing God's name you used to immerse yourself in water; now you immerse yourself in our blood."[50] Water is introduced in "The Judgment" in the opening paragraph as part of its symbolic setting, when Georg gazes at the water in which he later drowns himself (*PC* 49; *E* 53). If, as Sokel suggests,[51] Georg's death symbolizes the expiation of sin or the death of the scapegoat, then death in "The Judgment" is associated with purification by water. Georg's absorption in letter writing, which leads to his death by water, is reminiscent of Hershele's occupation as scribe, which, as demonstrated, is connected even more directly to water.[52]

In his analysis of "The Judgment" Erwin R. Steinberg connects Georg's drowning to the "death by water" mentioned in the Yom Kippur service, and he points to an important tenet of Jewish belief which holds that only the sins of man against

49. "LEYZER: Ir veyst dokh, ven baym shraybn di toyre kumt zum vort 'Adoshem' geyt er friyer in mikve....
"PESENIU: Shver lebn, ir kent dokh zogn, er geyt in vaser.
"LEYZER: Du vilst nit in mikve, zol zayn in vaser, abi er kumt aroys a naser.... Iz er zikh gegangen toyvl zayn" (*GMT* 18).
50. "Amol farn shraybn Adoshem flegst du zikh toyvl zayn in vaser un itst bist du zikh toyvl in unzer blut" (*GMT* 99).
In Hebrew, the root for the verbs meaning "to immerse," "to baptize," and "to drown" are related.
51. *Tragik und Ironie*, p. 76.
52. Politzer comments: "Georg Bendemann has an exaggerated respect for the written word" (*Parable and Paradox*, p. 54). The same could be said of Hershele Dubrovner.

God can be atoned for by the prayers of Yom Kippur.[53] Steinberg suggests that these theological concepts are relevant in explaining Georg's suicide. In "The Judgment," where no explicit mention of God occurs, if Georg has sinned, it can only be against man. But one need not rely on Kafka's knowledge (dubious at best) of the details of the Yom Kippur service in order to interpret Georg's suicide in terms of the doctrine of Yom Kippur, for this forms the explicit basis of Hershele's suicide in *God, Man, and Devil* and could have come to Kafka through his familiarity with this play. In the play Hershele sins against God and man, but he explains: "Our sages say: . . . Between God and man is Yom Kippur. But between Adam and Adam, what one man sins against another, there the tears, piety, penance, and prayers of Yom Kippur do not help."[54] Hershele's faith in God and Yom Kippur and his awareness of the inevitability of the Day of Judgment which permeate *God, Man, and Devil* may help to explain the sense of religious overtones in "The Judgment," an otherwise totally secular tale. Hershele's belief that he is carrying out God's judgment may also help to explain why old Bendemann seems to be transformed at the end of the story from a feeble old man to an Old Testament God.[55]

Jewish tradition may also be relevant in explaining another difficult detail in "The Judgment": the symbolism of the pockets in the father's shirt. As a final show of strength, the father boasts, "I have your customers here in my pocket!" to which Georg responds in wonder, "He has pockets even in his shirt!"

53. See Steinberg, "The Judgment," pp. 23–30. Yom Kippur is the Jewish Day of Atonement, a day of fasting (associated with the New Year) on which men beg forgiveness of God for the sins they have committed during the previous year.

54. "Unzere khokhomim zogn: . . . tsvishn Got un mentsh iz yom kipur. . . . Ober bin adam l'adam, vos eyn mentsh zindigt gegn andern, do helfn nit di trern, di tsitkes, di tkhines un tfiles fun yom kipur" (*GMT* 94–95).

55. Politzer calls him a "primitive war god" (*Parable and Paradox*, p. 61); Tauber remarks: "The father himself changes from a man in need of nursing into a God of Justice" (*Franz Kafka*, p. 15).

(*PC* 61).[56] These lines bring to mind the Yiddish idiom "Shrouds are made without pockets."[57]

White's interpretation of these lines—"the father controls the means of communication with the friend in Russia"—is not only unsatisfactory, but is also inaccurate. It seems to be based on a misreading of the text, which clearly separates the father's relationship to the friend from Georg's customers whom the father claims to have in his pockets. White erroneously combines the friend with the pockets—"[The] father informs [Georg] that he is in possession of 'die Kundschaft seines Freundes' ['the patronage of his friend']"[58]—while the text reads, "I've established a fine connection with your friend [*deinem Freund*] and I have your customers [*deine Kundschaft*] here in my pocket!" (*PC* 61).[59] White must have read *seine Kundschaft* for *deine*, which would alter the meaning of *Kundschaft* from "customers" to "patronage."

Georg *is* impressed with his father's pockets, but for quite another reason. It should not be difficult to see why, near the end of the father's unrelenting attack, Georg wishes his father were dead: " 'Now he'll lean forward,' thought Georg; 'what if he falls and smashes himself!' "[60] Combining this wish projection with the image of the old father in his none-too-clean underclothes, Georg, in his weakened psychological condition, already envisions his father in his shroud. If indeed "shrouds are made without pockets," we can understand Georg's amazement at his father's ability to obtain a shroud with pockets. The sense of the idiom is equivalent to the English "You can't take

56. "Deine Kundschaft habe ich hier in der Tasche!
"Sogar im Hemd hat er Taschen!" (*E* 66).
57. "Takhrikhim makht men on keshenes."
58. White, " 'Das Urteil,' " p. 217.
59. "Mit deinem Freund habe ich mich herrlich verbunden, deine Kundschaft habe ich hier in der Tasche!" (*E* 66).
60. "Jetzt wird er sich vorbeugen, dachte Georg, wenn er fiele und zerschmetterte!" (*E* 65).
The wording of this remark is deliberately ambiguous and expresses Georg's ambivalent feelings toward his father—fear ("what if he falls!") as well as secret wish ("if only he would fall!").

it with you!" but in Georg's exaggerated view of the old man's strength, Bendemann clearly assumes he can and will. For an instant Georg recognizes how absurd his father must appear, for the father alone does not seem to know what the whole community acknowledges: "Georg . . . believed that with this remark he could make him an impossible figure for all the world. Only for a moment did he think so, since he kept on forgetting everything" (*PC* 61).[61] But Georg's fear of his father obstructs his clearer vision, and his observation only further diminishes his already weakened image of himself.

This incident also involves a pun which Georg misses, for the son takes his father's figurative remark about clients in his pocket (that is, in his control) quite literally.[62] This kind of verbal play, integral to the comic method of the Yiddish plays, is particularly frequent in *God, Man, and Devil*. The father's trick on Georg with the word "covered" (*zugedeckt*) has a direct parallel in a trick played by the old jester in *God, Man, and Devil*, who, like Bendemann, deliberately misinterprets a statement he has put into the mouth of another character. By insisting on an answer to the question "Am I well covered up?" old Bendemann forces Georg to agree, "Don't worry, you're well covered up" (*PC* 59),[63] an answer Bendemann misinterprets to mean "you are as good as buried." In *God, Man, and Devil* Leyzer makes Hershele's wife (who repeatedly complains that her toothache is being ignored) say, "It doesn't hurt or bother me!" to which he replies, "So, fool, if it doesn't bother you, why should it bother me?"[64] In both instances, one character takes unfair advantage of the trust of another. But whereas the old jester's trick is harmless (even the butt of the

61. ". . . [Georg] glaubte, er könne ihn mit dieser Bemerkung in der ganzen Welt unmöglich machen. Nur einen Augenblick dachte er das, denn immerfort vergass er alles" (*E* 66).

62. White, " 'Das Urteil,' " pp. 220–23, discusses Kafka's extensive use of wordplay.

63. "Bin ich gut zugedeckt? . . .
"Sei nur ruhig, du bist gut zugedeckt" (*E* 63).

64. "PESENIU: Es hart mikh nit!
"LEYZER: Nu, shute, az dikh hart nit, far vos zol dos mir haren?"
(*GMT* 16)

joke joins in the laughter), Bendemann uses the joke as a weapon against Georg, who is unable simply to laugh it off.[65]

In addition to the element of humor, *God, Man, and Devil* and "The Judgment" share several technical devices. In both works setting and lighting function symbolically and serve either as a reflection of or as a contrast to the character's state of mind. In *God, Man, and Devil,* the more lavish the sets become, the greater the spiritual poverty enacted upon them; Hershele's dark chamber (at the end of the play) symbolizes the darkness of his despair. In "The Judgment" Georg's sunny room represents what he has managed to achieve since his mother's death, but he loses that in his father's dark "cell." Old Bendemann's room provides a visual contrast to Georg's and also reflects the father's closed attitude toward the son. The prayer books, the Torah scrolls, and the violin prominent in the first act of *God, Man, and Devil* and associated with Hershele's life as Torah scribe are conspicuously replaced in later acts by a large metal safe, which symbolizes Hershele's new devotion to business, money and worldly affairs. Objects described in "The Judgment"—the mementos of the mother, the uneaten breakfast, the newspaper, and the father's spectacles—function like the symbols of a play.[66]

In both works objects are used to accent a heightened moment in the action. At the height of his verbal attack, Georg's father whips out an old newspaper and flings it at his son,

---

65. I cannot agree with White when he suggests that Georg is unable to understand the pun because he is tied to the empirical world, while the father is associated with the absolute. In this connection White also remarks: "The father can play due to his distance from everything" (" 'Das Urteil,' " p. 223). It seems to me that the father's attitude in "The Judgment" is far from distant; in fact, he seems to be overly involved with his son. Fear, discomfort, or even sheer malice are equally plausible motives for the kind of play the father indulges in. Note, for example, the father in *God, Man, and Devil,* who quite literally hides behind his jesting.

66. White connects the unfinished breakfast to the "earthly nourishment" which cannot satisfy the hunger of the absolute father (" 'Das Urteil,' " p. 217). Pondrom suggests that the father's "defect of vision," symbolized by the glasses, prevents him from seeing his son objectively.

shouting, "Do you think I concern myself with anything else?
Do you think I read my newspapers? Look!" (*PC* 62).[67] The
sudden reappearance of the newspaper resembles a stage effect
used in *God, Man, and Devil* at a similarly crucial moment in
the action. To crown his accusation, Khatskel pulls his son's
bloody *talis* (prayer shawl) out from under his coat and
throws it at Hershele, shouting, "My dead son left you a talis;
put it on my bill."[68] In both works these sudden actions seem to
precipitate the suicide; the antagonist uses a prop to
strengthen his case against his opponent. Although it is clear
why the sight of the blood-stained prayer shawl would over-
whelm Hershele, it is less easy to understand why the newspaper which the father only pretended to be reading and which
the son does not recognize should so terrify Georg. The effect
of these highly theatrical actions on the reader or viewer is, in
both cases, surprise and heightened intuition of approaching
danger.

Like the dramatist, Kafka often assigns symbolic significance
to the names of his characters.[69] In the *Diaries* (*D*1 279; *T* 297)
Kafka calls attention to the similarity of the names Felice
Bauer and Frieda Brandenfeld. In view of Kafka's special interest in names, it is possible that the niece's name in *God,
Man, and Devil*—"Freydeniu," a diminutive of "Frieda"—pre-
disposed Kafka to choose the name Frieda for the fiancée in
"The Judgment." In general, names carry some symbolic significance in the Yiddish plays, often ironic. For example, in the
name given to Satan in human shape, Uriel Mazik, *Uriel* literally means "God is my light" and *Mazik*, "devil, conjurer,
harmer," although *Mazik* is also used humorously as a term of
endearment. Thematically, names play an extremely important
part in *God, Man, and Devil*: one entire scene is given over to

67. "Glaubst du, mich kümmert etwas anderes? Glaubst du, ich lese
Zeitungen? Da!" (*E* 66).

68. "Mayn geshtorbener zun hot dir ibergefirt a talis, fershrayb es
oyf mayn khezhbm" (*GMT* 100).

69. For an interesting discussion of the significance of names in Kafka,
see Margot P. Levi, "K.: An Exploration of the Names of Kafka's Central
Characters," *Names* 14 (1966): 1–10.

the old jester's forming anagrams from the names of the characters and analyzing their personalities in terms of the meanings of these words. Kafka's interest in the meaning of names is part of this Hasidic, Kabalistic tradition.

These many parallels in theme, character, action, and technique show that Gordin's play provided an important source for Kafka's story. It also seems likely that the exaggeration and tension that characterize "The Judgment" derive from the inherent theatricality of *God, Man, and Devil*.[70] But Gordin's fine play did not provide the only source for "The Judgment." We find in the story significant elements of a much lesser play, Avraham Sharkanski's *Kol Nidre*.

As Kafka himself observed, the work of Sharkanski was far inferior to that of Gordin. Nonetheless, Sharkanski's plays were frequently performed on the Yiddish stage, and Kafka was attracted enough by at least one of them to record his experience of it in the *Diaries*. On October 22, 1911, Kafka writes:

> Yesterday with the Jews. *Kol Nidre* by Scharkansky, pretty bad play with a good, witty letter-writing scene, a prayer by the lovers standing up beside each other with hands clasped, the converted Grand Inquisitor pressing himself against the curtain of the Ark of the Covenant, he mounts the stairs and remains standing there, his head bowed, his lips against the curtain, holds the prayer book before his chattering teeth. For the first time on this fourth evening my distinct inability to get a clear impression. (*Di* 106–7)[71]

70. An interesting perspective on Kafka's method in "The Judgment" is offered by Kafka's comments on acting. In answer to Janouch's objections that certain stage effects were too theatrical, Kafka replied: "So it should be. Actors ought to be theatrical. To create the desired effect their emotions and actions must be larger than the feelings and actions of their audience. If the theater is to affect life, it must be stronger, more intense than ordinary life. That is the law of gravity. In shooting one must aim higher than the mark" (*CwK* 44; J 37). Such a theory of acting (which corresponds to the style of the Yiddish theater troupe) could well explain the function of the exaggeration in "The Judgment."

71. "Gestern bei den Juden. 'Kol Nidre' von Scharkansky, ziemlich schlechtes Stück mit einer guten witzigen Briefschreibszene, einem

In spite of Kafka's low opinion of the play, he clearly found elements in the work that excited his imagination. We find a clue as to what attracted his imagination if we focus on the "good, witty letter-writing scene" that he singles out. On reading this play, however, we discover that *Kol Nidre* includes not one, but three letter-writing scenes, all of which are integral to the theme and structure of the play.

Kol Nidre is essentially a drama of intrigue, at the heart of which are two secrets: the love of Elvira for Bartelo and Bartelo's identity as Jew. The action occurs in Madrid fourteen years after the expulsion of the Jews. Elvira is the only child of the Grand Inquisitor, Paulus, a converted Jew who is dedicated to the extermination of all Jews. Bartelo is the king's favorite and a court singer. A nun and priest plot to reveal both secrets to Paulus. When the Inquisitor hears the secret of Bartelo's identity he vows to kill him, but since Bartelo is under the protection of the king, Paulus must show some evidence before he can carry out the execution. Paulus cannot completely restrain himself, however, and he accuses Bartelo publicly, deliberately using ambiguous language. The Inquisitor declares himself Bartelo's opponent and his sternest judge, before whom Bartelo will have to give account.

Through his spies Paulus discovers Bartelo visiting Elvira, and a furious fight ensues. Now doubly determined to get rid of Bartelo, Paulus plots to frame him with a letter supposedly written by other secret Jews. In this way Paulus soon discovers the secret meeting place of the Jews (in a church which can be converted into a synagogue) and interrupts their services on Yom Kippur. He finds the evidence he needs (a prayer book), and Bartelo's fate is sealed. But at this point Elvira enters; and on finding her father in the secret place, she openly declares her love for Bartelo and her eternal allegiance to the Jewish

---

Gebet der nebeneinander mit gefalteten Händen aufrecht stehenden Liebenden, dem Anlehnen des bekehrten Grossinquisitors an den Vorhang der Bundeslade, er steigt die Stufe hinauf und bleibt dort, den Kopf geneigt, die Lippen am Vorhang, stehn, hält das Gebetbuch vor seine klappernden Zähne. Zum erstenmal an diesem vierten Abend meine deutliche Unfähigkeit, einen reinen Eindruck zu bekommen" (*T* 111).

faith, curses her father, and stabs herself. She is only wounded, however, and Bartelo is jailed; both are to be tried and burned as Jews. Paulus now forces Bartelo to write a false confession admitting his guilt in seducing Elvira to Judaism. The last scene, the auto de fé, takes place in an empty, open space in which the Inquisitor's chair and the fire for execution are the only props. Paulus addresses the people, explaining that on this day it is his duty to judge his own child, and he begs them not to believe her words. But Elvira refuses to recant, and although Paulus vainly tries to prove her innocence by showing Bartelo's letter, the people demand her immediate death. As Elvira and Bartelo are led away by two executioners, Elvira voluntarily jumps into the fire, repeating the Jewish vow of faith, "Hear, O Israel"; Bartelo follows suit, completing the prayer, "The Lord is our God, the Lord is One."[72] In a brief final tableau Elvira and Bartelo appear among winged angels, and the people fall to their knees, while Paulus struggles with death.

From this synopsis it should be clear that the characters in the play are not fully motivated and that one cannot analyze their actions on the basis of psychology or even on the basis of character types. The play centers on intrigue, ambition, and revenge, which are contrasted to the pure ideals that bind the two lovers. It emphasizes sensational effects rather than character analysis or moral conflict. Yet, despite its limitations as art, the play no doubt presents an exciting spectacle, and it should not be unduly surprising that Kafka seems to have transplanted several elements from this play into the short story "The Judgment." The most obvious parallel is the significance given to letters and letter writing.[73] These dominate "The Judgment" to the same degree that they dominate the plot and structure of Kol Nidre. The entire first section of "The Judgment" is a scene of letter writing. The story opens with Georg sitting at his desk, sealing a letter he has just completed.

72. "Shma Yisroel, Adonoy Eloheynu, Adonoy Ekhod" (KN 40).

73. This is not to suggest that the device of letter writing is limited to the Yiddish plays. The parallel would of course be less striking or significant if this were the only device the two works shared.

In a sense, this letter seals Georg's fate as surely as the Inquisitor's letter seals Bartelo's. The Inquisitor refers to the letter he forces Bartelo to write as Bartelo's "death sentence" (*todes urtayl [KN* 30]). All the letters written or planned by the Inquisitor are literally "lying" or "false" letters. The father in "The Judgment" refers to all of Georg's letters to the friend as "your lying little letters" (*deine falschen Briefchen [PC* 59; *E* 64]), and there is a degree of truth in his accusation. Because Georg has been fooling himself about his ability to fulfill his plans for marriage, in the "lying" letter he commits himself to a line of action which he is ultimately unable to carry out.

The pattern of the first section of "The Judgment" repeats the pattern of the major letter-writing scenes in *Kol Nidre*. On three separate occasions in *Kol Nidre* a letter is dictated, discussed, and read aloud. This procedure calls attention to the significance of the letter for the character, it impresses the contents of the letter upon the audience, and it makes the scene dramatically viable. Kafka creates the equivalent of this dramatic technique in prose form. When "The Judgment" opens, Georg's letter is already written; but Georg's thoughts move from the letter to what has motivated it and slowly build back to the exact wording of the letter, which Georg repeats or "reads aloud."

In fact, *Kol Nidre* is not the only Yiddish play in which letters play a central role, although the letter-writing scenes in *Kol Nidre* are closer to "The Judgment" than are those in the other plays. Rikhter's *Moyshe the Tailor as Councillor* includes five scenes involving letters; Latayner's *Blimele*, three. A letter in Faynman's *The Vice-King* is significant, for it establishes its author as a secret Jew who is twice told by his accusers: "Then you have pronounced your own sentence."[74] The association of letters and letter writing with judgment or sentence of death in these plays bears directly on the theme and structure of "The Judgment." One wonders if even Kafka's choice of a title for the story was influenced by the frequent repetition of the words *urteil* and *urteiln* in the Yiddish plays.[75]

74. "Dan hast du zelbst dayn urtayl oysgesprokhn" (*VK* 18–19).
75. In German, the word *Urteil* carries several related meanings:

The device of letter writing is not the only significant element that *Kol Nidre* and "The Judgment" share. One of the most terrifying details of "The Judgment" is the idea of a father sitting in judgment over his child. Kafka was indeed haunted by his own father's authority, but *Kol Nidre* offers a literary precedent for this bizarre situation. Elvira's father, as Grand Inquisitor, is required to sit in judgment over his child, and because of her public espousal of Judaism, is forced to condemn her to death. In the play we are fully aware of the external pressures that force the father to condemn his child; his judgment is the inevitable result of all of the previous action. In "The Judgment" Kafka removes the framework which justifies and necessitates the judgment, leaving the reader without direct recourse to logic. Kafka does not spell out the conflicts within Georg—his inability to become an integrated person (to marry), his dependence on the approval of his father, his overattachment to the mother. He presents only the consequences of these facts in the interaction of the characters, relying on the intuition of the reader to pick up the cues and reconstruct the causative factors. All of the pressures which motivate the action in "The Judgment" remain partially hidden. Because they are internal, they seem more mysterious and more terrible.

We can go even further, and observe that Kafka repeats the rhythms of the language, the structure of the rhetoric, and even some of the very words of *Kol Nidre*. The father's accusation and judgment in "The Judgment" echo the words and pattern of the Inquisitor's ambiguous charge against Bartelo. The Inquisitor announces: "You are the darling of the King, you are the best singer of Spain, that is true. But one thing is not true—you are not the child that the Church took into its holy lap, you are far more the unworthy son of your unworthy father."[76]

"decision," "judgment," "sentence," and "verdict." In Yiddish, other words (derived from Hebrew) are more commonly used; but because the Inquisitors in these plays, as well as other characters in a position to judge others, are of a high rank, they speak a Yiddish that is close to standard High German (*Hochdeutsch*).

76. "Du bizt der libling des kenigs, du bizt der bester zenger Spaniens, dos ales izt var! Eyns ober iz nisht var—du bizt nisht dos kind

In "The Judgment" the father charges: "In truth, you were an
innocent child, but in greater truth you were a devilish human
being."[77] The logical structure of the two statements is similar:
this you are, but *that* you are not. In each case, what the person no longer is takes precedence over what he is or was. In
both statements there is a repetition of a key word: "unworthy"
(*unvirdig*) in *Kol Nidre*, "in truth, really, truly" (*eigentlich*)
in "The Judgment."

The implication of these charges is the same: you are not the
man you appear to be. In both works this crucial statement is
followed by a vital *darum* clause which leads to the death of
the hero. In *Kol Nidre* the Inquisitor declares: "Therefore, I
remain your opponent";[78] in "The Judgment" the father says:
"And therefore take note: I sentence you now to death by
drowning!" (*PC* 62–63).[79] Both Georg and Bartelo are addressed by their accusers with the familiar *du*. Except for the
formal tone and terrifying content of old Bendemann's words,
this is not unnatural between father and son. But in the case of
Bartelo and Paulus, the judgment itself occurs in a formal situation, in which the informal *du* is incongruous. It reflects
Paulus' contempt for Bartelo and his certainty of the power he
wields. The important word "child" is repeated by both judges,
as is the word meaning "to judge" or "to sentence" (*verur-
teilen*), which occurs several times in *Kol Nidre*. Bartelo is not
the *child* the Church took in; Georg was an innocent *child*.
Only submission to the Church would prove Bartelo's innocence; only in his submissive role as child was Georg innocent.
The father himself combines the two concepts in his choice of
words: "innocent child" (*unschuldiges Kind*). In *Kol Nidre* the
church will not tolerate what Bartelo *is* (a Jew); in "The Judg-

---

velkhe di kirkhe in ir haylige shos oyfgenumen hot, du bizt fil mer der
unvirdige zun daynes unvirdign faters" (*KN* 11).

77. "Ein unschuldiges Kind warst du ja eigentlich, aber noch eigentlicher warst du ein teuflischer Mensch!" (*E* 67).

78. "Darum blaybe ikh dayn gegner" (*KN* 12).

79. "Und darum wisse: Ich verurteile dich jetzt zum Tode des Er-
trinkens!" (*E* 67).

ment" the father cannot accept Georg *as he is*. (And, one is forced to conclude, neither can Georg himself.)

The lover chosen by the child in both works is rejected by the father. The word "seduction" (*verfirung*) occurs in connection with Bartelo's supposed seduction of Elvira to Judaism, but the sexual overtones of the word are implicit in the context. Old Bendemann implies that Georg's engagement is purely the result of lust.

Bartelo and Elvira are doomed to die whether or not they acquiesce in their deaths. By jumping into the fire voluntarily, by calling on the Jewish God, the two give ultimate proof of their faith. This melodramatic device has its exact parallel in the structure and language of the ending of "The Judgment." Georg rushes from the room to carry out his father's judgment. Before he jumps from the bridge he reaffirms his faith: "Dear parents, but I have always loved you."[80] In both works the strength of the judge is exhausted by his judgment.[81] Paulus struggles with death; old Bendemann collapses on the bed. The judicial powers of Paulus the Inquisitor are reflected in the psychological power of Bendemann. Although in both works the verdict is to a degree valid (Elvira and Bartelo are Jews; Georg is unable to carry out his plans), to a larger degree, it seems unjust.[82] *Kol Nidre* raises the question "Why need Jews be killed?" and one could equally reasonably ask of "The Judgment," "Why is Georg condemned to die and why does he accept the verdict?" Because of the external situation in which Elivra and Bartelo have become caught, they are unable to continue to live. Yet Georg is as trapped as they are by his own inability either to resolve his conflicts or to continue to live with them unresolved.

80. "Liebe Eltern, ich habe euch doch immer geliebt" (*E* 68).

Georg's words, however, are ambiguous in a way that Bartelo and Elvira's are not: his declaration of faith may also be read as an assertion of innocence.

81. Politzer discusses this point in *Parable and Paradox*, p. 62.

82. In fact, Georg is condemned not for his inability to succeed, but for daring to try.

The final tableau of *Kol Nidre* (Elvira and Bartelo among angels) suggests that the lovers are redeemed and that Paulus erred. Is there not perhaps the parallel suggestion in "The Judgment" that Georg was wrongly judged? *Kol Nidre* provides easy answers to the questions it raises, but no such definite conclusions can be reached for "The Judgment."

Aside from these specific thematic similarities between "The Judgment" and the two plays by Gordin and Sharkanski, Kafka's story also relates to the plays of the Yiddish theater in broad structural terms. A close examination of the structure of "The Judgment" shows that the story follows a basically dramatic pattern: an opening section of exposition (Georg's meditation over his letter) prepares the reader for the complications (the confrontation with the father) which build up to a point of climax (the moment of judgment) and are followed by a brief denouement (Georg's suicide).[83]

"The Judgment" falls into three distinct sections—two of approximately equal length and a brief closing paragraph—which differ from each other in setting, tone, pace, and method of narration. These sections may be better understood when viewed as if they corresponded to the separate acts of a play, each with its own rhythmic pattern which mirrors the dramatic structure of the whole. Each of the three parts of "The Judgment," like each act of *God, Man, and Devil,* is organized in a pattern of rising and falling action.

The first section of the story moves slowly and evenly, using several different modes of narration—third-person narration, indirect quotation, direct speech, and *erlebte Rede*.[84] Georg's rev-

---

83. Although the plays of the Yiddish theater are built along similar dramatic lines, Kafka's story is actually more tightly organized and more compact than any of these plays.

84. *Erlebte Rede* refers to passages which appear to be third-person narration, but are actually narrated in the language of one of the characters and convey his thoughts. For example, the statement in "The Judgment," "So he was wearing himself out to no purpose in a foreign country" ("So arbeitete er sich in der Fremde nutzlos ab" [*PC* 49; *E* 53]) is not the neutral observation of an impersonal narrator, but is Georg's interpretation of his friend's situation.

erie has the effect of a single long monologue.[85] Its function is
that of standard dramatic exposition, which it fulfills by introducing the characters (Georg, the friend in Russia, the father,
and the fiancée), establishing the nature of their relationship,
and making known the relevant facts of the past (the friend's
circumstances in Russia, the death of the mother, the changes
that have taken place in Georg's personal and business affairs).[86] The exposition, slow but not static, releases this information gradually, in an ascending order of interest. We start
from a point of rest, although in terms of the plot we are *in
medias res;* Georg's thoughts move from his friend, to his relationship with his friend, to the gossip he has written in previous letters, and finally to the important news (his own recent
engagement) which he had not been able to send. By the end
of the exposition our attention is firmly focused on the single
fact that provides the excuse for the quarrel with the father:
Georg's decision to send the news of his engagement to the
friend in Russia.

The first paragraph of the exposition serves the function of
stage directions: it relates time and place, gives details of the
setting, and places the characters. Because "The Judgment" is
a short story and not a play, it opens with direct narration: "It

85. Kate Flores refers to it as a soliloquy ("The Judgment," in *Franz
Kafka Today,* ed. Flores and Swander, p. 16).

86. Although he never appears in person, the friend functions as a
fourth character in the story. The use of a "felt presence" instead of a
seen character is a device often used by the dramatist: one is reminded
of the father in Strindberg's *Miss Julie,* Captain Alving in Ibsen's *Ghosts,*
Beata in his *Rosmersholm,* and "death" in Maeterlinck's *The Intruder.* In
a letter to Felice, Kafka comments on the function of the friend: "The
friend is hardly a real person, he is rather that which the father and
Georg have in common. Perhaps the story is a circling around father and
son, and the changing figure of the friend is perhaps the shifting perspective of the relationship between father and son." ("Der Freund ist
kaum eine wirkliche Person, er ist vielleicht eher das, was dem Vater
und Georg gemeinsam ist. Die Geschichte ist vielleicht ein Rundgang um
Vater und Sohn, und die wechselnde Gestalt des Freundes ist vielleicht
der perspektivische Wechsel der Beziehungen zwischen Vater und Sohn."
[*Fe* 396–97])

was a Sunday morning in the very height of spring. Georg Bendemann, a young merchant, was sitting in his own room on the
first floor" (*PC* 49).[87] The sparseness of the setting recalls the
staging of the Yiddish theater, with its single table and few
chairs. In Georg's room we see only the desk and chair and a
window out of which Georg can see the river, the bridge, and
the opposite shore.[88] In the father's room there is only a table,
a chair,[89] the bed, a cabinet, and a window whose light is
blocked by a high wall. The central action of "The Judgment"
is limited to a single space, which is transformed into two different rooms, first Georg's, then the father's. As in drama, this
space is redefined by means of setting and lighting.

In contrast to the form of the first section, the second is almost entirely dialogue and reads like the script of a play.[90]
Much of the interaction between the characters is in terms of
nonverbal communication, as in drama: "Georg ... tried to
meet his father's eyes"; "Georg made grimaces as if he didn't

87. "Es war an einem Sonntagvormittag im schönsten Frühjahr. Georg
Bendemann, ein junger Kaufmann, sass in seinem Privatzimmer im ersten
Stock" (*E* 53).

88. These function like the symbols of a play and recur at the end of
the story. Sokel (*Tragik und Ironie*, pp. 70–71), White ("'Das Urteil,'"
pp. 228–29), and Pondrom ("Coherence in 'Das Urteil,'") discuss the
meaning of these symbols.

89. *God, Man, and Devil* calls for a chair to represent God's throne,
called *kisey hakoved* ("chair of honor" or *kissey hamishpet* ("chair of
judgment"). This device may have suggested to Kafka the literal figure
of the father-judge seated in his chair of judgment. Furthermore, the
image of the Inquisitor's chair in *Kol Nidre* (and in Faynman's *The
Vice-King*), called by Paulus "der rikhter shtul" ("the chair of judgment"
[*KN* 39]) may also bear on the image of the seated father in "The Judgment."

90. It is not suggested that this dialogue, or any other in the work
of Kafka, ought to be staged, as it stands or in any other form. Friedrich
Beissner in *Der Erzähler Franz Kafka*, 2nd ed. (Stuttgart, 1958), rightly
deplores the dramatizations of Kafka's novels, which uniformly destroy
the complexity and intentional ambiguity of Kafka's prose. Although
Kafka adapted the method of the drama to prose form, he is first and last
a writer of fiction. The only play definitely known to be his, "The
Warden of the Tomb" (1916–17), attests to his lack of skill in writing
actual drama.

believe it. The father only nodded towards Georg's corner, affirming the truth of what he said."[91] Furthermore, almost all of the description of the characters is in terms of motion and gesture, which gives the effect of stage directions: "His father cleared away the breakfast dishes and set them on a chest. . . . [Georg] drew the letter a little way from his pocket and let it drop back again" (*PC* 55).[92] Thus, many of the actions of "The Judgment" are better understood when perceived as analogous to stage actions.

Except for his physical position, the father is not described, although some details of his dress ("his heavy dressing gown" [*PC* 54; *E* 59]) and appearance ("his . . . unkempt white hair" [*PC* 57; *E* 61]) are given as they become significant in the action. Here we see Kafka adapting another technique of the drama for the purposes of narrative prose. In drama, if the playwright describes the physical appearance of his characters at all, he does so only briefly, either in the stage directions that accompany the character's first entrance or in the *dramatis personae*. Likewise, Kafka drastically limits his description of the characters, but releases this information (as narrative form permits) whenever he deems it most effective.

There is no time gap between the two sections; the time spanned by the entire story is far less than Aristotle's "single revolution of the sun." The transition is marked by a significant change in lighting and set, however. Because "The Judgment" is a narrative, the shift from one section to the next is less abrupt than it would be in the drama: George is shown walking from one room into the next. In drama, the actual transition would not be depicted; the curtain would fall on Georg's exit from his room and open with his entrance into his father's. Kafka takes the opportunity of this transition to convey information concerning the relationship between Georg and his fa-

91. "Georg . . . suchte des Vaters Augen" (*E* 59); "Georg machte Grimassen, als glaube er das nicht. Der Vater nickte bloss, die Wahrheit dessen, was er sagte, beteuernd, in Georgs Ecke hin" (*E* 66).

92. "Der Vater räumte das Frühstücksgeschirr ab und stellte es auf einen Kasten. . . . [Georg] zog den Brief ein wenig aus der Tasche und liess ihn wieder zurückfallen" (*E* 59).

ther. It seems that Georg has not set foot in his father's room
for months, since the two see each other daily at work, at
lunch, and at home in the evenings. Yet despite the frequency
of their meetings, it becomes clear from the tone and imagery
of the prose that Georg and his father are hardly close. In a
play this information would either have to be incorporated into
the exposition, or it would be released in the second act. By
taking the prerogatives of narration, but keeping the structure
of drama, Kafka is able to focus more directly on the conflict
between father and son.

The objectification of an inner condition by using lighting to
create distortion on the stage is a familiar dramatic technique.
By means of described lighting, Kafka heightens our perception of the menacing nature of the father, who sits in a far corner of a dark room, waiting, it seems, for George to appear.[93]
Georg's comment—"My father is still a giant of a man" (PC
54)[94]—is in the nature of a stage aside; Kafka uses his words to
create a visual projection of Georg's perception of his father: a
man of gigantic proportions.[95] From his initial entrance into
the father's room there are two levels of speech: what Georg
says aloud and what he thinks to himself. All of his parentheti-
cal comments—for example, "In business hours he's quite different" (PC 55);[96] "Now he'll lean forward, ... what if he falls
and smashes himself!"—mirror the dramatic convention of the
aside, which was used liberally by all the Yiddish playwrights.

At the opening of the second section there is a brief exchange between father and son preceding Georg's announce-
ment of the reason for his visit. This exchange sets the tone for
the long interview which follows, for although the words themselves are ordinary and deceptively simple, there is a menacing

93. Sitting in a corner is also associated with the old father in God,
Man, and Devil, who retires into a corner whenever he is frightened or
when Hershele appears. But after Bendemann's initial outburst, it was
Georg who "stood in a corner, as far away as possible from his father"
("stand in einem Winkel, möglichst weit vom Vater" [E 64]).

94. "Mein Vater ist noch immer ein Riese" (E 59).

95. White makes a similar point (" 'Das Urteil,' " p. 221).

96. "Im Geschäft ist er doch ganz anders " (E 59).

quality underneath. The conversation opens with the father's greeting: "Ah, Georg." The son replies:

> "It is unbearably dark in here," he then said.
> "Yes, it certainly is dark," answered the father.
> "And you've also shut the window?"
> "I prefer it that way."
> "It is quite warm outside," said Georg, as if continuing his previous remark, and sat down.
> The father cleared away the breakfast dishes and put them on a chest.[97]

Because of subtle pressures beneath the surface of the words, we sense a tension developing between the characters. Georg's unspoken perception that his father is still a giant of a man colors his seemingly innocent remark "It is unbearably dark in here" and gives it a critical tone. In this context "unbearable" (*unerträglich*) connates "insufferable," "intolerable," and "overpowering." Georg apparently feels overpowered by the very atmosphere of his father's room. The father's answer—"Yes, it certainly is dark"—has an aggressive quality, in that the father himself acknowledges the capriciousness of his will. Since we know that it is a warm spring day, Georg's next question, "And you've also shut the window?" sounds like a reproach. "Also" suggests surprise, the question implies disbelief: not only is light shut out, but air also. The father now makes explicit what we have already surmised: "I prefer it that way."[98] Although Georg does not argue openly, his words betray his disapproval: "It is quite warm outside." "Quite" (*ja ganz*) calls attention to the foolishness of the father's whim, but Bendemann entirely

---

97. " 'Hier ist es ja unerträglich dunkel', sagte er dann.
" 'Ja, dunkel ist es schon', antwortete der Vater.
" 'Das Fenster hast du auch geschlossen?'
" 'Ich habe es lieber so.'
" 'Es ist ja ganz warm draussen', sagte Georg, wie im Nachhang zum Früheren, und setzte sich.
"Der Vater räumte das Frühstücksgeschirr ab und stellte es auf einen Kasten" (*E* 59).
98. In a similar situation in *God, Man, and Devil*, Hershele also refuses to have his dark room lit.

ignores his son's remark and calmly proceeds to clear the table. It is clear that the father has won the first round; the uneasiness engendered by this conversation foreshadows the disastrous outcome of the deeper confrontation that follows. The source of the pressure behind this first exchange is the latent hostility between father and son, which is allowed to die down at this point, only to flare up more violently later. Kafka here uses the method of the drama: he creates a tension which smoulders and upon which the action then builds.

At the close of the formalities Georg comes to the point of his visit, announcing his decision to send the news of his engagement "to Petersburg." By saying "to Petersburg" instead of "to my friend" Georg seems deliberately to avoid the word "friend." This omission suggests that Georg has some intuition that the subject of the "friend" will be a delicate one.[99] The father questions the son with interest and encourages him to explain his vacillation, while slowly leading up to the question (to which he already knows the answer) "And now you've changed your mind?" (*PC* 55).[100] Georg replies in the affirmative, repeating the words of the question in a fashion that makes him seem almost hypnotized. (It is at this point that the father removes his glasses and thus calls attention to his "defect of vision." Perhaps this action signifies a conscious decision "not to see too clearly.") In the atmosphere of increasing tension, the father's veiled accusations play an important part. When the father springs his first attack, the unexpected question "Do you really have this friend in ... Petersburg?" (*PC* 56) sounds like a challenge, and it represents the first complication leading to the climax.[101] Contrary to novelistic practice,

99. In this same sentence Georg also reveals his ambivalent attitude toward his engagement, for the verb he uses with "engagement" is *anzeigen,* suggesting *bei Gericht anzeigen* ("to report a crime to a higher authority"). He says: "I really only wanted to tell you . . . that I announced [reported] my engagement in Petersburg after all" ("Ich wollte dir eigentlich nur sagen . . . dass ich nun doch nach Petersburg meine Verlobung angezeigt habe" [*E* 59]).

100. "Und jetzt hast du es dir wieder anders überlegt?" (*E* 59).

101. "Hast du wirklich diesen Freund in Petersburg?" (*E* 60).

Sokel suggests that the father is not really questioning the existence

but typical of the drama, the author does not allow time for the reader to dwell on the implications of this peculiar question, but compresses the action so that the points of crisis occur very close to one another.

After the first high point, the tension temporarily levels off. Despite the father's accusations, Georg remains calm; he tries to avoid a quarrel by changing the subject, while reassuring his father: "Never mind my friends. A thousand friends wouldn't make up to me for my father" (*PC* 56).[102] The reader's attention is sustained while Georg undresses his father and carries him to bed. During this part of the scene, Georg seems to dominate; a plateau is maintained while Georg gently reminds his father of details concerning the friend, and it remains in effect while he tucks the father into bed.

This balance is abruptly shattered by the father's shout: "'No!' cried his father, cutting short the answer, threw the blankets off with a strength that sent them all flying in a moment and sprang erect in bed" (*PC* 59).[103] This surprising action represents the turning point and marks the end of Georg's attempt to control the situation. Visually, it is now the father who dominates the scene; towering above Georg, he literally becomes a giant.[104] The father's actions, which are highly theatrical, raise the tension to such a pitch that events are now forced to move directly forward, quickly building on a series of verbal blows. By accelerating the pace, as well as the intensity of the father's attack, Kafka makes a return to the previous "normal" condition impossible. The father's accusations and wild revelations have the effect which a sudden disclosure of

---

of the friend, but the nature of the friendship. He interprets the father's words to mean "Is this a *friend* you have there, or an enemy?" (*Tragik und Ironie*, p. 53). Ingenious though this interpretation is, I do not think it fits the text.

102. "Lassen wir meine Freunde sein. Tausend Freunde ersetzen mir nicht meinen Vater" (*E* 60).

103. "'Nein!' rief der Vater, dass die Antwort an die Frage stiess, warf die Decke zurück mit einer Kraft, dass sie einen Augenblick im Fluge sich ganz entfaltete, und stand aufrecht im Bett" (*E* 63).

104. Politzer makes a similar observation in *Parable and Paradox*, p. 61.

hidden facts might have in a trial or in a drama built around a mystery. These disclosures lead directly to the climax of the action: the father's judgment of Georg.

In this connection, Kafka's remarks in support of the detective story are illuminating. Janouch reconstructs a meeting with Kafka: "When Kafka saw a crime novel among the books in my briefcase he said: 'There is no need to be ashamed of reading such things. Dostoievski's *Crime and Punishment* is after all only a crime novel. And Shakespeare's *Hamlet?* It is a detective story. At the heart of the action is a mystery, which is gradually brought to light. But is there a greater mystery than the truth? Poetry is always an expedition in search of truth'" (*CwK* 93–94; J 99). Kafka's comments are entirely appropriate to the action of "The Judgment." At the center of the story stands a truth that is gradually revealed, both to Georg and to the reader. That the story is about hidden truth is implied by the father's early remark: "But it's nothing, it's worse than nothing, if you don't tell me the whole truth" (*PC* 56).[105] To push the legal comparison further, Georg's last words—"Dear parents, but I have always loved you"—ring like the final protest on the lips of the unjustly accused prisoner. Although Georg carries out his father's sentence, the pathos of his declaration leaves us uncertain. Does Georg really accept the fact of his guilt, as his actions suggest, or does he feel himself unjustly condemned, as his words imply? The words themselves are ambiguous and support both interpretations. Georg may believe in his own innocence, but possibly, *because* he has "always loved his parents" too much, he is unable to withstand the father's judgment.

105. "Aber es ist nichts, es ist ärger als nichts, wenn du mir jetzt nicht die volle Wahrheit sagst" (*E* 60).

Exactly what Kafka means by "truth" is an extremely complex question. In answer to Janouch's question "But what is the truth?" Kafka replied: "Truth is what every man needs in order to live, but can obtain or purchase from no one. Each man must reproduce it for himself from within, otherwise he must perish. Life without truth is not possible. Truth is perhaps life itself" (*CwK* 94; J 99). Many of the Yiddish plays concern some hidden truth which is revealed and punished.

By withholding judgment, by forcing the reader to view the events as if they were occurring on a stage, Kafka succeeds in putting the reader of "The Judgment" into the position of the spectator at the theater, who must determine the meaning of the stage action for himself. And that Kafka perceived the role of the theater audience as judge, not passive spectator, is shown by a long diary entry for October 26, 1911, in which Kafka writes (with reference to Gordin's *The Savage One*):

> The discreet impression made by the playbill. One learns not only the names but a little more, yet only so much as the audience has to know, even a very cool audience with the best intentions, about a family exposed to their judgment. . . . for one who judges honestly no decent relationship can be seen between the playbill and the play after its performance. (*D*ı 113–14)[106]

In this same entry, Kafka also reflects at length on the identification of characters on the playbills at the Yiddish theater:

> Shmul Leiblich is a "rich merchant," however, it is not said that he is old and infirm, that he is a ridiculous ladies' man, a bad father and an irreverent widower who remarries on the anniversary of his wife's death. And yet all these characterizations would be more accurate than that on the playbill, for at the end of the play he is no longer rich, because the Selde woman has thoroughly robbed him, he is also hardly a merchant any longer, since he has neglected his business. . . . Vladimir Vorobeitchik is only "Selde's lover," but not the corrupter of a family, not a drunkard, gambler, wastrel, idler, parasite. In the characterization "Selde's lover," much of course is betrayed, but considering his behavior it is the least that can be said. (*D*ı 113)[107]

106. "Der diskrete Eindruck des Theaterzettels. Man erfährt nicht nur die Namen, sondern etwas mehr, aber doch nur so viel, als der Öffentlichkeit, und selbst der wohlwollendsten und kühlsten, über eine ihrem Urteil ausgestzte Familie bekanntwerden muss. . . . für den ehrlich Urteilenden nach der Vorstellung zwischen Theaterzettel und Vorstellung nichts Erlaubtes mehr zu sehen ist" (*T* 118–19).

107. "Schmul Leiblich ist ein 'reicher Kaufmann', es wird aber nicht gesagt, dass er alt und kränklich, ein lächerlicher Weiberfreund, ein schlechter Vater und ein pietätloser Witwer ist, der am Jahrzeittag seiner Frau heiratet. Und doch wären alle diese Bezeichnungen richtiger

Kafka is here pointing to the disparity between the definition of the characters in superficial terms of social role, and
their actions, which reveal their inner being. Despite his criticism, Kafka obviously found this method of labelling characters useful, for his remarks concerning the Yiddish plays can be
applied with complete accuracy to the characters of his own
story. Georg Bendemann is delineated simply as "a young merchant," and although this is the very least one can say about
him, it is all we are told. More importantly, he is also a friend,
a fiancé, a son, and at the end of the story, a suicide. Nothing is
said directly about his immaturity, his self-involvement, or his
neglect of his aging father. His fiancée is referred to only as
"[Miss] Frieda Brandenfeld, a girl from a well-to-do family"
(*PC* 52).[108] The friend who plays so significant a role in the
story is not given a name; he is simply referred to as "a childhood friend who was living abroad" or "the Petersburg
friend."[109] The father is never called by his proper name (presumably Bendemann), but only "the father." Clearly Kafka
wanted the reader of "The Judgment" to assess the characters
for himself on the basis of their words and actions. Furthermore, by omitting details, Kafka was able to broaden the scope
of his characters—to suggest, for example, the combined qualities of Father, Judge, God, and Devil in the figure of the father.

It may seem odd to suggest that the paragraph which describes the carrying out of the death sentence acts as the denouement, but if we think once again of the stages of a trial, we
will see that it is the delivery of the verdict, and not the execution of the sentence, that is the climax of the proceedings. Vis-

---

als jene des Theaterzettels, denn am Ende des Stückes ist er nicht mehr
reich, weil ihn Selde ausgeraubt hat, er ist auch kaum ein Kaufmann
mehr, da er sein Geschäft vernachlässigt hat. . . . Wladimir Worobeitschik ist nur "Seldes Geliebter', aber nicht der Verderber einer Familie,
nicht Säufer, Spieler, Wüstling, Nichtstuer, Parasit. Mit der Bezeichnung
'Seldes Geliebter' ist zwar viel verraten, mit Rücksicht auf sein Benehmen
aber ist es das wenigste, was man sagen kann" (*T* 118).

108. "Fräulein Frieda Brandenfeld, [ein] Mädchen aus wohlhabender
Familie" (*E* 56).

109. "Einen sich im Ausland befindlichen Jugendfreund" (*E* 53);
"Der Petersburger Freund" (*E* 64).

ually, all the events which follow the moment of judgment take a sharp downward turn.[110] The release of the tension built by the previous section is signalled by the crash of the father's body onto the bed. This crash is literally followed by a series of declining motions.

Yet, in terms of its own structure, even this brief closing section has the self-enclosed quality of a scene or an act of a play and follows a clear pattern of rising and falling action. It begins with the relative calm of Georg's reaction ("Georg felt driven from the room"),[111] which is immediately translated into action: "The crash with which his father fell on the bed behind him followed him from the room."[112] Georg's exit is implied, though not described. Although the narrative form permits the author to dwell at length on the character's feelings, Kafka does not choose this method, but instead chooses that of the drama, in which emotion is revealed directly through gesture and action. Georg's motives in fleeing from the room are at first unclear, although the speed with which he rushes down the steps is ominous, for it reveals the full intensity of Georg's feelings: "On the staircase ... he ran into his charwoman on her way up." The narrative dwells briefly on their moment of meeting— "'Jesus!' she cried, and covered her face with her apron"—but Georg does not stop even for an instant—"but he was already gone" (*PC* 63).[113] The charwoman's gesture is more fully dramatized by Kafka's choice of the verb *überrumpelte* in place of the more common *überraschte*. Georg does not merely star-

110. The falling nature of the action is reflected not only in the image created by the words "down whose steps [the staircase] he rushed as if it were an inclined plane" ("über deren Stufe er wie über eine schiefe Fläche eilte" [*E* 67]), but in the flow and sound of the words. The idea of *über* (motion over and down) is echoed in the paragraph by the repetition of *ü* sounds in words like *fühlte, stürzte, Schürze, würde, Brücke* ("felt," "rushed," "apron," "became," "bridge").

111. "Georg fühlte sich aus dem Zimmer gejagt" (*E* 67).

112. "Den Schlag mit dem der Vater hinter ihm aufs Bett stürzte, trug er noch in den Ohren davon" (*E* 67).

113. "Auf der Treppe . . . überrumpelte er seine Bedienerin, die im Begriffe war, hinaufzugehen. . . . 'Jesus!' rief sie und verdeckte mit der Schürze das Gesicht, aber er war schon davon" (*E* 67).

tle the charwoman, he takes her by surprise or catches her un-
awares. The gesture and cry of the charwoman express greater
fright than the incident itself would dictate. By her overly
large, public gesture, she foreshadows our feelings at the end of
the story, and thus acts as a kind of chorus.

The sense of motion put into effect by the first sentence of
the denouement is sustained throughout the entire sequence
and helps to create tension and urgency. "On the staircase"
progresses logically to "out the front door" and "across the
road."[114] The urgency of the motion is carried by the verb
"driven" (*trieb es ihn*) which directly combines feeling with
action: he does not run, he is driven. Speed and intensity are
suggested by the adverbs "already" (*schon*) and "still" (*noch*)
which precede and follow the action "he swung himself over":
"Already he was grasping at the railings. . . . With weakening
grip he was still holding on" (*PC* 63).[115] At each step suspense
is created by the tension between our growing intuition of
what will occur (Georg's suicide) and our hope that it will
not. The climax of the denouement—"and let himself drop"
(*PC* 63)[116]—coincides with the final release of the tension for
the entire narrative. After *hinabfallen* the downward motion
levels off, visually by the flow of traffic across the bridge, linguistically by the sense and sound of the two final words "un-
endlicher Verkehr" ("an unending stream of traffic" [*E* 68; *PC*
63]).[117] The story ends, as it began, at a point of complete rest.

114. "Auf der Treppe. . . . Aus dem Tor. . . . über die Fahrbahn" (*E*
67).

115. "Schon hielt er das Geländer fest. . . . Er schwang sich über. . . .
Noch hielt er sich mit schwächer werdenden Händen fest" (*E* 67).

116. "Und liess sich hinabfallen" (*E* 68).

117. *Unendlich* means "immense" and suggests the unlimited and
infinite; *Verkehr* echoes this duration into infinity by the repetition of
the flat *e* sound. Kafka's connection of *Verkehr* with ejaculation (in
German the word has a double meaning)—reported by Brod and commented upon by other critics, particularly Ruhleder ("'Das Urteil,'" pp.
13–14)—does not bear on this analysis, and neither supports nor contradicts it. It is possible to conjecture, however, that by this rather earthy
metaphor, Kafka was simply describing the collapse of tension in the
story.

This pattern mirrors the typical pattern of drama, in which the action begins with order and moves through chaos to restored order.[118]

Structurally and thematically the denouement of "The Judgment" almost exactly parallels that of *God, Man, and Devil*. After the accusation Hershele returns to his prayer books and violin (symbols of his unity with God), Georg turns to thoughts of his youth (when, as gymnast, he had been at one with himself and especially with his parents). In both works a brief glimpse of the continuing world follows the death of the hero.

It is interesting to note that one can even speak meaningfully of Aristotelian *anagnorisis* and *peripeteia* in "The Judgment," as well as in *God, Man, and Devil*. In the course of the action, Georg, like Hershele, comes to recognize the truth of his condition; with this "recognition" comes the inevitable tragic reversal that leads to death.[119] Georg had expected to marry, to succeed in business, to live a normal life; instead, by his recognition that this can never come to be, his expectations are completely reversed and he ends his life by drowning. The element of dramatic irony that such a structure of events suggests is evident in the story. Early in the action, Georg recounts to himself the areas of his success and concludes: "F[u]rther progress lay just ahead" (*PC* 51).[120] In fact, nothing could be farther from the truth, and throughout, Georg remains oblivious to the disaster in store for him.

In this story Kafka uses yet another device of the drama, one that is now entirely out of fashion, but which was popular on the Yiddish stage in the early years of this century. This is the

118. Sokel interprets "The Judgment" in terms of Nietzsche's theory of tragedy (*Tragik und Ironie*, pp. 69–73). Politzer also observes that "the harmony of the world is restored by the death of the hero" (*Parable and Paradox*, p. 60).

119. Sokel makes a similar observation: "The ending of the story presents an ironic reversal, which is identical to the tragic irony in Sophocles' Oedipus" (*Tragik und Ironie*, p. 58). Politzer also refers to the story as a tragedy in *Parable and Paradox*, p. 60.

120. "Ein weiterer Fortschritt stand zweifellos bevor" (*E* 55).

vision that the father's accusation conjures forth in Georg's mind: "His friend in ... Petersburg, whom his father suddenly knew too well, touched his imagination as never before. Lost in the vastness of Russia he saw him. At the door of an empty, plundered warehouse he saw him. Among the wreckage of his showcases, the slashed remnants of his wares, the falling gas brackets, he was just standing up. Why did he have to go so far away!" (*PC* 59).[121]

This image, so visual in its detail, is akin to the visions that were common in Jacobean drama and which found their way into the plays of the Yiddish theater. Avraham Goldfaden, a dramatist of whom Kafka was particularly fond, uses this device conspicuously in two of his best-known plays, *Shulamit* and *Bar Kokhba*. In the Yiddish plays these visions serve as warnings to the characters and are instrumental in restoring order. Gordin adapts a similar warning device in *God, Man, and Devil*, for when Hershele hears the cry of his friend's wounded son, he suddenly recalls the human values he had long forgotten, and he rejects Mazik. Is it not possible to interpret Georg's vision of his friend, lost in the vastness of Russia, as such a dramatic "vision" meant to signal Georg that he has lost control? Georg is so completely trapped in his relationship with his father, however, that he is powerless to heed the warning.

Loss of control (associated with interest in material gain) is the theme of another Yiddish play, Gordin's *The Savage One*, which also has parallels in "The Judgment." The play begins with the marriage of a lecherous old man to a vulgar young

---

121. "Der Petersburger Freund, den der Vater plötzlich so gut kannte, ergriff ihn wie noch nie. Verloren im weiten Russland sah er ihn. An der Türe des leeren, ausgeraubten Geschäftes sah er ihn. Zwischen den Trümmern der Regale, den zerfetzten Waren, den fallenden Gasarmen stand er gerade noch. Warum hatte er so weit wegfahren müssen!" (*E* 64).

The intensity of this description is striking. If we take into account Kafka's interest in Eastern European Jewry and his reading of the Jewish newspaper *Selbstwehr* (with its weekly reports of pogroms in Russia), and set these beside the connections we have shown between "the friend," Russia, and the Yiddish actor Levi, we might well conclude that in describing the friend's plight, Kafka is drawing on reports of pogroms in Russia.

woman and concerns the old man's "simple" son, Lemekh, who
is driven to insanity by his sexual attraction to the father's new
wife (combined with the hostility shown him by his father).
The son's progressive irrationality is shown by his inability to
remember what he wanted to say. In a conversation with his
sister he suddenly breaks off: "What did I want to tell you?
Oy, I forgot already. Do you hear, Lisa, I am all alone here.
Shimon [his brother] went away from here. . . . Oy, what did I
want to tell you? I forgot again."[122] This detail is parallel to
Georg's poor memory, twice mentioned in "The Judgment":
"Only for a moment did he think so, since he kept on forgetting
everything" (PC 61), and "Georg stood in a corner, as far
from his father as possible. A long time ago he had firmly determined to observe everything exactly, so that he could not be
surprised from behind or above by any ruse. Now he remem-
bered his long-forgotten resolve and forgot it."[123] Like Lemekh,
Georg feels himself alone and abandoned. Georg's inability to
keep watch and protect himself reflects the degree to which his
father touches him and is symbolic of his vulnerability. Georg's
failing memory not only reflects his loss of rational control; it is
also the cause of his further decline.

Despite his great age, the wealthy old father in *The Savage
One* quite obviously views his new wife as a sexual object,
while she blatantly plays upon his physical attachment to ex-
tract money from him. This marriage, which takes place on the
anniversary of his first wife's death, *is* a disgrace to her memory and may be linked to Bendemann's insistence that Georg's
engagement defiles his mother's memory. Like old Bendemann
(and like Leyzer Badkhan in *God, Man, and Devil*), the father
in *The Savage One* acts the comedian: he dances and drinks

122. "Vos hob ikh dir gevolt zogn? Oy, ikh hob shoyn fargesn. Herst,
Lisa, ikh bin itst aleyn do, Shimon iz avek fun danen. . . . Oy, vos hob
ikh dir gevolt zogn? Ikh hob vider fargesn" (DVM 38).
123. "Georg stand in einem Winkel, möglichst weit vom Vater. Vor
einer langen Weile hatte er sich fest entschlossen, alles vollkommen
genau zu beobachten, damit er nicht irgendwie auf Umwegen, von hinten
her, von oben herab überrascht werden könne. Jetzt erinnerte er sich
wieder an den längst vergessenen Entschluss und vergass ihn" (E 64–
65).

and makes a fool of himself. When he complains of feeling ill, his wife's lover taunts him: "Go be sick in good health. Who is bothering you? If a person can't fall asleep, he covers himself over with a blanket over his head and sweats."[124] The highly metaphoric language of this directive corresponds to Georg's covering up his father and may even have provided the idea of Bendemann's trick with the blanket. In *The Savage One* the father is wanted out of the way by the wife's lover and by at least one of his sons. This "no-good" son accuses the father of having lived with "dead ones" in a home that was like a grave which no one wanted to enter. These images suggest the setting of Bendemann's dark, grave-like room, literally lined with mementos of the dead mother. Bendemann shares with the father in *The Savage One* and *God, Man, and Devil* the desire to be young, which in all three is coupled with feeble health and a basic mistrust of their offspring. These characteristics link old Bendemann to the clichés of Jewish culture, according to which the aging, self-sacrificing parent pities himself for his mercenary, unfeeling children. No doubt Kafka's own father voiced these same feelings. In "The Judgment" Kafka plays on the ironic undercurrent often underlying the cliché by portraying the father as stronger than the son.

No one familiar with Kafka's continuing struggle to come to terms with the specter of his all-powerful, demanding, disapproving father can fail to see in old Bendemann some features of Kafka senior. In this respect, the father-son relationship, a dominant theme of the Yiddish theater, coincides with Kafka's personal difficulties (which provided the raw material for Kafka's narratives) and thus may explain his intense interest in these plays. It may also be that he was able to write "The Judgment" with such rapidity because he was hanging it on a pre-existing framework provided by the Yiddish plays.

"The Judgment" can properly be included among the best of Kafka's stories. It is one of the few which he himself prized

124. "Zayt aykh krank gezunterheyt. Ver tshepet aykh? Un az men ken nit dershlofn vern, dekt men zikh iber mit a koldere ibern kop un men shvitst" (*DVM* 40).

highly, perhaps for purely personal reasons: it was the first of his successful works, and it remained closely connected in his mind with Felice Bauer. In a letter to Felice, Kafka proposed an attitude for reading "The Judgment" which is highly illuminating, not only for this story, but for the entire *oeuvre*. He writes: "But you don't know your little story at all yet. It is a bit wild and senseless and did it not have inner truth (which never allows itself to be confirmed, but rather must always be granted or denied anew by each reader or listener) it would be nothing."[125] The continual reinterpretation which Kafka considered necessary and appropriate to "The Judgment" links the method of this story to that of the drama.

125. "Aber Du kennst ja noch gar nicht Deine kleine Geschichte. . . . Sie ist ein wenig wild und sinnlos und hätte sie nicht innere Wahrheit (was sich niemals allgemein feststellen lässt, sondern immer wieder von jedem Leser oder Hörer von neuem zugegeben oder geleugnet werden muss) sie wäre nichts" (*Fe* 156).

chapter six

The dramatic in
Kafka's work to 1914

"The Judgment" not only illuminates Kafka's narrative method, but it also allows us to link the development of his style to his experience of the Yiddish theater:
in its choice of theme, character, structure, and technique the
story reveals the direct impact of the Yiddish plays. Yet the
influence of these plays is not limited to the first of Kafka's
successful stories. It is also evident in work which Kafka began
before the breakthrough—for example, in the unfinished novel
Der Verschollene (*Amerika*), an important narrative which is
difficult to place in either the early or the later period[1]—
and in work written during the two years immediately following.

Although far more successful than anything else Kafka wrote
before "The Judgment," *Der Verschollene* is not as powerful or
convincing as the later work. As a whole, it does not apply dramatic method to narrative prose; it does, however, include
many sections that bear the mark of the later style.[2] The initial
meeting between Karl and the stoker (brought about by Karl's
chance knock on the cabin door) is an especially good example
of a "staged" scene, which, like the drama, is enacted in a limited space, develops character and action by means of terse dialogue, and is punctuated by large, significant gestures: " 'But

1. Hereafter referred to as *Der Verschollene* ("he who disappeared,
was forgotten, lost, never more heard of"), the name Kafka gave to the
novel (see D$_{II}$ 107; *T* 453). Brod is responsible for the title *Amerika*,
which Politzer calls a "misnomer" (*Parable and Paradox*, p. 124). I prefer to use the author's own title, especially as it is closer to the essence
of the novel; I keep the original German because I could not find a
concise English equivalent.

2. Politzer (*Parable and Paradox*, p. 125) describes Karl's seduction
by Johanna as an "early example of Kafka's mature prose style."

then I must go up and see about it at once,' said Karl, looking round for the way out. 'You just stay where you are,' said the man, giving him a push with one hand on the chest, quite roughly, so that he fell back on the bunk again. 'But why?' asked Karl in exasperation. 'Because there's no point in it,' said the man" (*Am* 5–6).[3] The menace inherent in this situation (Karl is essentially imprisoned in the cabin of a total stranger) is not analyzed by the author, but conveyed solely by means of word, gesture, and tone. Similarly, the stoker's self-imposed "trial" in the captain's office, which builds on the effects of the previous scene, is constructed like a melodrama in which mystery and suspense are introduced and embellished (Can the ineffectual stoker triumph over his powerful enemy, the hated Schubal?), only to be resolved unexpectedly with a great theatrical flourish (the stoker's case is completely overshadowed by Uncle Jakob's finding his nephew Karl).[4]

Begun sometime in early 1912, reworked between late 1912 and 1914, and finally abandoned in 1915 or 1916, *Der Verschollene* spans the years of transition and continues well into the later period.[5] The first chapter, "The Stoker" (published inde-

3. "'Da muss ich aber doch gleich hinaufschaun', sagte Karl und sah sich um, wie er hinauskommen könnte. 'Bleiben Sie nur', sagte der Mann, und stiess ihn mit einer Hand gegen die Brust, geradezu rauh, ins Bett zurück. 'Warum denn?' fragte Karl ärgerlich. 'Weil es keinen Sinn hat', sagte der Mann" (*A* 13).

4. Other staged scenes, all confined to a single setting, include the dinner at Mr. Pollunder's, Karl's encounter with Klara, Karl's "trial" at the Hotel Occidental, Karl's attempted escape at Brunelda's, and especially Fragment I, Brunelda's bath, a scene in which the main character (Brunelda) is presented only as a voice and a force, while in the foreground her "slaves" (Karl and Robinson) rush frantically around the room trying to serve and appease her.

For a detailed discussion of the function of gesture and costume in this novel, see Jahn, "Kafka und die Anfänge des Kinos"; and idem, *Kafkas Roman "Der Verschollene.*" In his discussion of *Der Verschollene* Jahn divides the novel into self-contained units (which he calls *Handlungszentren* [centers of action or plot]) whose structure corresponds to the individual acts of a play.

5. See Pasley and Wagenbach, "Datierung sämtlicher Texte," in *Kafka Symposion,* by Born et al., pp. 62–63; and Jürgen Born, "Vom 'Urteil' zum *Prozess:* Zu Kafkas Leben und Schaffen in den Jahren 1912–1914," *ZDP* 86 (1967): 186–96.

pendently in *Der Jüngste Tag*, May, 1913), appeared in the *Diaries* on September 25, 1912, only a few days after "The Judgment," while the next five chapters were completed by mid-November 1912. A substantial portion of Chapter 7 was written (though not completed) in late November of that same year; there is a large gap in time between it and what was probably to have been the last chapter, "The Nature Theater of Oklahoma."[6] In addition to these, only two fragments of intervening material remain.

Politzer persuasively summarizes the difficulties that must have beset Kafka in the writing of this novel. Having conceived the basic plan for the novel before the breakthrough, "he seems very soon to have become aware of the incompatibility of the material at hand with the new means now at his disposal."[7] Kafka's difficulties with the work are made clear in a letter to Felice (March 9/10, 1913) in which he alludes to two hundred manuscript pages of a "completely unusable" draft of the novel (*Fe* 332). Although it is not possible to compare the early formulation, which he probably destroyed, with the later one, it is clear that the broad scope and the descriptive style of much of *Der Verschollene* is far from the closed construction of "The Judgment." The novel is clearly a product of transition, although on the whole, its panoramic sweep brings it closer to the conceptions of Kafka's earlier work. Spilka has detailed the heavy debt that this novel owes to the work of Dickens. Wolfgang Jahn relates the style of *Der Verschollene* to the cinematographic method of the silent film.[8] The validity of these influence studies is in no way diminished by our linking *Der Verschollene* to the plays of the Yiddish theater that occupied Kafka intensely during this period.

The striking image in the opening paragraph of the novel—

6. H. Uyttersprot, *Eine Neue Ordnung der Werke Kafkas? Zur Struktur von "Der Prozess" und "Amerika"* (Antwerp, 1957), p. 73, suggests that the Nature Theater was not meant to be the final one, and that a chapter describing Karl's death was to follow.

7. Politzer, *Parable and Paradox*, p. 117.

8. Mark Spilka, *Dickens and Kafka: A Mutual Interpretation* (Bloomington, Ind., 1963); Jahn, "Kafka und die Anfänge des Kinos."

the Statue of Liberty holding a sword in place of a torch—and the strange figures of trumpet-blowing angels in the last chapter lead us directly to the prologue of Gordin's play, *God, Man, and Devil*, which opens with an allegorical portrayal of the heavens, replete with God, Satan, and hordes of angels. God finds it difficult to accept Satan's view that man has not progressed in the thousands of years since he ate of the Tree of Knowledge: "I chased him from the Garden of Eden, for thousands of years he wandered about, and you still find him in the same place, next to the gates of Eden? Nonsense!"[9] Satan counters (calling God "ancient master" [*alter her*]) that man has indeed moved from the gates of Eden, for if he still stood on the same spot he would certainly have returned to Paradise long ago: man did not find what he sought in the world, and the guardian angels whom God placed at the gates became old and weak, their swords rusted and blunt. Satan concludes that the ceaseless wandering was useless, for man carried with him his "wildness" and his "old rags," and remained at heart a robber and a beggar.

Satan's description of the two angels and his view of man are related to Kafka's vision in *Der Verschollene*. Karl, the seeker, the wanderer, expelled from his parental home (the first Eden) is sent to America (the Promised Land), which, ironically, he finds is guarded by Liberty holding aloft a sword.[10] Intrusion into this Eden is easy, not only because the sword which protects it is blunt and old, but because this Eden is no Paradise, as Karl is soon to discover. Like Satan's Adam, Karl

9. "Ikh hob im fortgeyogt fun gan-eydn, toyzender yor geyt et zayt dos als faroys un faroys, un du gefinst im nokh imer oyf demzelbn ort, nebn di toyren fun gan-eydn? Unzin!" (*GMT* 8).

10. In *Parable and Paradox*, pp. 122–23, Politzer discusses the meaning of this symbol. Although I agree that this sword "is not drawn against the social injustices bred by America's capitalism" (ibid., p. 123), I cannot agree so readily that it is pointed "against Karl Rossmann's conscience." The unwilling seduction in which Karl was more victim than victimizer would not merit so powerful a symbol. I believe that Kafka was here being playful, merging the Garden of Eden symbolism (angels guard its gates with swords) with that of the promise of freedom in the new land.

carries with him his old rags, "zayne alte lumpn" (his trunk), and his "vildness" (his impetuous, foolish, naïve, not always truthful, but essentially unguarded nature). Like Adam, Karl eats of the apple, although recognition of sexuality does not come to him through Therese, the giver of the apple, but through Brunelda, whose aggressive female sexuality he is forced to witness and finally to accept as a fact of life. Nevertheless, except for his "rape" by Johanna, the initial cause of his expulsion, Karl never experiences sex in any of his adventures. One might say he avoids it. It seems that Karl's search for maturity, sexual or otherwise, is to be as infinite and as useless as the wandering of the Jew through the wilderness. Like the sons of Adam, Karl's path leads not to salvation, but only to the farcical Nature Theater.[11]

The absurd image of the women angels with pasted wings in long white robes, blowing golden trumpets from high pedestals (later male devils dressed like Satan are to replace them) is reminiscent of the probable staging and costuming for the prologue in *God, Man, and Devil*. The stage directions read: "The chair of honor [God's throne] on high, clouds under the heavens, many stars. Many, many angels, young ones soaring in the air, old ones on the stairs leading to the chair of honor. Satan stands apart."[12] The improvised staging at the Savoy probably placed the angels who were to be "in the air" on pedestals, dressed in the long white robes traditionally associated with angels in the Yiddish theater.[13] Choruses of angels praise the

11. In interpreting this novel I cannot agree with Brod's assertion (see "Afterword," in *Am* 298), taken up by Klaus Mann and Mark Spilka, that the novel was to end happily. On this disputed point I side with Politzer, Uyttersprot, and Bergel, who conclude that the existing text in no way foreshadows a positive ending, and in fact, seems to take its hero steadily downhill. See Klaus Mann, "Preface," in *Am* vii–xviii; Lienhard Bergel, "*Amerika*: Its Meaning," in *Franz Kafka Today*, ed. Flores and Swander, pp. 117–26.

12. "Der kisey hakoved in der hoykh, untn himlen, volkns, fil shtern. Zeyr fil englen, yunge shvebn in der luftn, alte melakhim bay di trep fun kisey hakoved, der Satan shteyt bazunder fun dervaytn" (*GMT* 5).

13. See Lifson, *The Yiddish Theater in America*, pp. 48–51. Angels are also called for in the last scene of *Kol Nidre*.

natural order of the universe in which everyone has his proper
place. Whenever God speaks, a mighty blowing of the shofar
(the ram's horn) is heard. Because of the Jewish proscription
against images, God does not appear, and His voice merely
emanates from His throne. Could this elaborate, no doubt unintentionally ludicrous allegory of the heavenly spheres have
suggested the idea of the Nature Theater to Kafka? Sokel is
one of the few critics who relate the Nature Theater to the
Yiddish theater in Prague,[14] which (like the promise the Nature Theater held out to Karl) seemed to offer Kafka a new
vision of salvation, but which (like the fictional theater) ultimately failed to provide him with a sense of his own identity.
Karl, in fact, loses his identity altogether in the Nature Theater.

Der Verschollene can also be linked to another of the Yiddish plays, Rikhter's Moyshe the Tailor as Councillor, which,
like Der Verschollene, is the story of "one who disappears" into
the New World. The play concerns Khayit's son Nakhuml,
who, while on a business trip to Palestine, runs away to America, leaving behind him a pregnant young wife. Eventually,
Khayit's faithful servants bring Nakhuml's son to America,
where he is cared for by a wealthy, childless couple. Complications of the plot notwithstanding, one can see parallels in the
essential situation portrayed in the two works. Like Nakhuml,
Karl leaves his unborn child in Europe and "disappears" into
the New World, and like Nakhuml's child, Karl is himself
"adopted" in America by a wealthy patron.

America is an important symbol in Rikhter's play, and the
entire fourth act of Moyshe the Tailor is set in that country.
The themes of this act correspond to the details of Kafka's
America. The first scene of the fourth act takes place in the
home of Khayit's servant Yoshe, who soliloquizes on the many
difficulties he has experienced in America. Humor is mixed
with pathos. He begins by complaining about his poverty, for

14. Sokel, Tragik und Ironie, p. 507. I cannot, however, agree with
Sokel's assertion that the Nature Theater is romantic (ibid., p. 505).
Whatever serious intentions Kafka may have had in mind are lost in the
grotesque parody of Paradise that this theater represents.

despite extreme exhaustion and overwork, he is forced to eat
only one meal, in his own words, "dinner and supper in one":

> Oy, such a dinner should have beset Columbus before he came
> to this wasteland America. Why didn't he lead us back to Egypt?
> What is the difference between Pithom and Raamses and Brook-
> lyn and New York? There they fed us clay and bricks, and here
> they feed us machines and pressing irons. The difference is that
> in Egypt only the men worked and the women had rest, . . . and
> because the women had rest, every Jewish woman could really
> have six children at a time. It seems to me that if in Europe one
> were willing to be such a servant [slave] of Canaan, and work
> as hard as in America, one could more quickly become some-
> thing. There, if I worked, and my wife worked, we always saved
> up a few pennies. But where does a Jew run to find his fortune?
> To America. Here I've already worked six years with my bloody
> sweat, and I am still without a penny in my pocket.[15]

Aside from the broad similarities in Rikhter's and Kafka's views
of America as a false Promised Land, the most striking detail in
Yoshe's speech is the mention of the Biblical city Raamses,
which corresponds to the rather unusual name Kafka gave to
the city near which the Hotel Occidental is located. Chapter 4
of *Der Verschollene,* one of the chapters that Kafka himself
titled, is called "Weg nach Ramses."[16] In his soliloquy Yoshe is

15. "Oy aza a diner hot gezolt dershlogn Kolombusn, eyder er iz
gekumen in dem vistn Amerika. Far vos hot er unz nisht zurik gefirt
kayn Mitsrayim? Vos iz der khiluk fun Pitom v'Raamses biz Bruklin mit
Nu York? Dort hot men unz gehodivet b'khomer v'bilbaynim mit tsigl
un mit laym, un do hodivit men unz mit mashinen un bigel ayzns. Der
khiluk iz az in Mitsrayim hobn nur di mener gearbit un di vayber hobn
gehat ru, . . . un az di vayber hobn gehat ru hot take yede yidishe froy
gekent hobn 6 kinder mit eynmol. Mir dakht zikh az ven me vil in Yurop
zayn aza eved Kanani un azoy shver arbaytn vi in Amerika, volt men
gikher gekent tsu epes kumen. Dort az ikh hob gearbit un mayn vayb
gearbit, hot men zikh fort ershpart etlikhe guldn. Nur vi loyft a yud
zikhn glikn? Kayn Amerika, un do arbayt ikh shoyn 6 yor mit dem
blutign shvays, ober a sent in keshine lo" (*MK* 40–41).

Similarly ironic portraits of America dominate other works of Yiddish
literature with which Kafka became familiar in 1911 and 1912 through
his friend Yitskhok Levi.

16. I have used Kafka's spelling, "Ramses," in referring to his city;

clearly making a wry comparison between his labors as a Jew
and a newcomer to America and the slavery of the Jews in
Egypt. According to his understanding, Brooklyn is merely another Raamses, one of the Biblical treasure cities built for the
Pharaoh by the forced labor of the Israelites, and the point
from which they began their journey through the wilderness
(Exod. 1:11, 12:37). Such a wilderness is Kafka's America, and
such a treasure city is the Ramses in which Karl finds himself,
a city described strictly in terms of trade and commerce: "But
Karl and Therese stuck close together and hurried to the different offices, laundries, warehouses and shops" (Am 151).[17] Such
references suggest that Karl's journey parallels the wanderings
of the Jews through the desert.

Throughout this novel Kafka seems to be playing (albeit un-
systematically) with Biblical allusions. These may have come
to his attention through the Yiddish plays, for they are permeated with serious references to Jewish history as well as
with comic comparisons between modern and ancient times
that depend upon audience familiarity with Biblical themes.
Karl's expulsion from the Hotel Occidental recalls not only Ex-
odus, but also the story of Joseph and Potiphar. (The Joseph
story is also played upon in *Moyshe the Tailor*, when Nakhuml's supposed death is proven to his father by the return of
his prayer shawl and coat.) In the Hotel Occidental, Karl, like
Joseph in Potiphar's house, finds himself in service in a foreign
place where he is favored and given a position of responsibility. Joseph gets into trouble because of Potiphar's wife, Karl
because of Robinson. In his efforts to repel the advances of Potiphar's wife, Joseph rushes from her chamber, leaving his coat
in her hands. Angered by his rejection, Potiphar's wife accuses
Joseph to her husband, using the coat as evidence against him;

---

when I am speaking of the Biblical city, I use the spelling "Raamses."
(The English edition of *Der Verschollene* uses yet a third spelling—
"Rameses.")

Politzer (*Parable and Paradox*, p. 140) comments on the contradiction
inherent in the names Occidental and Ramses.

17. "Aber Karl und Therese eilten eng beisammen in die verschiedenen Büros, Waschanstalten, Lagerhäuser und Geschäfte" (A 148).

and on the strength of her word, Joseph is dismissed and thrown into prison. At the Hotel Occidental, Karl is (at least in part) falsely accused—the story of Karl's nights in town is a patent lie—and on the basis of this accusation is summarily dismissed. In his efforts to avoid the indecent approaches and the fury of the Head Porter, Karl escapes by leaving his jacket in the man's hands. Joseph is trapped in the wife's private chamber, Karl in the Head Porter's curtained booth. Kafka's reference to the Joseph story is here doubly ironic, since he reverses the male-female roles: the Head Porter takes the part of Potiphar's wife, while the manageress plays Potiphar. By locating Ramses in the Promised Land, Kafka creates a paradoxical image of bondage in freedom, which Karl does not fully comprehend: entering service as a lift boy, Karl replies to the manageress, " 'Yes, I'm free,' . . . and nothing seemed more worthless to him."[18] These allusions do not merge to form a coherent pattern in terms of which we can interpret the novel, however. Their main function is to widen the symbolic significance of the described world. In so doing, Kafka seems to build on Yoshe's ironic comparison of the Jew in Egypt and America by making these allusions concrete, first in Karl's servitude in the Hotel Occidental, then in his slavery or imprisonment in Brunelda's apartment.

Further parallels with *Moyshe the Tailor,* though unsystematic, are scattered through the novel. Yet other images in Yoshe's speech—for example, the machines associated with America and the clay and bricks of Egypt—are elaborated upon in *Der Verschollene.* In the hotel Karl is impressed with the machinery of the elevator and disappointed that he will not be allowed to observe it directly. In his naïveté, Karl does not recognize the oppressive, dehumanizing nature of the machine. Yoshe's description of the plight of woman in America and its associations with slavery, bricks, and building may be combined in the tragic story of Therese and her mother, whose suffering is also associated with bricks and building. The passage describing the death of Therese's mother is filled with the im-

18. " 'Ja, frei bin ich', . . . und nichts schien ihm wertloser" (A 130).

agery of bricks: the child is seated on a heap of bricks, the
building is filled with piles of bricks, bricks block the mother's
path, and bricks shower her as she falls.[19] The connection between the Jewish servant's speech and this episode is especially
compelling, not only because of Yoshe's reference to the bricks
that Jews were "fed" in Egypt, but because in both, bricks and
clay symbolize degradation and extreme privation. Therese's
story brings to Karl the lesson of human pain, which is also the
lesson of history and which Karl is soon to experience on his
own.

The discussion of origins between the manageress and Karl
brings to mind the Jewish emphasis on community, which is
particularly stressed in the Yiddish plays. The words for com-
patriot, *Landsmann* and *Landsleute* (in Yiddish, *landsman*
and *landslayt*), which occur three times in their conversation,
are common forms of greeting and recognition used by Jews
from the old country and reserved for those from the same
local area. Vienna (which is the manageress' home) and
Prague (Karl's) were very closely tied, and it seems that the
manageress had actually lived in Prague for a time. These greet-
ings may be veiled allusions to "being Jewish" and would account for her protective interest in Karl and for the precarious-
ness of her position in the hotel. Karl's reference to his com-
panions as "unclean" (*nicht rein* [A 121]) may be an allusion to
their being Gentiles, and therefore ritually unclean. This reference would explain their hostility to Karl and their ready
inclination to beat him. (Later they "save" Karl by taking him
into captivity.) It would also account for the warning against
the Irish which Karl had received in the old country, for legend reported that the Irish in America were heavy drinkers
and famous Jew baiters.

Another association which relates *Der Verschollene* to
Moyshe the Tailor, as well as to Jewishness, is the bearded stu-

19. The words for brick and brick-heap (*Ziegel, Ziegelhaufen*),
comparable to Yoshe's *tsigl,* occur eight times in close succession in the
denouement of Therese's story. Politzer's association of Therese's suffering with the martyrdom of Saint Therese is not compelling (see
Parable and Paradox, p. 141).

dent, Josef Mendel. His name may be a composite of several details from the America scene in Rikhter's play. Almost immediately we learn that in America Yoshe is called Joey. (In the play all the Jewish characters acquire new names in the New World, as does Uncle Jakob in *Der Verschollene*, who rids himself of his Jewish-sounding surname, Bendelmayer.) At the end of the first scene Joey and his wife, Asne, now Annie, sing a duet celebrating their newly found good fortune. In doggerel verse Yoshe calls himself "dein Mendele" ("your little man") to rhyme with "hendele" ("little chicken"). Mendel is a common Yiddish name, Mendele its diminutive. Neither the name nor the term is pejorative in Yiddish, as Politzer suggests it is in German.[20] It may be that Kafka combined the servant's name Joey (Joseph) with his poetic reference to himself as "Mendele" to form the name of the student Josef Mendel (whose nightly studying may be an ironic allusion to Jewish emphasis on learning). Josef Mendel may even be an ironic self-portrait of Kafka, who, like the student, was employed by day and wrote by night. Although the image of the disillusioned student is satiric, Karl takes his advice seriously, and on its strength decides to stay with Delamarche. Yoshe's experience in America may have served as a model for Josef Mendel, and through him, for Karl Rossmann. Since Kafka had never visited the United States, he was especially likely to need models in writing about American experiences.

Der Verschollene includes another detail which links Karl's difficulties in America to that of the Jew in Europe, the matter of identification papers. Twice Karl is asked to identify himself: the policeman in the suburb stops him on the basis of his looks, and even in the Nature Theater (which claims to accept everyone), Karl is asked to show his papers. Karl's precarious position in the world is not unlike that of the Jew who often did not have a legal entrance permit, and even if he did, often found himself totally unprotected against the malicious hostility of the police or other figures of authority.

The election motif in *Der Verschollene* also has a parallel in *Moyshe the Tailor* in the satiric portrait of the hero's father,

---

20. Politzer, *Parable and Paradox*, p. 154.

the nouveau-riche alderman who proudly explains how many thousands of rubles his election to office costs him each year. In America, as Josef Mendel explains to Karl, not even such vast expenditures of money can assure the candidate's election, despite the fact that he is well suited to the job. One might conclude that in the old country, at least "honest" corruption works. In America corruption is so universal that it proves ineffective.

Another technical device found in both these works is the act of peeping through a keyhole. In the Yiddish play, after the hero's wedding, there is a comic interlude during which the servant Yoshe peeks into his master's bedroom and gets very excited, shouting, "Quick, I want to get married." The joke is that when he invites the woman servant, Asne, to look too, she merely describes the lovely "concert" they are having, the wife playing the "fortepian," the husband the violin, and the father-in-law sitting by, enjoying the "music." The sexual allusions in this sequence are obvious.

They are less obvious, though definitely present, in the keyhole sequence in *Der Verschollene*, which occurs when Karl is brought up to Brunelda's room. Before Karl is allowed to enter the room, Delamarche bends down to the keyhole to see if Brunelda is sleeping. This spying is itself suggestive, and the dark room in which the fat woman lounges on the couch, her legs exposed to the knees, is even more so. Her first words to Delamarche—"Oh, this heat, Delamarche"[21]—sound like an open sexual invitation, especially in contrast to Karl's innocent observation that the heat in the room is not extraordinary. By means of stage techniques, the entire scene conveys the open sexuality that Brunelda embodies.

Kafka's two vagabonds, Robinson and Delamarche, have their counterparts in two characters in Gordin's play *The Savage One*. Alexander, one of the sons of the foolish old Shmul Layblikh, is characterized simply as "glat a gor nisht," just a nobody, a nothing; he joins forces with one Vladimir Vorobaytshik, who is also known as Fayvel Ganif (Fayvel the thief) and is Layblikh's wife's lover. Like Robinson and Dela-

21. "Das ist eine Hitze, Delamarche" (A 220).

marche, these two drink, loaf, sing, and pay attendance on Zelde, who bears a strong resemblance to Brunelda (the two names even sound alike). Like Brunelda, Zelde is totally amoral; for example, while she blatantly moves her lover into the family home, she continues to wheedle funds from her unsuspecting husband. Like Brunelda, she supports the two good-for-nothings on this money, and like her, has many whims, demands much attention, and frequently pretends to faint or feel ill. Both these undeserving, innately unlovable women reject doting husbands who remain "in love" with them and who even go to the extremes of taking keepsakes to remind them of their wives.

There are other parallels: Robinson and Delamarche send Karl to get beer, bacon, and bread. In *The Savage One* the two idlers send Lemekh, the "simple" son, for liquor; and later they themselves bring drink (rum is mentioned in both works) and *treyfe kalbes* (meat forbidden to Jews) into the house. The literal filth of Brunelda's house corresponds to the moral filth of Layblikh's establishment. Layblikh's "moral" son, Shimon, refers to it as a "dirty house" and to the two vagabonds as *shmuts* ("dirt").

Karl displays a simplicity of understanding akin to the limited perceptions of Lemekh in *The Savage One*. Both boys have father figures who reject them: Lemekh is beaten by his real father, Karl by his father-surrogate Delamarche. The behavior of the two good-for-nothings toward the young boys is similar. Both sets of idlers treat the boys with derision and hostility but make use of them whenever they can. Like Brunelda, Zelde teases and arouses the young boy, who cannot cope with his feelings of sexuality. Karl pushes Brunelda away, Lemekh begs Zelde to stop petting him. Some memory of Lemekh—the central character of Gordin's play, the "simple" son who is intensely attached to his dead mother and utterly confused by his feelings toward the young woman brought into the home as his "new mother"—may have influenced Kafka's conception of Karl—the young, simple boy who is both drawn and repelled by the open sexuality of the mother-figure Brunelda.

Despite Lemekh's murder of Zelde, *The Savage One* ends on

a note of hope: the entire family, Lemekh included, will mi-
grate to an unnamed faraway country to make a fresh start.
And, as Yoshe remarked in *Moyshe the Tailor*, "Where does a
Jew run to find his fortune?"—clearly, "To America." Kafka's
novel seems to pick up where *The Savage One* ends. Perhaps
Kafka blended Gordin's sentimental, naïve note of hope with
Yoshe's more realistic view of America and Satan's dark perception of man and fused the whole with Biblical allusions to
create the fantastic, symbolic image of the modern world to
which he gave the name "Amerika." The story, however, remains Karl's; it presents the adventures of "one who was lost,"
was never more heard of—Kafka's image of man. This image is
further developed (with grimmer pessimism and more sar-
donic humor) in "The Metamorphosis," a story which closely
follows Kafka's completion of the first six chapters of *Der Verschollene*.[22]

The fascination of "The Metamorphosis," the most widely
known and one of the most disturbing of Kafka's works, lies
chiefly in the horror of its central metaphor—a man awakens
one morning to find that he has become a giant bug—a situation which is presented with a matter-of-factness that is difficult
to accept or comprehend. Begun in November and completed
in December of 1912, only three months after the writing of
"The Judgment," "The Metamorphosis" also reflects the direct
impact of the Yiddish plays. Gordin's *The Savage One*, a clas-
sic of the Yiddish theater previously discussed in connection
with "The Judgment" and *Der Verschollene*, offered Kafka a
model for making concrete the insect metaphor which he origi-
nally conceived in 1907.[23] In the *Diaries* Kafka discusses *The
Savage One* at length and outlines its plot in some detail:

22. According to Pasley and Wagenbach, Kafka completed these on
November 12, 1912, and began to work on "The Metamorphosis" only
five days later ("Datierung sämtlicher Texte," in *Kafka Symposion*, by
Born et al.).

23. See the novel fragment "Wedding Preparations in the Country,"
DF 6–7; *H* 12.

Parts of the plot of *Der Wilde Mensch* are very spirited. A young widow marries an old man with four children and immediately brings her lover, Vladimir Vorobeitchik, along into the marriage. The two proceed to ruin the whole family, Shmul Leiblich (Pipes) must soon hand over all his money and becomes sick, the oldest son, Simon (Klug), a student, leaves the house, Alexander becomes a gambler and drunkard, Lise (Tschissik) becomes a prostitute and Lemech (Löwy), the idiot, is driven to idiotic insanity by hate of Mrs. Selde, because she takes the place of his mother, and by love, because she is the first young woman to whom he feels close. At this point the plot reaches a climax with the murder of Selde by Lemech. (*Di* 112)[24]

Accurate though Kafka's synopsis is, it fails to emphasize the centrality of Lemekh, the "defective" son who becomes "the savage one" and whose situation (but for Gregor's physical disfigurement) closely parallels that of Gregor Samsa in "The Metamorphosis." Like Lemekh, Gregor is barely tolerated in the home, and like him, is looked upon with disgust (particularly by the father) as an outcast whose very existence shames his family. In different ways, Gregor and Lemekh combine the same qualities of "thing" and "person." Both are presented as essentially simple, meek, self-effacing persons who become animal-like creatures because of a drastic transformation, which culminates in Gregor's death and Lemekh's murder of Zelde.

24. "Sehr mutig ist teilweise die Handlung des 'Wilden Menschen'. Eine junge Witwe heiratet einen alten Mann, der vier Kinder hat, und bringt gleich ihren Liebhaber, den Wladimir Worobeitschik, mit in die Ehe. Nun ruinieren die zwei die ganze Familie, Schmut [*sic*] Leiblich (Pipes) muss alles Geld hergeben und wird krank, der älteste Sohn Simon (Klug), ein Student, verlässt das Haus, Alexander wird ein Spieler und Säufer, Lise (Tschissik) wird Dirne und Lemech (Löwy), der Idiot, wird gegenüber der Frau Selde von Hass, weil sie an Stelle seiner Mutter tritt, und von Liebe, weil sie der erste ihm nahe junge Frau ist, in einen idiotischen Wahnsinn gebracht. Die so weit getriebene Handlung löst sich mit der Ermordung der Selde durch Lemech" (*T* 117).

The names in parentheses refer to the Yiddish actors who took the various roles in this performance of *The Savage One.*

Although Gregor's physical transformation is already completed when "The Metamorphosis" opens, while the change in Lemekh occurs more gradually, the process of progressive decay continues throughout both works. Thus, Gregor's metamorphosis parallels Lemekh's decline.

Each of the five characters in Kafka's story has a direct counterpart in Gordin's play. Besides Gregor and Lemekh, the two defective sons, there are the two fathers, Samsa Senior and Shmul Layblikh, who are "resurrected" (Samsa by his son's decline, Layblikh by his marriage); the two mother-figures, Mrs. Samsa and Zelde, who protect their sons and are adored by them; the two sisters, Grete and Liza, half-developed girls who eventually abandon the brothers to whom they are so closely attached; and the two housekeepers, who show no fear of the peculiar son and take charge of him.

The central metaphor of "The Metamorphosis" corresponds to the imagery which the housekeeper uses to describe Lemekh's position within his family: "They kill him if he comes in here, so he lies in his own room, days on end, with his eyes open, and stares, like an animal waiting to be sacrificed."[25] While Lemekh is said to stare at humans dumbly as if he were an animal, Gregor literally becomes an animal, and like Lemekh, is grateful to be allowed to look at and listen to his family from the darkness of his room: "He was sufficiently compensated for this worsening of his condition by the fact that

25. "Men harget im er zol nit aher nisht geyn, ligt er bay zikh, vi a hun in bney adam" (*DVM* 37–38).

The last words in this passage, *vi a hun in bney adam,* which I have translated "like an animal waiting to be sacrificed," literally mean "like a chicken [scapegoat] in a ritual." (In the Diaspora, the traditional sacrifice of a [scape]goat was replaced by a chicken.) *Bney adam* (literally, "sons of Adam") are the opening words of a prayer recited on Yom Kippur before the required sacrifice is made. The prayer calls upon "men [*bney adam*] who sit in darkness bound in misery and iron." The idiom *vi a hun in bney adam* stems from this prayer and generally refers to an unknowing, ignorant person (i.e., one as unknowing as the animal that is to be sacrificed). In *The Savage One,* however, the servant is calling attention to Lemekh's bewildered look, characteristic of the uncomprehending, instinctively frightened animal in the presence of men who are about to slaughter it.

towards evening the living-room door, which he used to watch intently for an hour or two beforehand, was always thrown open, so that lying in the darkness of his room, invisible to the family, he could see them all at the lamp-lit table and listen to their talk" (*PC* 110–11).[26] Whenever either Lemekh or Gregor tries to join his family, he is shooed into his designated quarters and beaten by an enraged father. Shmul Layblikh whips his son; Samsa uses a stick, a newspaper, and finally apples as weapons against Gregor. The two sons are described by similar epithets that set them apart from others, Lemekh as "the unsuccessful son" (*der nit gerutene zun*), Gregor as "the unfortunate son" (*der unglückliche Sohn*). Both epithets suggest misfortune, calamity, affliction, and conspicuous lack of success. The irrationality of Lemekh's behavior is paralleled by Gregor's confused responses to his changed physical condition. Gregor speaks of the morning's events as "foolishness," he feels "idiotic," he is described as "almost mad," "beside himself," and he believes that his solitary life "must have confounded his senses."[27]

The son's abnormal condition, which evokes parental fear and mistrust in both works, is at first interpreted (not only by the parents, but by the victim himself) as an illness that a doctor might cure. Layblikh shouts, "Woe, woe, help! help! . . . Quick, call people . . . , call a doctor . . . quick a doctor!"[28] Similarly, Gregor's mother responds with "For God's sake, . . . perhaps he is terribly sick. . . . You must go for the doctor this very minute. Gregor is sick. Quick, get the doctor," and "Help,

26. "So bekam er für diese Verschlimmerung seines Zustandes einen . . . Ersatz dadurch, dass immer gegen Abend die Wohnzimmertür, die er schon ein bis zwei Stunden vorher scharf zu beobachten pflegte, geöffnet wurde, so dass er, im Dunkel seines Zimmers liegend, vom Wohnzimmer aus unsichtbar, die ganze Familie beim beleuchteten Tische sehen und ihre Reden, . . . anhören durfte" (*E* 119).

27. "Narrheiten" (*E* 71); "blödsinnig" (*E* 72); "fast wild geworden" (*E* 76); "ausser sich" (*E* 83); "seinen Verstand hatte verwirren müssen" (*E* 110).

28. "Vay mir, gevald, ratevet! ratevet! . . . Geshvind, ruft mentshn . . . , ruft a doktor . . . geshvind a doktor!" (*DVM* 31).

for God's sake, help!"[29] In each case, the son is suspected of deliberate malice. Lemekh is blamed for "making himself crazy"; Gregor is accused of stubbornness (*Starrsinn*) for not opening the door of his room. Later, Samsa senior fears that his son will commit "an act of violence" (*eine Gewalttat*), a suspicion shared by Shmul Layblikh, which becomes a fact in *The Savage One*. In story and play alike, the son's transformation manifests itself in loss of the ability to communicate. Gregor's voice is described as "a squeaking" (*ein Piepsen*), while Lemekh's speech takes on the quality of a weeping groan ("er krekhtst vaynend"); Gregor's words become completely incomprehensible, Lemekh's barely coherent. Both heroes suffer from their families' false assumption that because they cannot *be* understood, they necessarily cannot understand. For this reason, both are forced to listen to many unflattering, painful remarks carelessly made in their hearing.

The Oedipal conflict and the broader theme of incest, presented in highly exaggerated form in *The Savage One*, are also played upon in "The Metamorphosis." In both works the son's love for the mother and sister becomes confused with sexual desire. Gregor's vision in which he imagines himself locked into his room with his sister, "protecting" her against all intruders, is clearly a sexual fantasy and parallels the scene in which Lemekh literally locks himself into a room with the sleeping Zelde and swears to keep her as his own.[30] Gregor's rivalry with the father, made clear by the shifting of their economic roles, parallels Lemekh's open jealousy of Shmul. In both works the son faints or becomes dizzy whenever the father embraces his wife. In context, this blacking-out is symbolic of the son's inability to accept the union of his parents. Because Zelde is only Lemekh's stepmother and because she is, at the same time, a provocative young woman ill-matched to the decrepit

---

29. "Um Gottes willen, . . . er ist vielleicht schwerkrank. . . . Du musst augenblicklich zum Arzt. Gregor ist krank. Rasch um den Arzt" (*E* 84). "Hilfe, um Gottes willen, Hilfe!" (*E* 91).

30. In an earlier scene Lemekh had literally tried to keep his brother's friends from his sister.

old man she marries, Lemekh's jealousy can more easily be accounted for than Gregor's, at least on the literal level. Because
Lemekh and Gregor are both sexually naïve but physically
adult, their sex drive expresses itself in ways which they can
neither control nor comprehend. When Lemekh feels aroused
by his new mother, he naïvely describes his feelings in rather
obvious fire and heat imagery: "When you [Zelde] touch me I
get hot"; "she touches me and I burn"; "a fire burns . . . I like it,
it's good, let it burn."[31] A similar expression of intense physical
desire, also phrased in terms of heat, is revealed by Gregor's
uncontrollable urge to "save" his picture of the lady in furs: he
"quickly crawled up to it and pressed himself against the glass,
which held him fast and soothed his hot belly."[32] Politzer correctly interprets Gregor's act as vicarious possession of the
woman in the picture, a parallel to Lemekh's symbolic possession of Zelde, which occurs when he stabs her, repeating the
words, "I have married . . . she is mine, my bride."[33]

But suppressed sexuality is only one among the many thematic and technical devices tying Kafka's story to Gordin's
play. Gregor's difficulties in getting out of bed produce in him
a fantasy that is very close to the literal events portrayed in
The Savage One. As he struggles, he imagines: "How simple it
would be if he could get help. Two strong people—he thought
of his father and the servant girl—would be amply sufficient;
they would only have to thrust their arms under his convex
back" (*PC* 73).[34] In Gordin's play, when Lemekh falls into a
faint he is literally rescued by two such helpers, his brother
and the housekeeper. Lemekh's confused behavior, associated

31. "Az ir rirt mikh on vert mir heys"; "zi tsindet mikh on un ikh
bren"; "es brent . . . es gefelt mir, es iz gut loz brenen" (*DVM* 17, 45).

32. "[Er] kroch eilends hinauf und presste sich an das Glas, das ihn
festhielt und seinem heissen Bauch wohltat" (*E* 113).

33. "Ikh hob khasene gehat . . . zi iz mayne, mayn kale" (*DVM*
46–47). See Politzer, *Parable and Paradox*, p. 72.

34. "Wie einfach alles wäre, wenn man ihm zu Hilfe käme. Zwei
starke Leute—er dachte an seinen Vater und das Dienstmädchen—hätten
vollständig genügt; sie hätten ihre Arme nur unter seinen gewölbten
Rücken schieben . . . müssen" (*E* 78).

with his loss of rational control—"he crawls on the floor" (*er krikht oyf der erd*)—provides a direct, visual statement of the extent of his degradation. This is paralleled in "The Metamorphosis" by Gregor's crawling, which signals his acceptance of his animal condition, particularly in the second section, where it is not only a means of locomotion, but a diversion as well. In another comparison, Lemekh's hiding behind the drapes when he hears Zelde's footsteps is paralleled by Gregor's hiding under the couch beneath a draped sheet whenever his mother or sister enters the room.

Fainting as a theatrical device recurs in both *The Savage One* and in "The Metamorphosis." In both works it serves to heighten the intensity of the action and to reveal strong emotion by direct, visual means. The staged quality of the scenes in which Gregor confronts his family—for example, the mother's melodramatic response to Gregor ("That made his mother scream again, she fled from the table and fell into the arms of his father, who hastened to catch her" [*PC* 85])[35] and her knocking over a pot of coffee as she flees from her son (*PC* 85; *E* 91)—creates a comic effect within the tragic circumstances that recalls the fusion of the tragic with the comic in the plays of the Yiddish theater.

Setting functions symbolically in both works. Lemekh expresses his feelings of isolation by reference to the furnishings of the newly redecorated family room, from which he is barred: "When there were not such [fancy] chairs and couches here, it used to be warm and friendly; now it is cold, gloomy, dark, sad, just as it is in here. (*Points to his heart.*)"[36] The condition of Gregor's room, filled with dirt, garbage, and cast-off furniture, perfectly reflects the family's disgust for their son and makes concrete Gregor's own feelings about himself by means a dramatist might employ. Lemekh's appraisal of his

35. "Darüber schrie die Mutter neuerdings auf, flüchtete vom Tisch und fiel dem ihr entgegeneilenden Vater in die Arme" (*E* 91).

36. "Ven do iz nit geven azelkhe shtuln un divanen, iz do geven varm un fraylakh, haynt iz do kalt, pust, finster, troyrig, azoy vi bey mir ot a do. (*Tsaygt oyf zayn harts.*)" (*DVM* 25).

family's attitude—"For me and for you it would be better if I died. . . . Who wants me to live?"[37]—parallels Gregor's evaluation of his position: "The decision that he must disappear was one that he held to even more strongly than his sister, if that were possible" (*PC* 127).[38]

Other symbols, central to story and play, further link "The Metamorphosis" to *The Savage One*. The image of the hospital is associated with the "illness" of the hero in both works. The bleak view of the gray hospital building which greets Gregor's vision as he awakens each morning is analogous to the institution in which Lemekh is eventually confined. The restraining power of the "iron jacket" into which Lemekh is locked parallel's Gregor's "armour-plated hard back," which literally imprisons him and is also symbolic of his spiritual limitation.[39] Such symbolic details as response to music and loss of appetite are associated with the son's condition in both works. Lemekh remarks that music helps him to forget that he is not a person like others: when he hears music he forgets the whip and the beatings and thinks that he is only as much of an idiot as all others are.[40] The pathos of Lemekh's humor is paralleled by the grim irony of Gregor's rhetorical question "Was he an animal that music moved him so?"[41] (Throughout the narrative Kafka makes use of dramatic irony based on Gregor's failure to

37. "Far mir un far aykh volt beser geven az ikh zol shtarbn. . . . Ver vil ikh zol lebn?" (*DVM* 20).

38. "Seine Meinung darüber, dass er verschwinden müsse, war womöglich noch entschiedener als die seiner Schwester" (*E* 136).

39. "Er lag auf seinem panzerartig harten Rücken" (*E* 71).

Politzer comments on the "encasing" quality of Gregor's plated back (*Parable and Paradox*, p. 69). Sokel observes that Gregor was "locked in" by his family—note the position of his room—even before the metamorphosis (*Tragik und Ironie*, p. 77).

40. "Zingt nokh, nokh, az men zingt ferges ikh az ikh bin nit aza mentsh vi ale yuden, ikh ferges in'm moment kantshik, un Shifras petsh un ikh mayn az ikh bin aza idyot vi ale mentshn" (*DVM* 10).

41. "War er ein Tier, da ihn Musik so ergriff?" (*E* 130).

The role of music and food in Kafka's work will be taken up in greater detail in the discussion of "A Hunger Artist" and "Josefine" (Chapter 7).

comprehend fully the seriousness of his situation.[42] For example, when he falls to the floor and suddenly feels physically comfortable for the first time since he awoke, he readily believes that "final relief from all his sufferings was directly at hand."[43] As events prove, he could hardly have been more mistaken.)

In handling setting in "The Metamorphosis" Kafka again adapts the techniques of the stage. Each section of the story is limited to a small, clearly defined area (Gregor's room and the living room); props are placed and accounted for as if they were to be made concrete on a stage. With the exception of Gregor, the characters are minimally developed and resemble the type characters of the drama, who fulfill one function or embody only a single trait. The movements of the characters are recorded with the precision of stage directions, and the exaggerated action often culminates in a grouping of characters that recalls the tableaux of the Yiddish theater. For example: "Now they were all watching him in melancholy silence. His mother lay in her chair, her legs stiffly outstretched and pressed together, her eyes almost closing for sheer weariness; his father and his sister were sitting beside each other, his sister's arm around the [father's] neck" (PC 126).[44]

Structurally, "The Metamorphosis" progresses like a drama, building through a series of crises (Gregor's three confrontations with the outside world) to a final denouement (Gregor's death and removal). The three chapters which make up "The Metamorphosis" correspond to the stages of Gregor's decline

42. An extremely interesting discussion of the comic methods of "The Metamorphosis" is provided by F. D. Luke ("The Metamorphosis," in *Franz Kafka Today*, ed. Flores and Swander, pp. 25–44).

43. "Und schon glaubte er, die endgültige Besserung alles Leidens stehe unmittelbar bevor" (E 90). The German also carries the more literal meaning "already he believed that a final recovery from his ailment was imminent."

44. "Nun sahen ihn alle schweigend und traurig an. Die Mutter lag, die Beine ausgestreckt und aneinandergedrückt, in ihrem Sessel, die Augen fielen ihr vor Ermattung fast zu; der Vater und die Schwester sassen nebeneinander, die Schwester hatte ihre Hand um des Vaters Hals gelegt" (E 135).

and relate to each other like the separate, self-contained acts of a play.[45]

In content and function, the sentimental ending of "The Metamorphosis" exactly parallels the epilogue of *The Savage One* (with the important distinction that in "The Metamorphosis" Gregor dies, while in *The Savage One* Lemekh is reconciled with his family). At the end, both families vow to forget the events of the past and to look to the promise of the future, which is symbolized for both by the prospective marriage of the young daughter. Like the epilogue of *The Savage One*, the ending of "The Metamorphosis" not only seems contrived and false, but ironically, its realistic action seems far less convincing than the truly fantastic events of the body of the story. One is tempted to discount the aesthetically unsatisfying endings of both works.[46]

A comparison of the role of the family in "The Metamorphosis" and *The Savage One* reveals that to a great degree the Samsas and the Layblikhs are similarly to blame for their sons' declines. Lemekh's all-consuming passion for his new stepmother is, at least in part, brought on by Zelde's carelessness in handling him, and is further aggravated by the father's total lack of compassion for his son. From the details that come to light in "The Metamorphosis," it becomes clear that Gregor has not been treated fairly, that his family has shown him little compassion, and that in addition they have seriously exploited his willingness to be their sole support.[47]

Although one would never assert that the metamorphosis can be fully explained as a metaphor for Gregor's subservience within the family or on the job, nevertheless, in order for the narrative to cohere, one must assume that Gregor's animal shape embodies some essential aspect of his previous human experience.[48] Kafka deliberately leaves the meaning of his cen-

45. Luke emphasizes the dramatic qualities of the story.

46. Politzer also finds the ending unconvincing (*Parable and Paradox,* p. 82). Kafka himself was dissatisfied with what he called its "unreadable ending." See *Dn* 12, *T* 351; and *Fe* 163.

47. The narrative makes clear that the members of the family are not as unable to care for themselves as Gregor had been allowed to believe.

48. Politzer comes close to this interpretation when he writes: "The

tral symbol partially obscure; Gordin, however, provides us with an explicit key to his work, which aids our understanding of the Kafka story as well. Near the end of the play Lemekh's brother explains: "What—where is this savage one? A savage who observes our behavior and our ways is buried deep within each of us. . . . When we improve ourselves, when the spirit in us wakens, when our souls reign over our bodies, then the savage one within us sleeps. But, when we strive only for material goals, when we have no ideals, when our spirit sleeps, then the savage one awakens and forces us to go against civilization, against the laws of humanity!"[49] This analysis of one who would fall prey to the animal instinct within him perfectly describes Gregor as he is shown to have been before the metamorphosis: a man of few ideals, devoted single-mindedly to material gain. His mother unwittingly reveals the paucity of his previous existence: "The boy thinks about nothing but his work" (PC 75).[50] Even the one ideal that Gregor seems to have lived for—his plan to send his sister to the music conservatory—is presented in terms of money ("despite the great ex-

metamorphosis has failed to change [Gregor]" (Parable and Paradox, p. 79). Although Politzer speculates that the metamorphosis may represent the hopelessness of Gregor's human situation, or that it may be a means of dramatizing Gregor's inherited parasitic traits, he concludes that the ultimate meaning of the metamorphosis can never be known. In Tragik und Ironie, Sokel links the metamorphosis to "The Judgment": " 'The Metamorphosis' is a judgment in advance" (p. 78); he views the metamorphosis as a punishment for Gregor's unconscious wish, fulfilled by the metamorphosis, to rebel against his employer. See also Walter H. Sokel, "Kafka's 'Metamorphosis': Rebellion and Punishment," Monatshefte 48 (1956): 203–14. Although this analysis is extremely convincing, one wonders why Sokel specifically excludes the family as a focus of Gregor's resentment. Were it not for the family's debt, Gregor would be free to leave his hated job.

49. "Vos? Vu iz der vilder mentsh? Der vilder mentsh zitst tif bagrobn bay yedn fun unz, betrakht alle unzer benemen, unzer oyffirung. . . . Ven mir bildn zikh, ven der gayst ervakht in unz, ven unzer zele hersht iber'n kerper, dan shloft in unz der vilder mentsh, ober farkert, ven vir shtrebn nur tsu matriele tsiln, ven vir hobn kayne idealn, ven unzer gayst shloft, dan vakht in unz der vilder mentsh, velkher tsvingt unz tsu geyn gegn tsivilizatsion, gegn di gezetse der mentshhayt" (DVM 51–52).

50. "Der Junge hat ja nichts im Kopf als das Geschäft" (E 80).

pense that would entail, which must be made up in some other way" [*PC* 95]).[51]

Gordin's play warns of the "beast" lurking in every man beneath the human facade. Similarly, Kafka seems to be pointing to the vermin which every man inherently embodies. While most readers will not be ready to accept Gregor as a universal symbol of man, it is difficult to escape the conclusion that in "The Metamorphosis" Kafka is portraying what was, at least at that time, his own despairing, tragi-comic vision of the human condition.[52]

During 1913, in the second year of his flood of letters to Felice, Kafka produced no new work. But in the last months of 1914 he began to write again and during this period produced the bulk of *The Trial* and the whole of "In the Penal Colony."[53] These narratives, fundamentally unchanged in character and style from the writing of the breakthrough period, not only relate to specific works of the Yiddish theater but are also closely connected to the aggregate of themes found in Yiddish plays. The single motif that dominates the plays of the Yiddish theater is the theme of obedience: that owed by child to parent, by man to temporal authority, and by man to God.[54] While most of the Yiddish dramatists accept the necessity of absolute obe-

51. "Ohne Rücksicht auf die grossen Kosten, die das verursachen musste, und die man schon auf andere Weise hereinbringen würde" (*E* 102).

Politzer sees in Gregor's plan a degree of spite or "faint rebellion" against the parents who opposed this "great expense" (*Parable and Paradox*, p. 76).

52. Politzer observes that because Gregor is, above all, "an average man, his incredible fate could befall any average man among the readers of this tale" (*Parable and Paradox*, p. 80).

53. The fragment "The Village Teacher" (erroneously titled "The Giant Mole" by Brod), a precursor of Kafka's animal fables, was also written at this time (December 1914). Politzer connects this fragment to the later story "The Burrow"; see *Parable and Paradox*, p. 385, n. 25.

54. Obedience owed by child to parent is prominent in *David's Violin*, *Mr. Harry the Aristocrat*, *The Savage One*, *Moyshe the Tailor*, and *The Slaughtering*; that owed by man to temporal authority, in *Kol Nidre*, *The Vice-King*, *Blimele*, and *Bar Kokhba*; that which man owes God, in

dience on all levels, some question and even condemn it. Yakov Gordin in *The Slaughtering* and particularly in *Elishe ben Avuya* challenges the virtue of blind obedience and urges the Jewish people to think for themselves, relying on reason (not ancient law) as a basic for action. Gordin stresses the fact that keeping the letter of the law is of no use if its spirit is not preserved and comprehended. This conflict between enlightenment and tradition, which is the specific concern of *Elishe ben Avuya,* is also central to Kafka's story "In the Penal Colony."

Stripped of its romantic subplot, Gordin's play presents the historic legend of the great Jewish scholar Elishe ben Avuya, who prevailed upon his people to accept enlightenment and to abandon the rigid laws of the Torah which bound them. For such blasphemy, Elishe was officially ostracized by the community of Jews, although he remained among them.

Kafka's nameless "explorer," who finds himself in a distant "colony" where he is asked to pass judgment on an "ancient system of law," resembles Gordin's scholar, Elishe. A similar awareness of the great disparity between the spirit of the ancient code and its enactment leads Elishe, the hero of Gordin's play, and the explorer, his counterpart in Kafka's story, to reject the old order. Both these men are uncommitted to any single system and stand apart from the law they judge—Elishe becomes "other" (*akher*), "the stranger" (*fremder*); the explorer is called "der Fremde." Both are associated with European learning and are guided by wide experience and reason. This last particularly sets them apart from their opposites, the head of the *yeshiva*[55] and the officer, the supporters of a decaying system who resemble one another in their priest-like devotion and fanatic loyalty to the ancient systems they serve.

While Gordin is careful to identify the Law that his hero rejects as the Torah, Kafka is equally careful not to give the Law

---

Bar Kokhba, Shulamit, Elishe ben Avuya, and *God, Man, and Devil.* In most of the plays these themes merge, and obedience in one form (particularly to the father) becomes symbolic of obedience to God.

55. Literally, the head of the academy. He is the elder of the community who combines within himself the role of rabbi, judge, and scholar. The officer in Kafka's story also serves as judge.

weighed by the explorer too specific a referent. Yet, as Politzer observes, the laws of the penal colony bring to mind the spirit and wording of the Ten Commandments,[56] while the ancient instructions left by the old Commandant recall the pages of an ancient Hebrew text: "The explorer . . . [saw] a labyrinth of lines crossing and re-crossing each other, which covered the paper so thickly that it was difficult to discern the blank spaces between them" (*PC* 202).[57] Like the Torah and the commentaries surrounding it, the old Commandant's writings are almost as difficult to decipher as to comprehend. "Yes, . . . it's no calligraphy for school children. It needs to be studied closely" (*PC* 202), and "it is not easy to decipher the script with one's eyes," the officer explains.[58] In addition, the officer's careful treatment of his manuscripts ("They are my most precious possessions" [*PC* 202])[59] and his eagerness to wash his hands before touching its pages (this occurs on two separate occasions) correspond to the restrictions concerning the handling of the Torah. Just as the old Commandant's instructions recall Scripture or the body of ancient Jewish law, so the unseen old Commandant suggests Moses, or an ancient Hebrew priest, if not Jehovah Himself. The soldier's reference to the old Commandant as the "ancient one" (*Der Alte*) recalls the prologue of *God, Man, and Devil*, in which God is addressed simply as "ancient one" or "ancient master" (*der alte, alter her*).

As previously noted in the discussion of *God, Man, and Devil* and "The Judgment," purification by water is central to Jewish law and is an important symbol in Kafka's work as well. The filthy water in which the officer is to wash his hands for a third time seems to be a grotesque parody of the Mikve, the

56. Compare "Honor thy superiors!" (*PC* 197; *E* 205) and "Be just!" (*PC* 219; *E* 228). For further discussion see Politzer, *Parable and Paradox*, pp. 106–7.

57. "Der Reisende . . . sah nur labyrinthartige, einander vielfach kreuzende Linien, die so dicht das Papier bedeckten, dass man nur mit Mühe die weissen Zwischenräume erkannte" (*E* 211).

58. "Ja . . . es ist keine Schönschrift für Schulkinder. Man muss lange darin lesen" (*E* 211); "es ist nicht leicht, die Schrift mit den Augen zu entziffern" (*E* 213).

59. "Sie sind das Teuerste, was ich habe" (*E* 210).

ritual bath, which is believed to cleanse the soul in spite of the fact that its water becomes filthy from common use.[60] The officer's substitution of sand for water corresponds to the Jewish laws of *kashrut* (ritual cleanliness), which permit a vessel that has become impure to be cleansed by being buried in sand. Kafka's general preoccupation with the symbols of dirt and cleanliness seems to be related to the concept of kashrut.[61] For example, the officer's complaint that the "apparatus" has been defiled (*verunreinigt*) clearly has symbolic as well as literal reference and reminds one of the defiling of Jewish temples portrayed in the Yiddish plays.[62]

Although this line of analysis explores only a single level of meaning of Kafka's story, it is an avenue suggested strongly by the text itself, which is permeated with details corresponding to and suggesting the symbols of Jewish ritual and tradition.

Thus, the isolation of the colony suggests the various forms of Jewish isolation (the ghetto, the Diaspora, clandestine worship)—a recurrent theme of all Jewish literature and particularly stressed in Gordin's plays. The quarrel of the old versus the new suggests the perpetual fight of Jewish Orthodoxy to maintain itself against voluntary assimilation or enforced conversion.[63] The attitude of disdain and ridicule which the officer

---

60. Kafka commented on this paradox in the *Diaries* (October 27, 1911): "The Jewish ritual bath . . . , which must only wash the earthly dirt from the soul, whose external condition is therefore a matter of indifference, that is, a symbol, therefore can be, and is, filthy and stinking" ("Das jüdische Reinigungswasser, . . . das nur den irdischen Schmutz der Seele abzuwaschen hat, dessen äusserliche Beschaffenheit daher gleichgültig ist, das ein Symbol, daher schmutzig und stinkend sein kann und auch ist" [*Di* 115–16; *T* 121]).

61. The similarity between Kafka's use of cleanliness as a symbol of purity and the Jewish concept of ritual cleanliness is noted by Robert Kauf, "Once Again: Kafka's 'A Report to an Academy,'" *MLQ* 15 (1954): 364.

62. Such defiling is described in great detail in Goldfaden's *Bar Kokhba*. It is also a prominent motif in many of the Yiddish poems and stories that had become familiar to Kafka.

63. In his discussion of "A Report to an Academy," Kauf describes how widespread this issue was in Prague in those years. The Jewish weekly *Selbstwehr* reflects this conflict.

claims to detect in the new Commandant resembles the derision typically shown to the Orthodox by the assimilated, the converted, or the hostile outsider. The officer's exaggerated insecurity corresponds to the historically legitimate Jewish fear of being ousted or attacked. The day of execution (*Hinrichtungstag*) combines the ceremonial quality of Yom Kippur (the Jewish *Richtungstag*) with the atmosphere of Roman gladiatorial combat. The conditions of Yom Kippur (fasting, atonement, and a full day of prayer) parallel the details surrounding the execution: the prisoner was to fast, the machine was to be in continuous operation for twelve hours, the procedure was to make clear to the prisoner the nature of his offense. The officer's description of a previous happier time when the old Law flourished and the valley was filled with people suggests the overflowing synagogues of the Orthodox, as well as the packed arenas and amphitheaters of the Romans. The festivity surrounding the executions of the past recalls a scene portrayed in Goldfaden's *Bar Kokhba*, in which the hero is pitted against a lion in the arena. In *Bar Kokhba*, as in Kafka's story, a life-and-death struggle is enacted; tension and excitement fill the air; women are prominent in the audience; military bands play; and iron spikes are prominently displayed. Both scenes end with a great theatrical flourish: Bar Kokhba rides off on the back of the beast that was to kill him; the prisoner provides a spectacle when he is "transfigured" in the sixth hour of his execution.

The officer repeatedly refers to the existence of adherents to the old who will not identify themselves under the new Commandant: "This ... method of execution ... has at the moment no longer any open adherents in our colony. . . . consequently the adherents have skulked out of sight, there are still many of them but none of them will admit it" (*PC* 207–8).[64] His description recalls the secret loyalty of the hidden Jews at the time of the Inquisition, and the soldier's reference to secret "adherents, who now must be nameless" (*PC* 226) reinforces

---

64. "Diese Hinrichtung ... hat gegenwärtig in unserer Kolonie keinen offenen Anhänger mehr. . . . infolgedessen haben sich die Anhänger verkrochen, es gibt noch viele, aber keiner gesteht es ein" (*E* 216–17).

the parallel to hidden Jews.[65] In this same vein, the teahouse containing the remains of the old Commandant—described as "a deep, low, cavernous space" in the "ground floor of the house" (*PC* 225)[66]—compares closely with the synagogues of the Orthodox, for they were often no more than dingy, ill-lit, stuffy, out-of-the-way shops or rooms made into places of worship. The sense of "a historic tradition" and the "power of past days" (*PC* 225; *E* 235) that the teahouse evokes for the explorer further connects the teahouse to an Orthodox house of worship. The full beards of the teahouse guests, their humility, and the shabbiness of their dress ("they were poor, humble creatures" [*PC* 226])[67] suggest the characteristics of Orthodox Jewry, while their whispering, evoked by the explorer's entrance ("It's a foreigner" [*PC* 226]),[68] recalls the fearful clannishness of the Jewish people, particularly the extremely Orthodox. The prophecy associated with the old Commandant—that he will return and help his followers reestablish the colony—resembles the promise of God to lead the Jewish people back to Zion. The epithet on the old Commandant's grave, "Have faith and wait!" (*PC* 226),[69] perfectly describes the passive attitude of the Orthodox, whose beliefs preclude all worldly activism.

Several other significant details link the colony and the officer to the traditions of Orthodox Judaism that Gordin specifically attacked in *Elishe ben Avuya*. The strange language of the colony is analogous to Hebrew and Yiddish, the sacred and profane languages by which the Jewish people set themselves apart. The officer's impractical uniform—which is admittedly ill-suited to local conditions and upon which the explorer is quick to comment—corresponds to the peculiar dress of the Or-

65. "Anhänger, die jetzt keinen Namen tragen dürfen" (*E* 236).

Hidden Jews provide the central conflict in *Kol Nidre* and *The Vice-King*.

66. "Im Erdgeschoss eines Hauses war ein tiefer, niedriger, höhlenartiger . . . Raum" (*E* 235).

67. "Es war armes gedemütigtes Volk" (*E* 235). The German word *Volk* more strongly suggests a people, nation, or tribe.

68. "Es ist ein Fremder" (*E* 235). *Fremder* is the German equivalent of the Yiddish word for nonbeliever or non-Jew, *Goy*.

69. "Glaubet und wartet!" (*E* 236).

thodox; and indeed, the officer's explanation for this costume echoes the reasoning behind the traditional caftan and hat: "But they mean home to us; we don't want to forget about home" (*PC* 192).[70] For the officer, as well as for the Orthodox Jew, his costume, his language, and especially his strict observance of the Law signify a direct avowal of faith. Although Gordin and Kafka both conclude that the ancient systems in question no longer serve and that they carry within themselves the seeds of their own destruction, Gordin does not, like Kafka, suggest that the system is in itself brutal or inhuman. But Gordin does suggest that, by their stubborn insistence on carrying out every detail of the Law as it was handed down to them, the Jewish people have made themselves responsible for the great suffering and the many tortures and indignities which, as a people, they have had to endure throughout history. In a grotesque and distorted fashion, Kafka's machine reflects this suffering.[71]

The parabolic nature of "In the Penal Colony" becomes clear when we compare Kafka's story to the parable by means of which Elishe ben Avuya explains his attack on Orthodoxy: "God and the Torah is exactly like a king who captures a bird and says to his servant, 'Keep it and guard it all your life; if you do not, you will pay with your life.' The servant does not know what kind of bird this is, or why he should keep it, but he keeps it anyway and guards it for years and years. Do you know why? Because he is a slave, because although he does not live, he fears to die... I have let the bird go free...."[72]

70. "Sie bedeuten die Heimat; wir wollen nicht die Heimat verlieren" (*E* 200). The German *Heimat* also suggests homeland, native place or country.

71. Politzer connects Kafka's interest in machines to his experience in the insurance company, where he had to make out elaborate reports on accidents concerning machines. One might also associate the machine to the torture apparatus of the Inquisition. In *Bar Kokhba* Eliezer describes some of these atrocities: "The skin was scraped off their bodies while they lived" ("Abgeshundn die Hoyt lebendig" [*BK* 109]). See also the Inquisitor's threats in *VK* 17.

72. "Got und di toyre iz punkt vi a kenig vos hot gekhapt a foygl un zogt tsu zayn diner, 'Halt es un hit es op dayn lebn lang, oyb nit betsolst

Because Gordin's fable is more allegorical than parabolic, its meaning is easy to grasp. The king represents Jehovah; the servant, the Jewish people; the bird, the Law. By means of this fable Gordin chastises the Orthodox for the futility of their efforts in keeping a Law which is neither reasonable nor comprehensible, and which does not even result in the justice promised to those who uphold it.

Although the meaning of Kafka's story cannot be discovered so easily, it is not difficult to see in Gordin's fable the basic elements of "In the Penal Colony." The king and the bird clearly correspond to the old Commandant and the old Law. The faithful servant of Elishe's parable becomes the disobedient soldier who in Kafka's story finds himself a prisoner (in place of the bird) in what may be interpreted as a grotesque distortion of Gordin's cage (the machine). The senseless orders given to the soldier (he was to salute his superior's door every hour all night long) matches in absurdity the king's command to guard the bird. The punishments for disobedience are the same in the two works, although Kafka greatly embellishes the king's simple warning "You will pay with your life." While Gordin clearly offers Elishe (the servant who would release the bird) as a model of human dignity and worth, Kafka presents his characters with varying degrees of irony and ridicule. The mute soldier who disregards the Law is not exemplary, for he is a helpless being who comprehends neither his imprisonment nor his sudden release. As Politzer suggests, not even the explorer, the most rational being in the story, can serve, for although he has dignity, he lacks warmth and compassion.[73] As previously noted, the officer, chief advocate of the old Law, corresponds to Gordin's head of the yeshiva, for whose benefit the parable is told.

Thus, although we cannot expect to explain all of the psycho-

---

du mit dayn lebn.' Der diner vayst nit, vos iz dos far a foygl, nokh vos hot men zi gekhapt un varum darf men zi haltn, un halt zi dokh zayn lebn lang, vayst ir far vos? Vayl er iz a shklaf, vayl er lebt nit un hot dokh moyre zu shtarbn... Ikh hob di foygl avekgelozt in der frayhayt..." (EbA 69).

73. *Parable and Paradox*, pp. 111–12.

logical complexities of "In the Penal Colony" (particularly its rather obvious sadism) by reference to Gordin's *Elishe ben Avuya,* we can nonetheless widen the possibilities of its interpretation by tracing some of the symbols of the story and conception of the characters to what is perhaps their original context.

Like "The Judgment" and "The Metamorphosis," "In the Penal Colony" has an extremely staged quality. In spite of its symbolic nature, the "apparatus" is described as if it were to be given a literal, fixed, three-dimensional existence. Except for the brief epilogue in the teahouse, the action of the story is confined to a single setting, which recalls the desert scene in the first act of Goldfaden's *Shulamit.* Not only the stark setting, but also the stripped quality of the nameless characters (the officer, the soldier, the prisoner, the explorer, and the hovering presence of the old Commandant) recalls the single-dimensioned characters of the medieval morality play or of twentieth-century Expressionist drama. In addition, the emphasis given to the spoken word (the story is essentially a dialogue between the officer and the explorer), the importance given to timing, the inclusion of speeches and monologues that function like stage asides, the reliance on gesture and tableau, the suspense surrounding the execution, the theatricality of the officer's plea, and the melodrama of the ending (the swift reversal between officer and prisoner and the sudden breakdown of the machine) link "In the Penal Colony" to the themes and techniques of the Yiddish stage. Such parallels are abundant not only in Kafka's short works, but in the novels as well.

Kafka's abstract concern with the Law and the court in *The Trial,* his inquiry into the relationship of the individual to the absolute, and his exploration of the nature of guilt and innocence are also the major problems raised by the dramatists of the Yiddish theater, who interpreted these broad questions in terms of their specific relevance to Jewish life. Several different images of the Law and the court recur in the Yiddish plays. The feared and hated Inquisition, which made merely being Jewish a crime punishable by death, provided a central symbol of hos-

tile law, while the atrocities associated with Roman rule presented another. Within the Jewish community itself, the elders
constituted a court (known in early times as the Sanhedrin)
which held the power to try any Jew suspected of being a trai-
tor or an enemy of the people. As in *Elishe ben Avuya,* this
Jewish court was often also shown in an unfavorable light and
was associated with bigotry, narrow vision, and passive acceptance of the status quo. In addition, in almost all of the plays,
even in those most critical of authority, there occurs some reference to man's relationship to God and the ultimate judgment
that will fall on man from God. Kafka's picture of the battle Josef K. wages against the unknown court in *The Trial* seems to
be a distillate of the various specific instances of "man against
the powers" represented in the Yiddish plays. Although *The
Trial* as a whole cannot be linked to any single work of the
Yiddish theater as strongly as can "The Judgment" or "The Metamorphosis," the novel contains many fragments of scenes and
conversations, technical devices, conceptions of character, attitudes and points of view that can be traced to the Yiddish plays.
Kafka so removes these details from the particularity of their
original contexts, however, that their function in his work becomes highly ambiguous and frequently ironic.

The seminal scene of *The Trial,* Josef K.'s arrest, corresponds
to a brief but important sequence in one of the Yiddish plays,
the arrest of Don Sebastian in Faynman's *The Vice-King.* Like
Sharkanski's *Kol Nidre* (discussed in connection with "The
Judgment"), *The Vice-King* takes place at the time of the Inquisition and is the story of a secret Jew, Don Sebastian, who is
arrested by the authorities and brought before the high court
of the Inquisition. The following are the details of his arrest:
Two masked servants of the Inquisition come to Don Sebastian's home and announce that they have been sent to arrest
him on suspicion of being a secret Jew. Although Sebastian is
willing to comply with the law, he asks to be informed of the
nature of the evidence against him, and is told by the deputies
that they do not have the authority to give him any further information. Following this exchange, Sebastian is taken away.

Stripped of its particularity (i.e., the Inquisition and secret

Jews), Don Sebastian's arrest is a model for that of Josef K. and exhibits those qualities which take the firmest hold on the imagination of the reader. Like Sebastian, Josef K. is arrested in his room by two warders, who, according to their own testimony, are the lowest representatives of a large and powerful organization that sounds very much like an abstraction of the machinery of the Inquisition.[74] Josef K.'s warders, like Don Sebastian's guards, are entirely unable to enlighten him concerning his arrest. The wording and the pace of the dialogue in the two scenes is remarkably similar. In *The Vice-King* the deputy announces, "I have been sent . . . to arrest you"; in *The Trial* the warder informs Josef K., "You are arrested" (*Tr* 5).[75] In response to his inquiry about the evidence against him, Sebastian is told, "I am not permitted to give you information"; Josef K. is similarly informed, "We are not authorized to tell you that" (*Tr* 6).[76] In *The Trial*, however, this exchange between the arrested and his arrestors occurs not once, but twice, with only minor changes in wording. "You're under arrest. . . . We don't answer such questions" (*Tr* 9), the warder reiterates.[77] By repeating this sequence, Kafka undermines the seriousness of K.'s arrest and makes his hero look slightly ridiculous, for only a fool would "forget" such vital information.

In this entire sequence, Kafka seems to parody the details of *The Vice-King*. While Sebastian fully understands the seriousness of the charge against him and the nature of the organization that arrests him, Josef K. is given only useless information that confuses more than it explains. But for Josef K., as well as for Don Sebastian, the arrest marks the beginning of a sharp

74. K. describes it as "an organization . . . of servants, clerks, police, and other assistants, perhaps even hangmen" ("Eine Organisation . . . von Dienern, Schreibern, Gendarmen und andern Hilfskräften, vielleicht sogar Henkern" [*Tr* 57; *P* 61]).

75. "Bin ikh geshikt gevorn . . . dikh tsu verhaftn" (*VK* 13). "Sie sind ja verhaftet" (*P* 11).

76. "Mir iz nit geshtatet dir erklerung abstugebn" (*VK* 13). "Wir sind nicht dazu bestellt, Ihnen das zu sagen" (*P* 11).

77. "Sie sind doch verhaftet. . . . Solche Fragen beantworten wir nicht" (*P* 14).

personal decline and signals the end of the hero's existence as a respectable citizen of the community. Sebastian's loss of position is dictated entirely by external circumstances which make it seem inevitable; K.'s decline, on the other hand, stems almost entirely from within K. himself, who thus appears to be a more foolish than tragic victim. Furthermore, whereas Don Sebastian knows that he was denounced by a personal enemy, Josef K. (from whose perspective the novel is narrated) has no such information and is allowed to speculate lamely, without any visible frame of reference: "Someone must have accused Josef K. falsely, for without his having done anything wrong, he was arrested one morning."[78] However unjust the laws described in *The Vice-King* may be and however crudely the characters may be constructed, Sebastian's arrest follows logically from the given facts of the plot. In contrast, K.'s arrest remains unexplained and unmotivated to the end. The resulting mystery and ambiguity mitigates its seriousness somewhat and gives to the situation a slightly comic cast.

It is not to be thought, however, that Kafka transformed a piece of straight tragedy into the comic idiom. *The Trial* is as far from comedy as *The Vice-King* is from tragedy. Although the situation in *The Vice-King* is extremely serious, the scene of Sebastian's arrest is interlaced with comic elements which, in this instance, take the form of colorful insults made by Sebastian's servant Pedrilo against the arrestors. These highly idiomatic asides are designed to make the agents of authority

78. "Jemand musste Josef K. verleumdet haben, denn ohne dass er etwas Böses getan hätte, wurde er eines Morgens verhaftet" (*P* 9).

Like the Orthodox Jews in the Yiddish plays who interpret persecution as punishment for sin, K. assumes that his arrest must be attributable to some cause which is as yet unknown to him. Neither K. nor the Jews entertain the possibility that their misfortune is gratuitous, incomprehensible, and without meaning.

One might note in passing that from 1911 on, Kafka was continuously exposed to news items concerning false accusations against Jews, followed by absurd trials whose outcome had been determined in advance. (See the Jewish periodical *Selbstwehr* for 1910–24.) It is possible that Kafka's conception of K.'s arrest and subsequent trial (the entire proceedings of *Der Prozess*) was influenced by such reports.

look foolish, and thereby, less threatening. The wording of Pedrilo's insults—"You swollen bellies, you eaters of sacrifices. Like wild dogs they fell on us and we cannot drive them away with a hundred sticks"[79]—matches the actions of the warders in *The Trial*. These fall on Josef K. like "wild dogs" (K. complains: "First these gentlemen fell upon me");[80] one bumps into K. with his fat belly ("swollen bellies"), the other claps him familiarly on the shoulder. Together they steal his clothes and eat his breakfast ("eaters of sacrifices"), as if his food and belongings were the offerings and he, the sacrifice. The punishment to which K.'s warders are later subjected (in the whipping scene) corresponds to the curses of Pedrilo, who wishes Sebastian's arrestors every evil: "You should only become dumb yourself," he says; "You should be burned and tortured, you stuffed pigs."[81] The court's representatives in *The Trial*, particularly in their inclination toward lechery and vengeance, show the same characteristics that Yiddish dramatists attributed to the enemies of the Jewish people, who are always shown to be lascivious, dishonest, unreliable, and untrustworthy.[82]

Among other analogous details in the two scenes of arrest are the black outfits of the arrestors and the knocking on the door that precedes their entry. In both works the knocking is a device used to build suspense and call attention to those entering, while the black clothing is symbolic of hostile authority. The black masks and costumes worn by the deputies of the Inquisition may, in fact, have provided the model for the

79. "Ir geshvolene baykher, ir korbonot freser. Vi di bayze hint zenen zay unz befaln un es iz zay nisht avektsutraybn mit hundert shtekns (*VK* 13)."

It is possible to relate these deputies to the assistants in *The Castle*, who also represent a form of absolute authority and who are almost equally difficult to get rid of, even with beatings.

80. "Die Herren haben mich zuerst überfallen" (*P* 22).

81. "Az vershtump zolstu shoyn aleyn vern"; "az verbrent un versarfet zolt ir vern, ir ongefresene trelbukhes" (*VK* 13). Literally, *trelbukhes* are paunches.

82. The only exceptions are those who only appear to be enemies, but are in fact, secret Jews in high positions, working to help other Jews.

warder's "closely fitting black suit, which was furnished with all sorts of pleats, pockets, buckles, and buttons, as well as a belt" (*Tr* 4).[83] In the light of the similarity between this "traveling suit" and the costumes of the deputies, Kafka's comment on the suit's apparent purpose—" [it] looked eminently practical, though one could not quite tell what actual purpose it served" (*Tr* 4)[84]—seems to be a gross understatement and an irony largely lost on the reader unaware of the underlying comparison that evoked it. In this detail, Kafka takes over the theater's emphasis on costume, while distorting its function. Instead of permitting the uniform to establish the identity of the warders (a function it normally fulfills in the drama), Kafka allows it only to suggest possibilities. In describing the outfits, as in building the scene of arrest, Kafka seems to abstract elements from the Yiddish play to create images which are detailed without being specific.

Such analysis may help to explain the peculiar nature of K.'s "First Interrogation," which combines the atmosphere of a hidden synagogue with the attitudes of a court of Inquisition and the disputations of a political debate. On one level, the interrogation of Josef K. is a parody of Sebastian's trial in *The Vice-King*. The high seriousness of the Holy Inquisition is transformed into the apparent apathy and disorder of K.'s examination. The Grand Inquisitor's formal inquiry (name, place of birth, etc.) becomes the examining magistrate's single, carelessly framed question "Well, then, . . . you are a house painter?" (*Tr* 50).[85] In *The Vice-King*, the questioning of the defendant proceeds in an orderly fashion until Sebastian swears (falsely, we know) that he is a believing Christian, at which point he is challenged by witnesses and proven guilty. In a comic parallel, Josef K.'s self-identification as "chief clerk

83. "Anliegendes schwarzes Kleid, das . . . mit verschiedenen Falten, Taschen, Schnallen, Knöpfen und einem Gürtel versehen war" (*P* 9).

84. "Ohne dass man sich darüber klar wurde, wozu es dienen sollte, besonders praktisch erschien" (*P* 9).

85. "Also, . . . Sie sind Zimmermaler?" (*P* 54). The casual quality of K.'s examination is highlighted by the magistrate's remark, which provides for itself a false answer to the question it purports to ask.

of a large bank" provokes not opposition, but laughter, which, like the witnesses' challenge to Sebastian, suggests disbelief. Nevertheless, as there is no indication in the text of *The Trial* that K. is lying about the facts, one must assume that he is misrepresenting himself in some other, perhaps more essential aspect of his being. Possibly, while Sebastian openly lies to others, K. lies only to himself.[86]

Several minor details also link K.'s hearing to Sebastian's. In both cases the court makes a major concession to the defendant. Don Sebastian is given special permission to visit his family; Josef K.'s hearing is allowed to take place despite his tardy arrival. In *The Trial*, however, this detail provides a note of irony, for K. is pardoned for a breach he did not knowingly commit (he had not been told when to arrive). Structurally, both hearings are brought to a close by a shriek which is associated with the entry of a woman into the all-male courtroom.[87] In *The Vice-King* the woman is a servant in the pay of Sebastian's enemies; in *The Trial* she is similarly associated with K.'s opponents, the men of the court.

In another parallel, the "password" which K. invents in order to find the court chambers without divulging his mission ("As he could not inquire for the Court of Inquiry he invented a joiner called Lanz" [*Tr* 45])[88] recalls the passwords used by the secret Jews to gain entry into the hidden synagogues in plays like *Kol Nidre* and *The Vice-King*. Josef K. is as secretive about the court and his trial as the secret Jew was forced to be about Judaism and the synagogue. The source of K.'s obvious reticence remains obscure, however, and one cannot determine whether he was ashamed, afraid, or if his secrecy was at all

86. To support this assertion one can point to K.'s overblown estimate of his importance on the job and his misjudgment of his strength against the court. By describing the facts of K.'s previous life, the text urges us to relate these details to the question of K.'s guilt.

87. In *The Trial* a man actually makes the sound while he is embracing the woman.

88. "Da er doch nicht nach der Untersuchungskommission fragen konnte, erfand er einen Tischler Lanz" (*P* 49).

necessary. We have come to recognize the resulting ambiguity as an integral part of Kafka's method.

But K.'s first examination not only calls to mind synagogues, hidden Jews, and the Inquisition; as K. himself observes, it also resembles a political meeting, characterized by factions and disorder. The prologue to Goldfaden's historical drama *Bar Kokhba* includes such a combination of elements; and in addition, its setting and structure resemble those of the courtroom scene in *The Trial.* When *Bar Kokhba* opens, the Jews of Jerusalem are met in prayer on the holy day commemorating the destruction of the temple in Jerusalem. The opening tableau shows a podium with the Holy Ark and a pedestal on which there stands a nearly burnt-out lamp. To the right and left of the ark Jews are seated, their heads bent in mourning, their hands clasped. On the bottom step of the podium sits the old scholar Eliezer, holding a holy scroll from which he recites. It is not difficult to see in this scene the essential features of the attic court which meets on another kind of holy day (the Christian Sunday) in *The Trial.* Like the synagogue, the court is crowded, stuffy, dimly-lit, and filled with an all-male audience which appears to be composed of two groups, physically separated by a narrow aisle. Like the Orthodox Jews in *Bar Kokhba,* many of the men in the courtroom are old, white-bearded, and dressed in long, black "holiday coats" (*Feiertagsröcken*), a fact that strikes K. as particularly odd. K.'s speculation that these older men are perhaps the most influential members of the community corresponds to the facts of *Bar Kokhba,* for there the elders constitute the Sanhedrin, the high court governing Jewish life. The bent posture of those in the gallery in *The Trial* resembles the bowed heads of the Jewish elders, who are shown humbling themselves before God. These elders live by traditional values and fully accept the age-old explanation for Jewish suffering, which is based on the premise that God is just, and concludes that if Jews suffer, they must have sinned. The passivity that K. attributes to the men of the court is like the ingrained passivity of the Jewish elders. The yellowed books of the court, held together by only a few threads, suggest ancient Jewish prayer books, and correspond to the ancient scroll from which Eliezer recites.[89]

But the prayer and penance in the synagogue quickly turn into a political debate when Bar Kokhba challenges the elders' passive acceptance of Roman oppression. This division among the Jews in the synagogue may be mirrored ironically in K.'s assumption that the court is divided into two opposing groups, one of which is favorable to him. While K. assumes audience division only to discover unity, in *Bar Kokhba* the congregation is, in fact, united (in being Jewish) *and* divided (on the political issue).

The prologue to *Bar Kokhba* is built around a series of speeches by means of which Bar Kokhba and Eliezer try to sway the audience to their respective points of view. This disputation (the speeches are long and full of rhetorical devices) finds its parallel in K.'s address to the court, by means of which he too hopes to win the favor of the audience: "He[K.] considered what he should say to win over the whole of the audience once and for all, or if that were not possible, at least to win over most of them for the time being" (*Tr* 49).[90] Like Bar Kokhba, K. becomes highly emotional and is carried away by the sound of his own voice. But, while Bar Kokhba actually succeeds in swaying the congregation, K. manages to convince only himself. The shaking of heads and pulling of beards, the clapping, pointing, and general murmuring which greet the pauses in K.'s speech correspond exactly to the stage directions for the congregation in the prologue to *Bar Kokhba*.

The Trial also seems to parody some of the stage devices of *Bar Kokhba*. For example, the tremulous music which accompanies the more impassioned parts of Bar Kokhba's speech cor-

---

89. In Jewish tradition prayer books are never thrown away or destroyed, and they actually gain in value as they age. For an interesting discussion linking the obscenity in the books of the court to orthodoxy, see Malcolm Pasley, "Two Literary Sources of Kafka's *Der Prozess*," *FMLS* 3 (April 1967): 143.

90. "Er dachte nach, was er sagen könnte, um alle auf einmal oder, wenn das nicht möglich sein sollte, wenigstens zeitweilig auch die anderen zu gewinnen" (*P* 53).

responds to the buzzing K. hears as he reaches the climax of his address: "In that stillness a subdued hum was audible which was more exciting than the wildest applause" (*Tr* 57).[91] In both works this signal gives the hero false confidence in a victory he ultimately fails to achieve. To a great degree, K.'s struggle mirrors Bar Kokhba's. While Bar Kokhba rebels against the brutality of Roman rule and the authority of the Jewish elders, K. challenges the authority of the court. Both publicly claim to represent not only themselves, but the "many" who are in a similar predicament; and both are determined not to give up without a fight. Bar Kokhba's cry "Nothing can come of sitting and waiting"[92] well describes K.'s developing attitude toward his trial. Like Bar Kokhba, K. is anxious to show his adversary that he is a man "who [knows] how to protect his rights."[93]

The conflicting views of the rebellious Bar Kokhba and the tradition-bound Eliezer, central to Goldfaden's play, are mirrored in the opposing attitudes of Josef K. and Lawyer Huld. Huld's advice on how to deal with the court—"The only proper thing was to acquiesce in the existing circumstances. . . . By no means to attract attention! To keep quiet, no matter how little sense things make"[94]—corresponds exactly to Eliezer's attitude of servility and compromise toward the Romans: "Let us obey the new rulers, whatever they will ask of us."[95] Huld's warnings about "vengeful officials," who, if offended, would become even more severe and ruthless, echoes the substance of Eiezer's warnings about the Romans. In addition, Eliezer's conviction that suffering is itself proof of guilt is reflected in the bitter logic of the Law in *The Trial*, according to which the court is attracted only to the guilty, so that being arrested, like being

91. "In dieser Stille entstand ein Sausen, das aufreizender war als der verzückteste Beifall" (*P* 60).

92. "Fun zitsn un vartn kon gor nisht geshen" (*BK* 114).

93. "Der sein Recht zu wahren verstand" (*P* 153).

94. "Das einzig Richtige sei es, sich mit den vorhandenen Verhältnissen abzufinden. . . . Nur keine Aufmerksamkeit erregen! Sich ruhig verhalten, selbst wenn es einem noch so sehr gegen den Sinn geht!" (*P* 146).

95. "Lomir folgn di naye Hershers, vos zey veln unz gebitn" (*BK* 111).

persecuted, becomes synonymous with guilt. While Josef K.'s attitude is the opposite of Eliezer's, the two men share a basic optimism. Eliezer's faith that Jewish suffering is not gratuitous parallels K.'s firm belief that the cause of his arrest can be explained, that he will be cleared. Thus, K. combines the faith of Eliezer with the activism of Bar Kokhba, and like the rebellious hero of Goldfaden's play, determines to take his defense into his own hands. Although Goldfaden clearly views Bar Kokhba's rebellion as a sin against God and an act of pride doomed from the start, he nonetheless admires his hero's courage. In contrast, Kafka cannot really be said to judge K.'s efforts, for he presents them with irony, an attitude which precludes genuine admiration as well as unqualified condemnation. As a result, one cannot interpret K.'s unsuccessful rebellion as easily as Bar Kokhba's.

While Bar Kokhba is the prototype of the tragic hero, the good man drawn larger than life who errs and falls, Josef K. is usually cited as the typical anti-hero, the small man who takes on the posture of the hero, but lacks the hero's strength and vigor. From this perspective Josef K. is a parody of Bar Kokhba. Where Bar Kokhba is fearless and bold, K. is meek and unable to assert himself; only in his impetuousness and pride does K. match Bar Kokhba. Throughout the play, and particularly in death, Bar Kokhba displays the kind of heroism which, according to the values of the play, raises him above the ordinary. By choosing an honorable death in the face of certain defeat Bar Kokhba attains tragic stature:

> The power of the enemy is great...
> It's difficult to defend oneself—all is over, lost!
> (*With fire.*) No, enemy, do not rejoice.
> If I can take nothing from you—
> *One* thing I can rob you of: your pride over me!
> Not *your* arrow will pierce the breast of the hero;
> By *my own* hand I would rather die.
> (*He pierces his heart with a sword and falls down dead.*)[96]

96. "Di makht fun dem soyne iz zeyr groys...
    Shver zikh tsu haltn, farloyrn iz alts—oys!

The theatrical ending of *The Trial* seems to be a direct parody of Bar Kokhba's elaborately prepared, heroic death. Bar Kokhba's sword, the weapon of the soldier-hero, becomes the coarse double-edged butcher's knife the warder plunges into K.'s heart. Not only does K. not die by his own hand, he allows himself to be slaughtered passively, "like a dog." Yet K. retains some memory of a "code" according to which a man "ought" to take his own life. That he does not do so, K. interprets as his own weakness and the fault of "him who had not left him the strength necessary for the deed" (*Tr* 285).[97] But as the opposing interpretations of Politzer and Sokel show, even on this crucial point the text is ambiguous. While Politzer interprets K.'s refusal as an act of strength, Sokel interprets it as a deficiency.[98] If, however, one views K.'s death as a parody of heroism, then the reference to the necessity of suicide appears more ironic than serious. Kafka seems to suggest that to take one's life as the culmination of an incomprehensible trial is a futile and empty gesture that would imply approval of the "senseless proceedings." In Goldfaden's play, Bar Kokhba's defeat is meaningful, for through it, the hero learns humility: "If God does not will it, the hero's strength is in vain."[99] In contrast,

---

    (*Mit fayer.*) Neyn, soyne. Fray dikh nit!
    Az ikh ken shoyn gor nit nemen bay dir—
    Ayns vel ikh bay dir roybn: dayn shtolts iber mir!
    Nit *dayn* fayl zol durkhboyrn di brust fun dem givur—
    Fun *mayn* hant aleyn iz mir tsu shtarbn liber.
    (*Er shtekht zikh arayn in hartsn a shvert, falt um oyf der erd toyt.*)" (*BK* 204–5)

97. "Der, der ihm den Rest der dazu nötigen Kraft versagt hatte" (*P* 271).

98. Politzer writes: "By surrendering the responsibility for his case to the Court, he assumes paradoxically the full responsibility for himself as a free man" (*Parable and Paradox*, p. 216). Sokel's view is that K. "was incapable of fulfilling his duty and stabbing himself with the knife. He knows perfectly well that he should have died as a free man" (*Tragik und Ironie*, p. 290).

In another of the Yiddish plays, Gordin's Elishe ben Avuya makes much of the fact that he not only lived as a free man, but that he also is dying as one—by his own choice.

99. "Az Got vil nit, iz umzist dem givurs koyakh" (*BK* 204).

K.'s death can teach nothing, and even the last "vision" permitted him (the figure in the lighted window) remains inconclusive. This mysterious figure, which seems to reach out to K., may well be a parody of the ghost of Eliezer, which appears on a high tower in the moments before Bar Kokhba's death and brings him to recognize his guilt.[100]

K.'s struggle against the court may also be linked to Gordin's *Elishe ben Avuya,* a work previously discussed in connection with "In the Penal Colony," which also examines the nature of man's relationship to the Law. In Gordin's play, Elishe is subjected to the anti-Semitism of the Romans and to the bigotry of the Jews, two injustices which merge in Kafka's abstract, universalized image of the injustice of the court in *The Trial.* By his emphasis on reason, Elishe resembles not only the explorer, but Josef K. as well, for K.'s actions are strongly predicated on the belief that through reason he can discover the nature of the Law that accuses him. Elishe's philosophy, "A man must think," and "The only path to salvation is the way of reason,"[101] corresponds to K.'s attitude toward his trial. At the beginning K. asserts: "Far more important to him was the necessity to understand his situation clearly" (*Tr* 7); and at the end he still maintains: "The only thing for me to go on doing is to keep my intelligence calm and analytical to the end" (*Tr* 282).[102]

It is one of the ironies of *The Trial* that K.'s reason is often overruled by impulse (a trait he shares with Bar Kokhba) although there is no indication in the text to suggest that the Law would have been any more accessible had K. been less impetuous. Furthermore, K.'s assertion "it is only a trial if I recognize it as such" (*Tr* 51) corresponds to Elishe's dictum

100. Bar Kokhba had not only assumed that he could rely entirely on his own strength and had let himself be crowned as Messiah (King of the Jews), he had also killed Eliezer in an impetuous fit of rage and grief over his fiancée's death (for which he erroneously blamed Eliezer).

101. "A mentsh darf denkn"; "der eynzige veg fun erlezung iz der veg fun vershtand" (*EbA* 9, 11).

102. "Viel wichtiger war es ihm, Klarheit über seine Lage zu kebommen" (*P* 12); "das einzige, was ich jetzt tun kann, ist, bis zum Ende den ruhig einteilenden Verstand behalten" (*P* 269).

"Man punishes and rewards himself."[103] For K., as for Elishe, each man stands at the center of his world. K.'s continued avowal of innocence in the face of presumed guilt echoes El- ishe's reaction in an analogous situation: "So long as I say I am right, there is no law and no judgment that can make me wrong."[104] Like Elishe, K. never ceases to doubt the verdict or the system that judges him. But Elishe and K. differ in one im- portant respect. While Elishe refuses to justify himself to those who wrong him ("Only he who does not stand higher than the accusation must answer [it]"),[105] the entire thrust of K.'s effort is meant to gain him the opportunity to *prove* his innocence. It is as if Kafka were determined to show that K. does not stand higher than the accusation.

In addition to the connections in the characters of Elishe and Josef K., these two works share an important structural de- vice that links them even more closely. At the center of each, there stands a parable representing a compressed, more intense statement of the essential problem raised by the larger work. As noted in the discussion of "In the Penal Colony," Elishe ex- plains his rejection of Jewish law by means of the fable of the king, the bird, and the cage. In *The Trial* the priest tries to enlighten K. by means of the parable "Before the Law," famil- iar to all students of Kafka, in which a man from the country tries to gain entry to the Law, but is prevented by a door- keeper whose sole responsibility seems to be to keep the man out. In contrast to Elishe's simple, easily interpreted fable, the priest's story is inconclusive, ending with the doorkeeper's cryptic statement to the man from the country: "No one else could gain entry here, for this door was meant only for you. I am now going to shut it."[106] As shown by K.'s subsequent re-

103. "Es ist ja nur ein Verfahren, wenn ich es als solches anerkenne" (*P* 55). "Mentshn beshtrofn un beloynen zikh aleyn" (*EbA* 13).

104. "Zo lang Elishe ben Avuya zogt, az ikh bin gerekht, iz nito aza mishpet, aza bet din, velkher zol mikh ungerekht makhn" (*EbA* 35–36).

105. "Ferentfern darf zikh nur der, ver es shtayt nit hekher fun der bashuldigung" (*EbA* 28–29).

106. "Hier konnte niemand sonst Einlass erhalten, denn dieser Eingang war nur für dich bestimmt. Ich gehe jetzt und schliesse ihn" (*P* 257).

sponse to the story, he is utterly confused by it and fails to recognize himself in the man from the country. Thus, far from clarifying the larger work, the priest's parable serves to reinforce the ambiguity already surrounding the Law and K.'s arrest. While both parables concern man and the Law, they differ considerably in emphasis: Gordin questions man's relationship to the Law; Kafka describes the paradoxical nature of the Law itself.

Politzer links the man from the country to the *am ha'arets* (*amkhorets*) of Jewish tradition, the ignorant man who has no genuine understanding of scripture and no patience for the intricacies of the Law.[107] *Elishe ben Avuya* provides a model of such a man in one of the important comic characters associated with the head of the yeshiva. This Jew (who is specifically listed in the cast of characters as an ignoramus, or *amkhorets*—clearly a well-known type) parrots the sages and speaks as though he were expert and scholar, quoting the thoughts and experiences of others as if they were his own. Like the amkhorets of Gordin's play, K. leans heavily on the experiences of others. He readily admits to ignorance of the Law which arrests and judges him: "I don't know this Law" (*Tr* 10), he tells the warders.[108] The words of Gordin's amkhorets—"I know all because I rub shoulders with learned men and am almost a sage myself"—seem to be echoed ironically by the manufacturer who flatters K.: "For you are almost a lawyer. I'm always saying: 'Chief Clerk K. is almost a lawyer.' "[109] By means of this device, Kafka makes both K. and the manufacturer look foolish, for K. hears only what he himself believes. The bigoted and uncharitable amkhorets provides a foil for Elishe, who accepts all men as equals. Elishe's attitude seems to be reflected in the humility of K.'s credo—"We are all simply men here, one

107. Politzer, *Parable and Paradox*, pp. 174–76. *Am ha'arets* is the Hebrew expression, *amkhorets* its Yiddish equivalent.

108. "Dieses Gesetz kenne ich nicht" (*P* 15).

109. "Ikh vays ales, varum ikh rayb zikh arum di talmidi khakhomim un bin kimat aleyn a talmid khokhem gevorn" (*EbA* 57). "Sie sind ja fast ein Advokat. Ich pflege immer zu sagen: Prokurist K. ist fast ein Advokat" (*P* 164).

as much as the other" (*Tr* 264)—but this view also echoes the comic tag line of the amkhorets—"I'm just an ordinary person in this world."[110]

In substance and function, K.'s interview with the priest parallels Elishe's interview with the head of the yeshiva. During these interviews, the representatives of the Law tell the protagonist that his case is going badly. Both protagonists argue candidly against the Law. K. describes the corruption of the court; Elishe points to the inconsistencies and contradiction in the Law. The head of the yeshiva angrily calls Elishe a "blind man," an epithet that corresponds closely to the priest's cry, "Can't you even see two steps ahead?" K.'s interpretation of this call—"It was . . . [like the cry] of one who sees another fall"[111]—echoes what Elishe is told explicitly—he is a fallen Jew for whom there is no hope. K.'s speculation that the priest could show him how to live outside the jurisdiction of the court ("how one could live outside the trial")[112] forms an ironic parallel to what Elishe *does* learn from the head of the yeshiva, who, by expelling Elishe from the community, teaches him how to live outside the Law.

Both works end abruptly with the death of the hero. The ambiguity surrounding K.'s death is analogous to the contradiction inherent in Elishe's suicide. Though innocent in his own eyes, Elishe, like K., is exhausted and crushed by his struggle against the Law. Gordin's play, like Kafka's novel, ends with a series of questions addressed to the Absolute. Elishe's sole defender eulogizes: "I cry to the heavens and ask if they will call you guilty without a judgment? Yes, you must be judged, but who is worthy to be your judge? Not I, not I."[113] In

110. "Wir sind hier doch alle Menschen, einer wie der andere" (*P* 253). "Vi ir zet mikh a mentshn oyf der velt" (*EbA* 57).

111. "'Siehst du denn nicht zwei Schritte weit?' Es war . . . wie von einem, der jemanden fallen sieht" (*P* 254).

112. "Wie man ausserhalb des Prozesses leben könnte" (*P* 254). The German word *Prozess* implies a long process or procedure as well as a lawsuit, proceedings, operation, or trial.

113. "Ikh shray tsu di himlen un freg, oyb zay veln vagn dikh dort shuldig tsu makhn on a mishpet!? Yo, mishpetn darf men dikh, ober ver di vos zenen vert dayne rikhter tsu zayn? Mir nit, mir nit" (*EbA* 71).

substance, these questions parallel the thoughts which come to K. in the moments before his death: "Where was the Judge whom he had never seen? Where was the High Court that he had never reached?"[114] For Gordin, as for Kafka, these questions remain unanswered and unanswerable.

In structure and in technique, the theatricality of the Yiddish plays runs through the fabric of *The Trial*. Although the novel is not complete and the ordering of its chapters remains uncertain, an element of mystery and suspense is sustained throughout. Not only the work as a whole, but each scene mirrors the rising and falling action associated with the drama. The individual chapters of *The Trial* are among the most staged and most "dramatic" of Kafka's works. The scene of K.'s arrest, the interview with Fräulein Bürstner (during which K. literally stages or reenacts the arrest), K.'s first interrogation, his interviews with the artist and the priest (including the priest's parable), and the scene of K.'s elaborately prepared, ritualistic murder all adapt the major elements of the drama to the narrative form. As was shown in detail in the discussion of "The Judgment," the setting for each of these scenes is also confined to a single space, the furnishings are handled and described as if they were stage properties, character is revealed chiefly through word, gesture, and costume. In addition, Kafka's apparent lack of interest in discursive psychological analysis corresponds to the crude, rather obvious motivation of the characters in the Yiddish plays. Although Kafka makes more frequent use of interior monologues in *The Trial* than in the earlier narratives (which in some passages tends to work against the inherent theatricality of the work), one can easily see in these extended monologues the reflection of the long soliloquies which characterize the Yiddish plays.

Yet a few other details in the novel can be attributed to the influence of the Yiddish plays. The student with the reddish beard, who carries the washerwoman to the high Judge and whom K. views as a villain, resembles the red-headed villain

---

114. "Wo war der Richter, den er nie gesehen hatte? Wo war das hohe Gericht, bis zu dem er nie gekommen war?" (*P* 272).

Papuz, who is commissioned by a Roman general to woo Bar Kokhba's fiancée Dina. The scene that the washerwoman describes to K. (the Judge's gazing on her as she lay sleeping) closely resembles a scene in which Papuz enters Dina's prison room and admires her as she sleeps. The Judge's present of stockings to the washerwoman corresponds to Papuz' wooing of Dina with jewels. Although these details are minor, they show that the melodramatic scenes of the Yiddish plays remained in Kafka's memory as impressions upon which he drew in writing his own narratives.

chapter seven
The remaining work

Although, as one might expect, Kafka's writing is less directly related to the plays of the Yiddish theater the farther one moves from 1912, the abundant evidence present in his earlier work should enable us to see in the later narratives continued reliance on the motifs, techniques, vivid impressions, and central themes of that theater. One can discern many significant elements and devices from the Yiddish plays in the highly symbolic stories Kafka produced in the winter of 1916/17.

The essential elements of the complex story "A Country Doctor" correspond to specific details of Latayner's play *Blimele*. In both, an official doctor is unexpectedly summoned to answer an urgent call from which he never returns. But while it is clear that the Jewish doctor, Daniel, is detained by the intrigue of his enemies, the country doctor's failure to return remains unexplained. Although Kafka's doctor is a bachelor, while the Jewish doctor is newly wed, there is a close correspondence in the names and functions of the female figures in the two works. Daniel's wife, "Blimele" (a diminutive of "flower"), is the counterpart of "Rosa," the country doctor's servant girl. When the doctors leave, these women are of necessity left alone, weeping and unprotected.

The secondary characters in these works provide additional parallels. Kafka's brutish groom, who appears from the depths of the pigsty and assaults Rosa, plays the same role as the enemies of the Jews who plot to dishonor Blimele. Such a pattern of assault on virtue—always a Gentile villain versus an honorable Jewish girl—was standard in the Yiddish plays and must have been familiar to Kafka through his experience of the Yiddish theater. The country doctor's unexplained, extreme pessimism ("Never shall I reach home at this rate; my flourishing

172

practice is done for; my successor is robbing me. . . . Betrayed! Betrayed!" [*PC* 143])[1] may be compared with the "betrayal" inherent in the plot against Daniel. The paradox of the country doctor's dilemma, which Politzer describes as "the helplessness of a man whose profession consists in helping,"[2] corresponds exactly to the paradox inherent in Daniel's position at Court. Though doctor to the king, he is helpless against the ills which anti-Semitism brings.

A sense of the supernatural, treated ironically by the narrator, permeates the action of "A Country Doctor" (for example, "in cases like this the gods are helpful, send the missing horse" [*PC* 139]).[3] Likewise, the theme of divine intervention, given serious and comic emphasis, figures in Latayner's play. In a serious vein, the Jews pray together for Daniel's safe return, while in a comic contrast the Gentiles call on both God and the Devil to aid their plot. The irony of Rosa's remark concerning the groom in the pigsty—"You never know what you're going to find in your own house" (*PC* 137)[4]—corresponds to the irony of the situation in *Blimele,* for the Jewish doctor is literally surprised by what he harbors in his house (the plot against Daniel is carried out with the help of a brother and sister, raised in the doctor's home as members of his family). The peculiar name Kafka gives to the sinister horses which emerge from the pigsty, "Brother" and "Sister," may derive from this unsavory brother-and-sister team.

Other elements in "A Country Doctor" bring to mind scattered details of Latayner's play. The mysterious, blood-red wound in the patient's side recalls gunshot wounds which the Jewish doctor in *Blimele* is called upon to tend. A scene involving public stripping occurs in both works. The schoolchildren who, in "A Country Doctor," chant doggerel verse to "an ut-

1. "Niemals komme ich so nach Hause; meine blühende Praxis ist verloren; ein Nachfolger bestiehlt mich. . . . Betrogen! Betrogen!" (*E* 153).

2. *Parable and Paradox,* p. 89.

3. "In solchen Fällen helfen die Götter, schicken das fehlende Pferd" (*E* 149).

4. "Man weiss nicht, was für Dinge man im eigenen Hause vorrätig hat" (*E* 147).

terly simple tune" (*PC* 142; *E* 151) recall the choruses prominent throughout *Blimele* and other Yiddish plays, which voice
the sentiments of the community in correspondingly simple
verse and melody.[5]

Although the mood of "A Country Doctor" recalls the atmosphere of a grotesque fairy tale, the story is constructed with
the precision of a drama. Its individual scenes seem to set forth
the actions of characters performing on a stage. The story is
easily divided into three separate sections whose themes are
closely tied. The opening scene—which introduces the doctor,
Rosa, and the groom—establishes mood, provides necessary
background information, and leads directly to the central confrontation between doctor, patient, and family. The third section (which takes place in the patient's bed) consists of the
strange interview between the now-naked doctor and his patient, and culminates in the doctor's hasty and presumably ill-
fated retreat.

Throughout the narrative, tension is created by the mysterious nature of the events portrayed and heightened by the implied danger to the doctor (which is reinforced by his fears of
Rosa). Technical devices such as lighting (the dim lantern
light of the first scene, the moonlight of the second), sound
effects (the sudden whinnying of the horses), stage whispers,
exaggerated emotion, stylized gesture, pantomime, and tableau
further link the method of "A Country Doctor" to the Yiddish
plays. The following narrated sequence conveys the immediacy
and tense expectation usually associated with the stage:

> ... moonlight all around ... [I] want ... to see the patient.
> Thin, ... with vacant eyes, without a shirt, the boy lifts himself
> from under the feather bedding, puts his arms around my neck,
> whispers into my ear: "Doctor, let me die." I look around; no
> one has heard it; his parents stand silent, bent forward ...; his
> sister has brought a chair for my handbag. I open the bag and
> search among my instruments; the boy keeps feeling for me from

5. Choruses also play a central role in *Shulamit, Bar Kokhba, The
Vice-King, Kol Nidre, David's Violin*, and in the prologue to *God, Man,
and Devil.*

the bed . . . ; I take hold of a pair of tweezers, examine them in the candlelight and put them down again."[6]

This described scene is analogous to a stage tableau, in which the actions of each character are accounted for and emotions suggested largely through word and gesture.

The telescoping of time which allows the country doctor to reach his destination in "a moment" suggests the dropping and lifting of a curtain on stage. Such swift changes of scene were particularly favored by the playwrights of the Yiddish theater, who relied upon them to create maximum suspense.

But because these parallels between *Blimele* and "A Country Doctor" are largely only surface similarities which do not penetrate into the symbolism of the narrative, their value in interpreting the story is rather limited. Whether, as Basil Busacca suggests, "A Country Doctor" dramatizes the paradox of the medical man, the plight of the homosexual, the ironic history of the Jews, or the false pride of the professional (or a combination of these) remains an open question that cannot be answered on the basis of the Yiddish plays.[7] The symbolism of this difficult story, even more private than is usual for Kafka, remains largely impenetrable.[8]

"A Fratricide," written in the same months as "A Country Doctor," is a short narrative which closely resembles the script

6. ". . . Mondlicht ringsum; . . . [Ich] will . . . den Kranken sehen. Mager, . . . mit leeren Augen, ohne Hemd hebt sich der Junge unter dem Federbett, hängt sich an meinen Hals, flüstert mir ins Ohr: 'Doktor, lass mich sterben.' Ich sehe mich um; niemand hat es gehört; die Eltern stumm vorgebeugt . . . ; die Schwester hat einen Stuhl für meine Handtasche gebracht. Ich öffne die Tasche und suche unter meinen Instrumenten; der Junge tastet immerfort aus dem Bett nach mir hin . . . ; ich fasse eine Pinzette, prüfe sie im Kerzenlicht und lege sie wieder hin" (*E* 148–49).

7. Basil Busacca, "A Country Doctor," in *Franz Kafka Today*, ed. Flores and Swander, pp. 45–54.

8. Recently I have come upon new evidence which decisively links this story (as well as much of Kafka's later work) to other specific works of the classical Yiddish literary tradition. A detailed analysis is in preparation and will appear soon.

for a play. Its stylized action takes the form of a grotesque pantomime set on a darkened stage. It is night; knife in hand, Schmar, the aggressor, awaits Wese, the victim. From windows above, the citizen Pallas watches, Frau Wese waits. As Wese passes Schmar, the murder occurs. In quick succession, a crowd gathers, a policeman appears, Frau Wese collapses, Schmar is led away. To give credence to these strange events, Kafka once again relies heavily on such stage devices as costume, lighting, sound effects, suspense, timing, exaggerated gesture, pantomime, and soliloquy. Throughout, the spoken word is used primarily as a means of punctuating the action and heightening its theatricality: " 'Wese!' shrieks Schmar, standing on tiptoe, his arms outstretched, the knife sharply lowered; 'Wese! Julia waits in vain!' And right into the throat and left into the throat and a third time deep into the belly Schmar stabs."[9]

Although the meaning of this apparently unmotivated murder cannot be explained solely in terms of the acts of violence that were part of the Yiddish plays, it seems likely that "A Fratricide" is related to the scenes of stabbing central to two works of the Yiddish theater, Gordin's The Savage One and The Slaughtering.[10] In these plays, as in Kafka's story, the act of murder is the point of climax toward which the work builds. In both plays the murder weapon is a kitchen knife; in Kafka's story the tool is described as "half a bayonette, half a kitchen knife" (PC 168).[11] The murder in "A Fratricide," as also in The Trial and "In the Penal Colony," takes on the quality of a ritual affair (Wese is referred to as das Opfer) and thus relates to the theme of ritual slaughtering which domi-

9. " 'Wese!' schreit Schmar, auf den Fusspitzen stehend, den Arm aufgereckt, das Messer scharf gesenkt, 'Wese! Vergebens wartet Julia!' Und rechts in den Hals und links in den Hals und drittens tief in den Bauch sticht Schmar" (E 180).

10. Four other plays in the repertoire end in suicide. In addition, God, Man, and Devil, Bar Kokhba, and Kol Nidre include sensational scenes of attempted murder.

11. "Halb Bajonett, halb Küchenmesser" (E 179). Esterke, in The Slaughtering, uses a slaughtering knife which might resemble Schmar's weapon.

nates *The Slaughtering*.[12] Gordin's play gives literal as well as symbolic significance to this occupation. The heroine, though driven to commit murder, is herself symbolically "slaughtered"; one of the important secondary characters is shown training to be a *shoykhet* (ritual slaughterer). His continual recitation of the laws governing slaughter provides ironic counterpoint to the main action of the play.

The spilling of blood, central to Kafka's story, occurs not only as part of the action of Gordin's plays, but is emphasized by the language of the texts as well. Lemekh, in *The Savage One*, cries out: "I want to see how the warm red blood flows from your wound. . . . I want to see your blood. . . . oh, blood, blood!"[13] Esterke, in *The Slaughtering*, raves: "And I cut with the sharp knife, and the hot blood flows . . . the hot blood flows and I cut."[14] In "A Fratricide" Schmar cries: "The soaring ecstasy from the shedding of another's blood! . . . Why aren't you simply a bladder of blood" (*PC* 169).[15] In all three the bloody weapon is prominent. Lemekh wipes the blood-drenched knife on his shirt; Esterke waves the murder weapon; Schmar flings his knife away.

In addition to these details of theme and rhetoric, "A Fratricide" resembles these staged murder scenes in broad, structural terms. In all three the aggressor brandishes his weapon as he prepares to kill and accompanies the act with passionate words addressed to the victim. After the murder (again, in all three instances) the murderer is overwhelmed by a sense of relief which he expresses publicly. Lemekh admits: "I feel good. A stone has fallen from my heart."[16] Esterke triumphantly repeats

12. The German word *Opfer* is ambiguous and may be used to suggest offering, sacrifice, victim, or martyr. Kafka seems deliberately to play on this ambiguity, for Wese is both victim and sacrifice.

13. "Ikh vil zen, vi dayn varm royt blut vet flisn fun dayn vund. . . . ikh vil zen dayn blut. . . . oy, blut, blut!" (*DVM* 46).

14. "Und ikh shnayd mitn sharfn khalef und dos heyse blut gist. . . . dos heyse blut gist un ikh shnayd" (*DSh* 79–80).

15. "Beflügelung durch das Fliessen des fremden Blutes! . . . Warum bist du nicht einfach eine mit Blut gefüllte Blase" (*E* 180).

16. "Es iz mir gut. A shtayn iz mir arop fun mayn hartsn" (*DVM* 46–47).

the Laws of slaughter. Schmar cries: "The bliss of murder! The relief" (*PC* 169).[17] Not surprisingly, while the sense of release experienced by the protagonists in Gordin's plays is easily explained by their desperate condition, which the murder remedies, Kafka's work provides no explanation for either the murder or the relief that follows it. Furthermore, Schmar's murder of Wese differs from those enacted in Gordin's plays in that Lemekh and Esterke act in the heat of passion, while Schmar, seemingly unprovoked, kills with cold premeditation.

Nonetheless, all three acts of murder (as well as the relief that follows them) have unmistakably sexual overtones. Lemekh declares himself "aroused"; Esterke cools her burning cheeks with the knife, itself a sexual symbol. Kafka's "A Fratricide" is particularly suggestive of sexuality in its imagery: although the murder occurs on a cold night, Schmar is "glowing hot"; his murder weapon is "naked" or "exposed"; Frau Wese's clothing consists of nothing but a fur coat over a nightgown; Pallas, the eager observer, seems a voyeur.

Though the tale is brief, the apparently gratuitous violence of the action described in "A Fratricide" is both puzzling and disturbing. Politzer relates the method of this story to the techniques of dramatic Expressionism and interprets its action as a debunking of the "myth of human dignity."[18] But even this analysis does not adequately explain the mystery behind the unmotivated murder Kafka describes in such literal detail. The many parallels in theme, action, mood, rhetoric, and overall structure suggest that in "A Fratricide" Kafka was drawing on his memory of the highly theatrical murder scenes enacted in Gordin's plays, without deriving his meaning from them. Thus, "A Fratricide" may be more closely related to the methods of melodrama than to those of Expressionism.[19]

17. "Seligkeit des Mordes! Erleichterung" (*E* 180).

18. *Parable and Paradox*, p. 93. Politzer associates the name "Wese" with the German *Wesen* or *gewesen*, "being," "been," and the name "Schmar" with the Hebrew *shomair* (verb and noun), "to watch, to be on guard."

19. In some respects, of course, Expressionist drama is itself highly melodramatic. But it often uses melodramatic methods for purposes outside the aesthetic experience, and thus, to a different effect.

"The Hunter Gracchus," written between January and May 1917, concerns a dead man who, for reasons unknown, is doomed to wander among the living. Both versions of this story are essentially question-and-answer dialogues confined to a single, circumscribed space. The longer of the two fragments is embedded in a narrative of broader scope, while the shorter dialogue stands alone, though it was no doubt also intended as part of a larger work. In both versions the two main characters, the dead hunter and the burgomaster, are given the single dimensions of stage characters and described only in terms of costume and gesture. The burgomaster is "a man in a top hat tied with a band of black crepe," the hunter "a man with wildly matted hair and beard, tanned skin."[20] In the early moments of their meeting, the characters respond to each other without words: "The gentleman [burgomaster] stepped up to the bier, laid his hand on the brow of the man lying upon it, then kneeled down and prayed.... The man on the bier nodded, indicated a chair with a feeble movement of his arm" (*GWC* 208).[21] Although one cannot attribute the specific theme or situation described in "The Hunter Gracchus" to the Yiddish plays, one is nonetheless struck by the theatricality of the action and dramatic quality of its form.

Like "The Hunter Gracchus," "Jackals and Arabs" (January/February 1917) is essentially a dramatic encounter. Asleep in a desert oasis, the narrator is woken by a pack of jackals who surround, hold, and beseech him to help them by slitting the throats of their enemies, the Arabs, with small, rusty scissors. This strange meeting is interrupted by the appearance of an Arab, who drives the jackals away, scoffs at their pretensions, and throws them carrion upon which they fall wildly (contrary to their previous disclaimers). The tension created by these

20. "Ein Mann im Zylinderhut mit Trauerband"; "ein Mann mit wild durcheinandergewachsenem Haar und Bart, gebräunter Haut" (*B* 103).

21. "Der Herr trat zur Bahre, legte eine Hand dem Daliegenden auf die Stirn, kniete dann nieder und betete.... Der Mann auf der Bahre nickte, zeigte mit schwach ausgestrecktem Arm auf einen Sessel" (*B* 104).

Kafka's hunter has been linked by Binder to the universal figure of the wandering Jew ("Franz Kafka and *Selbstwehr*," p. 144).

"staged" events and the interplay of conflict among the three parties (narrator, jackals, and Arabs) resemble the effects created by staged drama.

In an extremely interesting article entitled "Kafka's 'Jackals and Arabs,'" William C. Rubinstein suggests that this story is based on the Old Testament legend of the coming of the Messiah-Warrior, who, it was said, lived among the Jews, but did not reveal Himself because the people proved themselves unworthy of His coming.[22] Rubinstein identifies the narrator of "Jackals and Arabs" with such a hidden Messiah. The jackals he associates with the Jews, the Arabs with Gentiles, and the scissors with tools of circumcision. Many details of "Jackals and Arabs," otherwise difficult to explain, become coherent in the light of Rubinstein's analysis. Particularly convincing is his association of jackals with Jews, for like the Jewish people, the jackals are "exiled" and involved in an "old quarrel" and an "ancient tradition." And like the Jews, the jackals have for centuries been awaiting outside help. The jackals' plaintive song and the rocking motions accompanying it bring to mind the Orthodox Jewish mode of prayer and recall as well Kafka's description of the singing at the Savoy (Di 80; T 81). In choosing jackals to represent the Jewish people, Kafka may be employing a pun on the Hebrew word for jackals, *tan* (plural *tanim*), and the word for teachers of *Mishna*, *tana* (plural *tanoyim*).[23] Although Kafka's adult Hebrew lessons did not begin until the spring of 1917, we may assume that as a result of his early Hebrew training, his close association with the actor Yitskhok Levi, and his interest in the Yiddish plays (all abundantly laced with Hebrew), many Hebrew words were familiar to Kafka even before his formal study of that language began.[24]

22. *Monatshefte* 59 (1967): 13–18.

23. *Mishna* refers to a collection of post-Biblical discussions of the second century B.C., forming part of the Talmud.
A second pun is also possible here: the Hebrew word for betrothal or engagement contract, *tnoyim*, is very close in sound to the other two Hebrew words in question. Betrothal was very much on Kafka's mind in these years; he was engaged to Felice for a second time in July 1917.

24. See Hartmut Binder, "Kafkas Hebräischstudien: Ein biographisch-interpretatorischer Versuch," *JDSG* 11 (November 1967): 527–56 for

The word *tana* is repeated in key speeches in *Elishe ben Avuya* and *Bar Kokhba;* Elishe's only friend among the Orthodox is a tana. Kafka's extremely biting and satiric portrait of the jackals coincides with the characteristics attributed to Orthodox Jews by Levi and the Yiddish playwrights, and observed by Kafka himself. In creating such a portrait, Kafka seems to echo Bar Kokhba's derision of the Jews' passivity and Elishe's scorn for their insularity.

Although Kakfa's narratives are entirely devoid of specific references to Jewish themes, his diaries and letters reveal a keen interest in the problems of the Jewish people. This interest, reflected obliquely in "Jackals and Arabs," is also discernable in the story of Rotpeter, the "humanized" ape. A lively discussion concerning "A Report to an Academy" (May/June 1917) began in 1952 when William C. Rubinstein suggested that Rotpeter, the narrator-ape of the "Report," was quite possibly "a Jew who has allowed himself to be converted to Christianity in order to escape persecution."[25] While Rubinstein's hypothesis received some support, it was challenged by Leo Weinstein in 1962 and by Schulz-Behrend in 1963.[26] In contrast to Rubinstein, who asserts that Rotpeter's obsequiousness to the academy makes him a "despicable figure," both Weinstein and Schulz-Behrend interpret the ape as one of the few positive characters Kafka ever created. In his recent study of Kafka, Walter Sokel not only fully accepts Schulz-Behrend's refutation of Rubinstein's theory; he also interprets the ape in a

---

detailed documentation of Kafka's Hebrew studies throughout his adult life. Kafka was prepared for the Bar Mitsvah; the ceremony took place on June 13, 1896, at the Zigeuner Synagogue. See Wagenbach, *Biographie,* p. 59.

25. William C. Rubinstein, "A Report to an Academy," in *Franz Kafka Today,* ed. Flores and Swander, p. 58. The kernel of this idea was proposed by Heinz Politzer, ed., *Vor dem Gesetz,* by Franz Kafka (Berlin, 1934), p. 78, cited by Leo Weinstein, "Kafka's Ape: Heel or Hero?" *MFS* 8 (1962): 75.

26. Rubinstein's work was extended by Robert Kauf, "Once Again: Kafka's 'Report.'" It was challenged by Weinstein, "Kafka's Ape," and by G. Schulz-Behrend, "Kafka's 'Ein Bericht für eine Akademie': An Interpretation," *Monatshefte* 55 (1963): 1–6.

generally positive light as a successfully integrated being.[27]
But an examination of "A Report to an Academy" in the light
of the Yiddish plays reveals an extraordinarily close connection
between Kafka's ape, Rotpeter, and Berele, a converted Jew
who plays a prominent part in Latayner's play *Blimele*. While
some important modifications of Rubinstein's theory are called
for, in the main this connection between *Blimele* and "A Report" supports the assertion that Kafka's ape is an ironic counterpart of a converted Jew.

Because Berele is not merely an unallayed villain, but a tragi-
comic figure trapped by circumstances into apostasy, Latayner
takes pains to mitigate the scorn and derision which are the
stock response of the Jewish audience to the convert by allowing Berele to explain himself. With wry humor Berele summarizes his plight: "I feel almost as if I were half-fish and half-
human: one half cannot live in the water and the other half
cannot live in the air.... That is to say, I am no more than half
a human."[28] Rejected as an apostate by the Jews, the convert is
not accepted by the Christians either, who viewed baptized
Jews with great suspicion. In an extremely long expository
speech which may have suggested to Kafka the form of the
"Report," Berele describes the history of his unwilling conversion with ironic wit and humor. At an early age he was or-
phaned and taken in by a family who placed him in the yeshiva (the academy) to be trained, like his father before him, as
a scholar and judge. As he became older, however, he no
longer wished to endure the difficulties of this training and
refused to study further. As a result he was beaten: "They
broke my bones on God's account."[29] He swears that to his dying day he will not forget the "Hasidic slaps with the slippers."[30]

27. Sokel writes: "He is completely what he became.... his metamorphosis was successful, because it made him into an integrated self, in
every sense a 'new person' " (*Tragik und Ironie*, pp. 330–31). I cannot
agree with this interpretation. The ape's body alone contradicts Sokel's
argument; the portrait of "successful conversion" is clearly ironic.

28. "Ikh fil mikh epes azoy vi halb fish un halb mentsh, die helfte kon
in vaser nisht lebn un di andere helfte kon in luft nisht lebn.... Dos
heyst, ikh bin nisht mer vi eyn halber mentsh" (*Bl* 25).

29. "Hot men mir gebrokhn di beyner oyf Gots konto" (*Bl* 26).

30. "Di Khasidishe petsh mit de pantofln" (*Bl* 26).

When, as a youth, he was unable to fast on Yom Kippur, no Jew would take pity on him and give him even a dry crust of bread, so he was essentially forced to turn to the Gentiles, in whose homes he had no choice but to eat unclean food, without covering his head or washing his hands, as is demanded by Jewish ritual. When his defection was discovered, Berele was severely beaten by the Jews and publicly shamed: "They beat me and broke me like a winey apple. And on top of that, they even shamed me by putting me in a pillory and spitting in my face."[31] When, soon thereafter, Berele was thrown out of the yeshiva, he was so thoroughly disheartened that he gave up Judaism entirely and became an apostate.

In addition to providing an explanation for his defection from Judaism, Berele's speech contains a biting indictment of the yeshiva in particular and of Orthodoxy in general, which corresponds to the criticism of the human condition and institutions implicit in Kafka's "Report." The pleasure the Hasidim derive from tormenting a being they consider "less than human" is analogous to the pleasure the sailors obtain from teasing Rotpeter.

The details of the ape's experiences in captivity are very similar to Berele's account of what he suffered at the hands of the Jews. Rotpeter, who is literally only half-human, and Berele, who perceives himself as only "half-a-person," are parallel figures.[32] Berele introduces his speech with the question "[You ask] what has become of me?" Rotpeter refers to "what I became."[33] Both are trapped beings who seek a compromise solution or an expedient "way out"; real freedom is as impossible for Berele as for Rotpeter. "I had no other choice," explains

---

The Hasidim are adherents of a Jewish religious movement founded in the eighteenth century, stressing pious devotion and ecstasy.

31. "Men hot mikh tseklapt tsebrokhn vi a veynign epel. Un nokh alemen hot men mir nokh aza buse ongeton, men hot dokh mikh in kiene geshtelt un ale hobn mir in punim arayn geshpugn" (Bl 26–27). The expression "veynign epel" probably refers to the bruising of a juicy apple when it falls from the tree or is made into cider.

32. Berele is also associated with an animal; his name means "little bear."

33. "Vos oys mir gevorn iz?" (Bl 26). "Was ich geworden bin" (E 189).

Berele. "I had no way out [alternative]," says Rotpeter.[34] The
yeshiva and the Orthodoxy that fosters it are as imprisoning
and oppressive as the bars of Rotpeter's cage, while the pillory
in which Berele was imprisoned provides a more literal parallel. The beatings of the Hasidim which nearly crippled Berele
("To this very day I cannot straighten out my legs from those
beatings")[35] are reminiscent of the shots which maimed Rotpeter ("It is the cause of my limping a little to this day" [PC
175])[36] and of various other tortures he had to endure. The
comic remark "I did not wish to squeeze the bench any
longer,"[37] which symbolizes Berele's spiritual discomfort as
well as his physical pain, corresponds to the pain inflicted on
Rotpeter by the bars of his cage ("While the bars of the cage
cut into my flesh behind" [PC 176]).[38]

Being spat upon while imprisoned behind bars is a symbol
central to both works. For Berele, this treatment represents the
worst humiliation imposed upon him. Rotpeter views it ironically, as a typically human characteristic which he happily
learns to imitate: "It was so easy to imitate these people. I
learned to spit in the very first days. We used to spit in each
other's faces" (PC 180).[39] Spitting is also part of the comic by-
play of Blimele. In a scene near the end of the play, Berele, by
then half-crazed,[40] sprays his Gentile masters (the real villains
of the play) with wine they had urged upon him. The idiom

34. "Hob ikh dokh kayn andere brere gehat" (Bl 26). "Ich war . . .
ohne Ausweg" (E 187).

35. "Ikn ken mir nokh haynt di beyner fun di shlek nisht oysglaykhn"
(Bl 26).

36. "Er hat es verschuldet, dass ich noch heute ein wenig hinke"
(E 186).

37. "Ikh volt nisht mer di benk kvetshn" (Bl 26).

38. "Während sich mir hinten die Gitterstäbe ins Fleisch einschnit-
ten" (E 187).

39. "Es was so leicht, die Leute nachzuahmen. Spucken konnte ich
schon in den ersten Tagen. Wir spuckten einander dann gegenseitig ins
Gesicht" (E 191).

40. Note that Rotpeter's mate is described as half-crazed: "She has
the insane look of the bewildered half-broken animal in her eye" ("Sie
hat nämlich den Irrsinn des verwirrten dressierten Tieres im Blick"
[PC 184; E 196]).

by which Berele expresses his disgust for the Orthodox Jews—
"Even then I wanted to spit on it all"[41]—is a play on the verb
"to spit" and may be related to Kafka's use of spitting as a symbol of degradation. The ape's ability to mimic (by means of
which Kafka mocks the human condition) recalls the inclination toward mime displayed by Berele, who taunts his Gentile
masters by mimicking their actions.

Rotpeter's strange assertion, referring to his decision to give
up being an ape—"a fine, clear train of thought, which I must
have constructed somehow with my belly, since apes think
with their bellies" (PC 177)[42]—sounds like an ironic reference
to the emphasis on food which permeates Jewish culture and is
reflected in the Yiddish plays. Berele was punished because of
his inability to keep the fast. Significantly, it was his search for
food which drove him to the Gentiles. In the same context,
drinking has negative associations and is a trait generally associated with Gentiles. In Jewish tradition, alcohol is consumed
moderately; wine is drunk ritually on the Sabbath and on other
holy days. Thus, the ape's learning to drink may well be an
oblique reference to Rotpeter's (the Jew's) "conversion." Such
reference, however, does not reside, as Rubinstein suggests, in
the symbolic association of spirits (Schnaps) with the sacra-
ment of Communion, but in the negative association of drinking with the enemies of the Jewish people.[43] The decidedly
positive response of Rotpeter's captors to his "learning to
drink" parallels the obvious satisfaction the Gentiles derive
from Berele's conversion.[44]

Although the academy that Rotpeter addresses probably
represents an ironic reference to the yeshiva (which literally

41. "Nokh damols hob ikh gevolt oyf ales a shpay gebn" (Bl 27).
42. "Ein klarer schöner Gedankengang, den ich irgendwie mit dem
Bauch ausgeheckt haben muss, denn Affen denken mit dem Bauch"
(E 188).
43. Robert Kauf, "Once Again: Kafka's 'Report,' " also argues this
point.
44. Note the teacher's satisfaction when Rotpeter dirties himself in his
cage: "I ... befouled myself in my cage, which again gave him [the
teacher] great satisfaction" ("Ich ... verunreinige mich in meinem
Käfig, was wieder ihm grosse Genugtuung macht" [PC 181; E 192]).

means "academy"), Kafka does not confine himself to ridicul-
ing the Jews in "A Report"; he also adapts and ridicules some
elements of the non-Jewish figures in the Yiddish plays. The
vulgarity and rowdiness of the crew on shipboard corresponds
to the behavior (typical of all the anti-Semites portrayed on
the Yiddish stage) of Berele's Gentile employers, who, like the
sailors in "A Report," drink heavily, smoke, and gamble. They
tease Berele, their converted Jew, much as the sailors tease
Rotpeter, their captive ape.

Because Rotpeter's tone suggests that he is not entirely taken
in by his "success," Schulz-Behrend maintains that he recognizes the shabbiness of his expedient.[45] The text, however, remains ambiguous on this point. Like many of Kafka's heroes,
Rotpeter stops short of seeing himself; his irony is directed
chiefly at his captors, teachers, and the members of the academy. The ambiguity of the ape's position parallels the ambiguous role given to Berele in Latayner's play, for Berele is clown,
villain, and martyr-hero, who renounces his conversion in the
end. Throughout, he is a figure of contempt for the Jews and of
ridicule for the Christians, who use him for their own purposes.
Does not Rotpeter's position in the variety show (symbolic of
his position in the world) correspond to Berele's role as "show"
Jew?

Rubinstein assumes that if Rotpeter is indeed modelled upon
the converted Jew, his implied apostasy necessarily stems from
the Jew's desire to escape Christian persecution. But Kafka nowhere suggests that Rotpeter chooses to leave the tribal life; on
the contrary, he makes clear that "conversion" is essentially
forced upon the ape. In this, possibly, "A Report" reflects and
distorts the irony of Berele's unwilling conversion, forced upon
him, even more ironically, by the behavior of his own people.
Thus, if, as Rubinstein concludes, Rotpeter is "despicable" (because of his conversion), those who have driven him to it must
be held at least equally so. Possibly the greatest irony in "A
Report" lies in the fact that the humans portrayed are hardly
more civilized than the ape and certainly not worthy of imita-
tion.

45. "Kafka's 'Ein Bericht,' " p. 4.

Ironically, both Rotpeter and Berele turn to their natural enemies as a way out, an expedient which in both instances is only partially successful. Berely runs from the Jews only to discover the greater inhumanity of the Christians; Rotpeter cannot return to the jungle and must choose between the circus and the variety show. While Latayner vindicates the Jewish people by the example of his noble heroes, Daniel and Blimele, Kafka gives us no model of worthiness; his story demands that we form our own judgment concerning the value of the ape's success. The platitudes by means of which Latayner neatly divides "real humans" from "spoiled beings" at the end of the play seem to be reflected (again, ironically) in Kafka's portrait of the "converted" ape who, by holding a distorting mirror up to man, makes it impossible to separate clearly the human from the bestial.

Some elements of Yitskhok Levi's biography, particularly his experiences at the yeshiva, coincide with what happens to Berele in *Blimele* and may have contributed to Kafka's portrait of Rotpeter.[46] In an essay on the Yiddish theater, which Kafka framed from notes he made while the actor talked, Levi remarks: "My purpose is quite simple: to present a few pages of memories of the Jewish [Yiddish] theater, with its dramas, its actors, and its public . . . , or to put it differently, *to raise the curtain and show the wound.* Only after the disease has been diagnosed, can a cure be found and, possibly, the true Jewish theater created" (*DF* 129; italics mine).[47] Although it is difficult to know if it was Kafka or Levi who supplied the metaphor, the wound Levi speaks of is clearly connected (in his or Kafka's mind) to Judaism in general, more specifically to the "sickness" ailing the Yiddish theater.[48] From what we know of

46. See *Di* 217–20; *T* 236–40.
47. "Meine Absicht ist ganz einfach: einige Blätter Erinnerungen an das jüdische Theater mit seinen Dramen, seinen Schauspielern, seinem Publikum . . . , hier vorzulegen oder, anders gesagt, *den Vorhang zu heben und die Wunde zu zeigen.* Nur nach Erkenntnis der Krankheit lässt sich ein Heilmittel finden und möglicherweise das wahre jüdische Theater schaffen" (*H* 154; italics mine).
48. This metaphor may help to explain the significance of the wound Rotpeter displays. Kauf discusses the symbolism of the wound and connects it to the wound Jacob received when wrestling with the Angel

Levi's skill as an actor and of the kinds of roles he usually portrayed, it is highly probable that he played the role of Berele when *Blimele* was performed. It is also likely that Levi's experience (which reinforced the material in the Yiddish plays) helped to shape Kafka's image of Orthodox Judaism, a theme Kafka played upon in many of his narratives.[49]

"A Crossbreed," written in the same months as "A Report to an Academy" (May/June 1917), also portrays a being composed of two irreconcilable parts; the creature is half-cat and half-lamb. In his illuminating essay "Franz Kafka: Jüdische Existenz ohne Glauben," Baruch Benedikt Kurzweil suggests that this strange animal is Kafka's symbol for the Jew in the Diaspora, who still retains vestiges of the lamb (the Biblical symbol of sacrifice) but has already become part beast of prey.[50] While Kurzweil relates the lamb part of the animal to the Jew, he associates the cat part to the wolf in the idiom "As a lamb among wolves," traditionally used to describe the position of the Jew among Gentiles. By virtue of its uneasy fusion of disparate elements, the beast in "A Crossbreed" resembles the narrator-ape of "A Report." If, as seems likely, Kurzweil's association of "A Crossbreed" with a half-assimilated Jew is valid, one may conjecture that Berele, the converted Jew who viewed himself as a hybrid, was the model not only for Kafka's ape, but for his mysterious crossbreed as well.

As Kurzweil suggests, the crossbreed becomes identified with its owner, the narrator of the story, and thus, to a degree,

("Once Again: Kafka's 'Report,' " pp. 362–63). For a full discussion of Kafka's use of the wound image, see Bluma Goldstein, "A Study of the Wound in Stories by Franz Kafka," *GR* 41 (1966): 202–17.

49. Apostasy from Judaism occurred frequently among Westernized Jews from the turn of the century until Hitler's rise to power. Almost every issue of *Selbstwehr* carried a column devoted to departures or apostasies from Judaism and included as well emotional essays on subjects like "Is Assimilation of Jews Possible?" (May 13, 1910, p. 1), and "Czech-Jewish Assimilation is Becoming Rusty" (December 29, 1911, p. 4). In contrast, the *Prager Tagblatt* favored conversion; on November 24, 1911, *Selbstwehr*, p. 5, reported "Das *Prager Tagblatt* rät zur Taufe" ("The *Prager Tagblatt* advises baptism").

50. *NRs* (1966), pp. 418–36.

with the author himself. On this basis, Kurzweil relates the narrator's casual suggestion of killing the beast—"Perhaps the butcher's knife would be a release [salvation] for this animal"[51] —to Kafka's self-hatred, which cannot be entirely separated from his Orthodox Jewish heritage.[52] One of Kafka's comments about the Jews, included in a letter to Milena, bears a striking resemblance to Berele's avowed feelings toward his former brothers, the Jews. Kafka wrote: "Sometimes I'd like to cram them all as Jews (including myself) into the drawer of the laundry chest, then wait, then open the drawer a little, to see whether all have already suffocated, if not, to close the drawer again and go on like this to the end" (*LM* 59).[53] Berele remarks, "The Jews? Oh, if I could drown them in a spoonful of water, I would do it."[54] Although these references do not exhaust the possible readings of this little story, they help to clarify some of its otherwise obscure symbolism.

"The Cares of a Family Man," which coincides with the writing of "A Report" and "A Crossbreed," has at its center the creature Odradek, who, Kurzweil suggests, is Kafka's symbol for decaying Judaism: "Only old, broken-off bits of thread, knotted and tangled together, of the most varied sorts" (*PC* 160).[55] This interpretation merits some attention, especially as Emrich connects the name "Odradek" with the Czech

51. "Vielleicht wäre für dieses Tier das Messer des Fleischers eine Erlösung" (*B* 112).

52. On his mother's side Kafka stemmed from pious, learned Jews. See *D*i 197–98, *T* 212–13; Wagenbach, *Biographie*, pp. 20–22; and "Letter to His Father," *DF* 140, *H* 164, in which Kafka discusses the disparate Löwy-Kafka elements in his own makeup. (Löwy was his mother's maiden name.)

53. "Manchmal möchte ich sie eben als Juden (mich eingeschlossen) alle etwa in die Schublade des Wäschekastens dort stopfen, dann warten, dann die Schublade ein wenig herausziehn, um nachzusehen, ob sie schon alle erstickt sind, wenn nicht, die Lade wieder hineinschieben und es so fortsetzen bis zum Ende" (*Mi* 57).

54. "Di yudn? Akh, ikh zol zey kenen in eyn lefel vaser dertrunkn, volt ikh es getun" (*Bl* 15).

55. "Nur abgerissene, alte, aneinandergeknotete, aber auch ineinanderverfitzte Zwirnstücke von verschiedenster Art" (*E* 170–71). In German, the language is itself tangled and onomatopoetic.

odraditi, "to warn away from,"[56] an attitude which describes at least a part of Kafka's ambivalence toward Orthodox Judaism. The narrator's association of Odradek with something childlike ("one . . . treats him . . . like a child")[57] recalls the oft-used appellation "Jewish children" ("Yidishe kinderlakh") with which Frau Klug warmly greeted the guests at the Savoy.[58] But this quality was not interpreted by all Jews as a positive trait. In *Bar Kokhba* Eliezer reprimands his people: "Children? Oy, precisely this is bad, that we are called *children,* not *people.* Oh, we should already be known as Jewish *people,* not *Jewish children.*"[59] The childlike quality which Kafka attributes to Odradek (as well as to Josef K., to Georg's friend in Russia, to Josefine and her community, to the assistants, and of course, to himself)[60] may be related to this popular concept of the Jewish people as the children of God. Could it not be that the family man alluded to in the story's title constitutes an ironic reference to such a heavenly Father, while Odradek's star-shape represents an allusion to the Star of David, symbol of Judaism?[61]

The stories "The Great Wall of China," "An Old Manuscript" (March/April 1917), "The Problem of Our Laws," and "The

56. Emrich, *Franz Kafka,* p. 103.

57. "Man . . . behandelt ihn . . . wie ein Kind" (*E* 171).

58. See *D*i 80; *T* 81. The word *kinderlakh* is a diminutive intended not merely to reflect but also to affirm the closeness and unity of the Jewish people.

59. "Kinder? Oy ot dos iz schlekht, vos mir heysn *kinder,* nit *mentshn.* O, men zol unz shoyn rufn yidishe *mentshn,* nit *yidishe kinder*" (*BK* 110).

60. Kafka was painfully aware of the fact that he always looked much younger than his years. In 1911, at the age of twenty-eight, he described himself as "a young man whom everyone takes to be eighteen" (*D*i 139).

61. This interpretation is supported by the fact that Kafka first published "The Cares of a Family Man" in the Jewish weekly *Selbstwehr* (December 19, 1919). According to Binder, this paper "proclaimed as its editorial objective the will to secure the present and future of the Jewish *people* and to make Jewishness a vigorous force" ("Franz Kafka and *Selbstwehr,*" p. 136). Three other of Kafka's short pieces—"Before the Law," the first version of "An Imperial Message," and "An Old Manuscript"—also appeared first in *Selbstwehr.* See ibid., pp. 146–47.

Refusal" (Fall 1920), though separated by three years, are related thematically by their common emphasis on the relationship of the individual to the community and of the community to its ancestors and to distant, unseen rulers. These stories, all first-person narrations, include the experiences of the people, as well as the private speculations of the narrator who is established as their representative. With the exception of "The Problem of Our Laws," these narratives are pervaded by a sharp sense of division between "us" (the group described, carriers of an ancient tradition) and "them" (the attackers). This sense of isolation and fear of attack correspond to the historical situation of the Jewish people, portrayed so vividly in *Elishe ben Avuya, Bar Kokhba, The Vice-King,* and *Kol Nidre.* All four stories are set in the distant past in remote places, as, for example, China.

Hildegard Platzer Collins interprets China as Kafka's image of human life, a vast, remote region wherein the Emperor is so elevated he becomes God. Clement Greenberg identifies China (on one level) as "Kafka's figure of speech for Diaspora Jewry" and the Great Wall as "the 'fence' of Jewish Law or the Torah."[62] Greenberg's argument is extremely convincing, for Kafka was very much aware of his Jewish heritage, and for a time tried (without success) to find his spiritual identity in the Orthodox Jewish tradition.[63] While "The Great Wall of China" is not an especially "dramatic" story, many of the characteristics attributed by the narrator to the Empire in which he dwells—its stagnation, its lack of unity, its confusion of past and present, and especially its fear of the present—echo criticism levelled at the Jewish people by playwrights like Gordin,

62. Hildegard Platzer Collins, "Kafka's Views of Institutions and Traditions," *GQ* 35 (November 1962): 492–503; Clement Greenberg, "At the Building of the Great Wall of China," in *Franz Kafka Today,* ed. Flores and Swander, p. 77.

63. Kafka despised the half-hearted Judaism he associated with his father; see "Letter to His Father," *DF* 171–74, *H* 197–200. This brand of Judaism is still common in half-assimilated Jews the world over. It involves a minimal attachment to the outer forms of the religion, e.g., occasional attendance at the synagogue and formal enactment of the more important rituals.

whose aim it was to revitalize Judaism. Whatever the symbolic significance of the Chinese Empire, it seems likely that a model for this image lies in the portrait of the Jewish people made familiar to Kafka through the Yiddish plays. If one analyzes Kafka's story substituting "Judaism" for "Empire," one can point to many other details which seem to describe the Jews of the Diaspora.[64]

In "An Old Manuscript" (a page of history, perhaps), the narrator, a modest cobbler whose shop fronts the Emperor's palace, describes an invasion of the capital by armed soldiers, who endanger the populace and bring "pollution" to the usually scrupulously clean town. These nomads resemble the Roman Legions who, in *Bar Kokhba*, viciously slaughter the Jews and defile their places of worship. (The invasion also resembles the pogroms against Jews frequent in Russian and Polish villages.) Kafka's description of the linguistic gulf that separates the natives from the invaders corresponds to the facts of Jewish experience portrayed in the Yiddish plays. The populace in "An Old Manuscript" is said to placate the enemy for the same reasons put forth by Eliezer in *Bar Kokhba* and by the head of the yeshiva in *Elishe ben Avuya:* "Who knows what they might think of doing" (*PC* 146–47).[65] The central position given to the butcher of the community recalls the emphasis placed on proper butchering (ritual slaughter) in Jewish tradition. Possibly, the climax of "An Old Manuscript"—the in-

64. Like the Jews, the Chinese in Kafka's story prize education and "architecture" (the art of building arguments) above all. In both groups almost every educated man is an expert: "Almost every educated man of our time was a mason by profession and infallible in the matter of laying foundations" ("Fast jeder gebildete Zeitgenosse war Maurer vom Fach und in der Frage der Fundamentierung untrüglich" [*GWC* 155–56; *B* 71]). In the schools young children are trained to build "structures" (arguments) which their teachers promptly "knock down." In their dislike of war, their veneration of the old, and their emphasis on learning and ancient tradition, the "overseas" Chinese are often compared to the Jews of the Diaspora. *Selbstwehr* carried many articles about the Chinese, and in one issue, even took up the question of the language spoken by Chinese and Japanese Jews (October 12, 1912).

65. "Wer weiss, was ihnen zu tun einfiele" (*E* 157).

vaders' barbaric devouring of a live ox—represents an ironic allusion to the Jewish prohibition against eating "bloody" meat.[66]
"An Old Manuscript" raises and leaves unanswered the question "How long can we endure this burden and torment?"
(*PC* 147),[67] which is the same question asked by Jews throughout history and repeated frequently by characters in the Yiddish plays.

The Laws described in "The Problem of Our Laws" also
seem to have the Torah as their point of reference. Like the
Torah, the Laws in the story are ancient; and like the Talmud,
the commentary which grew up around the Torah, the conflicting interpretations of this Law have themselves acquired legal
status. Freedom of interpretation, although still existent, is now
said to be very restricted. The nobility in whose hands these
Laws rest correspond to the sages of Jewish tradition, who
were also given an elevated position in the community; their
interpretations gain the force of Law. Few people, says the
narrator, doubt the wisdom of the ancient Laws, though some
(like Gordin's Elishe ben Avuya) actually deny their existence.
The study of the records in "The Problem of Our Laws," like
the study of the Torah, is often described as useless, "perhaps
only a game of the mind,"[68] especially by those who stand outside the community. The self-deprecation evidenced by the
people ("We are more inclined to hate ourselves, because we
have not yet shown ourselves worthy of being entrusted with
the laws" [*GWC* 257])[69] resembles the Orthodox Jews' habit of
accusing themselves, instead of God or their enemies, for their
sufferings (as, for example, in *Bar Kokhba*). With obvious de-
light in irony, the narrator sums up the problem arising from

66. See Rubinstein's "Kafka's 'Jackals and Arabs,' " in which the emphasis on raw meat is interpreted as a parody of Gen. 9:4 and Lev.
17:14. Kafka's emphasis on butchering and bloody meat may also be a
reflection of his vegetarian preference. Butchers are also important in
"A Hunger Artist" and "A Crossbreed."
67. "Wie lange werden wir diese Last und Qual ertragen?" (*E* 157).
68. "Vielleicht nur ein Spiel des Verstandes" (*B* 91).
69. "Eher hassen wir uns selbst, weil wir noch nicht des Gesetzes
gewürdigt werden können" (*B* 91–92).

even the mere possibility of repudiating either the Laws or the nobility: "The only visible, unquestionable Law imposed upon us is the nobility, and should we want to deprive ourselves of this only Law?"[70] This argument may be compared to the playful ambiguity characteristic of Jewish parables, while the cadence of the question echoes the tone and inflection of the Yiddish language.

Like "An Old Manuscript," "The Refusal" describes a remote town far from the frontiers governed by orders issued in the distant capitol, which, like the Temple in Jerusalem, has been twice destroyed. The humility of the citizens of this town corresponds to the humility of the Jewish people in the face of their foreign rulers. The highest officer in the village, the tax collector who holds himself aloof from the people and who almost ritually denies their requests, resembles the Roman officer in *Elishe ben Avuya* who imposes heavy taxes on the Jews. The sight of armed, official soldiers who speak a language not understood by the people creates fear and terror in the village. The revolutionary ideas of discontent that the narrator observes in local youths between the years of seventeen and twenty is reminiscent of the promulgation of new ideas and the subsequent rejection of Orthodoxy rampant among the older youths in the yeshivas of Russia and Poland, described by Levi and recorded by Kafka (*Di* 218; *T* 237).

The relationship between the chief officer of the town and the people (whose request is always refused) ties "The Refusal" to Kafka's most complex novel, *The Castle* (January–September 1922). This novel not only emphasizes the distance between the people and the authorities, but adds a complicating factor; for K., the hero of the novel—unlike the narrator of "The Refusal," who is of the people—belongs neither to the Castle nor to the village. K's position of outsider resembles that of Elishe ben Avuya, who becomes estranged from the community of Jews as well as from his friends among the Romans. The uncertainty surrounding K.'s relationship to the Castle re-

70. "Das einzige, sichtbare, zweifellose Gesetz, das uns auferlegt ist, ist der Adel und um dieses einzige Gesetz sollten wir uns selbst bringen wollen?" (*B* 92).

calls the extreme unreliability attributed to the Roman authorities. Elishe's struggle to create a personally meaningful relationship with God is paralleled by K.'s futile efforts to establish contact with Klamm and the Castle, both of whom clearly symbolize some kind of Absolute.[71] In K.'s attack one can also see a similarity to Bar Kokhba's attempts against the Romans. "Impudent" is a word often applied to K., and it is the word used to describe Bar Kokhba's actions as well.[72]

In Hebrew, the word meaning "Messiah," *Moshiakh*, and the word meaning "land surveyor," *Moshoakh*, are almost identical, and the one could easily be used as a pun on the other. If, as parallels indicate, K. is (like Josef K.) in some degree modelled on Bar Kokhba, who was crowned as Messiah by his people, could not Kafka's choice of occupation for his hero be a play on Bar Kokhba's sense of mission? Erich Heller relates K.'s profession as land surveyor (*Landvermesser*) to the German *vermessen*, "audacious," *Vermessenheit*, "hubris," and *sich vermessen*, "to commit an act of spiritual pride" or "to take a wrong measure"—attributes which describe Bar Kokhba as well as K.[73] The implications of such allusions would be ironic, for although Bar Kokhba was guilty of pride, his battle was undertaken on behalf of an entire people, whereas K.'s struggle clearly concerns only himself; in addition, he is perfectly willing to use others to accomplish his ends.

Overall, *The Castle* is considerably less "dramatic" than *The Trial:* its scope is broader, its action is less confined, its charac-

71. Politzer writes: "Kafka has found in K.'s antagonist, the Castle, the perfect image to conceal his own uncertainties about man's ultimate destiny" (*Parable and Paradox*, pp. 280–81). In "The World of Franz Kafka" Erich Heller writes: "The castle represents neither divine guidance nor Heaven. It is for K. something that is to be conquered, something that bars his way into a purer realm" (*Kafka: A Collection of Critical Essays*, ed. Ronald Gray [Englewood Cliffs, N.J., 1962], p. 118). Homer Swander, "*The Castle:* K.'s Village," concludes that the Castle represents "that unimaginable territory of the spirit which signifies some strange metaphysical—not social—integration" (*Franz Kafka Today*, p. 192).

72. In the last scene of *The Castle*, the Herrenhof landlady applies the words "impudent" and "audacious" (*keck, Keckheit*) to K. six times.

73. Heller, "The World of Franz Kafka," in *Kafka*, ed. Gray, p. 111.

ters are more numerous. Even so, individual sections of the novel still display the exaggeration and melodrama associated with the Yiddish theater—for example, the opening sequence at the inn, the confrontation scene in the schoolroom, and K.'s interview with Hans. In addition, many minor elements in *The Castle* can be traced to the Yiddish plays. The story of Amalia's attempted seduction by Sortini, which brings ruin to her family, corresponds to a theme of *Bar Kokhba* (previously discussed in connection with *The Trial*), in which Papuz, a rich Gentile merchant, attempts to buy the heroine's affection with jewels. Dina's furious rejection of what she considers an indecent offer, symbolized by her throwing the jewels into the merchant's face, is a major factor responsible for the eventual defeat of the Jewish people in the play.[74] The same spirit of disgust, evoked by similar circumstances, informs Amalia's tearing up of Sortini's "indecent" letter and throwing the pieces into the face of the waiting messemger.[75] The ostracism of her family which follows Amalia's rejection of the Castle also parallels the predicament of Elishe ben Avuya, who was ostracized by his people (the equivalent of the village folk) when he rejected the authority of Jewish Law. Elishe's renown as a scholar makes his rejection a greater threat to the community; similarly, Olga (Amalia's sister) speculates that her family's punishment was so severe because of the father's prominence in the community. In both works money and provisions are secretly supplied to the "outcasts." Furthermore, Amalia's stance of silent suffering resembles Elishe's stoic acceptance of deprivation.

In some details K.'s mistress, Frieda, resembles the young girl Beata in *Elishe ben Avuya,* who becomes devoted to Elishe because of all men, only he shows kindness to her. When Elishe's house is destroyed by a mob of angry Jews, it is she who makes his room comfortable for him, a deed which parallels Frieda's "fixing" the maids' bare chamber for K. at the Bridge Inn. And like Frieda, Beata ultimately leaves her man. But in

74. Papuz takes his revenge by plotting against the Jews.
75. Tearing up a letter to show contempt for its contents was a device often employed in the Yiddish plays.

sharp contrast to K., who willingly uses sex with Frieda as a means to gain his ends (Klamm), Elishe rejects Beata's offer of friendship because he realizes that it would involve a sexual attraction which he does not care to mask and to which, as a married man, he is unwilling to succumb. "I hate masked means," he remarks.[76] K.'s willingness to use just such "masked means" could even be a deliberate, ironic reversal of Elishe's heroism on this point.

Amalia's brother, Barnabas, the messenger from the Castle, resembles a character in *Elishe ben Avuya*, Shimon Hanzir, a fanatic whose entire existence is governed by the idea of repentance, a motive that describes Barnabas with equal accuracy. The white costume Shimon wears, which he calls his "dress of repentance," not only resembles Barnabas' white outfit, but describes its function as well. Barnabas introduces himself, "Barnabas is my name. . . . A messenger am I."[77] Like Barnabas, Shimon announces himself as a messenger: "I have come to you in the name of our Father in heaven... He alone has sent me."[78] While Elishe's response is ironic—"Quite a long mission... I fear I may have to send you back to Him..."[79]—K. responds with obsessive seriousness, manifest in his sending long letters, to which he expects serious and speedy replies, to the Castle through Barnabas.

Kafka's representation of the ledgers and files in which Castle records are kept relates to Elishe's ironic image of what he describes as a false perception of the Absolute, according to which, God is a shopkeeper who sits in his store and writes man's debts in his ledgers.[80] Possibly, this limited, naïve per-

---

76. "Ikh hob faynt vermaskirte mitln!" (*EbA* 30).
The names Beata ("giving happiness") and Frieda ("peace") are symbolic and serve similar functions in their respective works.
77. "Barnabas heisse ich. . . . Ein Bote bin ich" (*S* 34).
78. "Ikh bin gekumen tsu dir in'm numen fun unzer fater in himl... Er aleyn hot mikh geshikt" (*EbA* 11).
79. "Zeyr a vayter shlikhot... Ikh hob moyre ikh vel dikh darfn shikn tsurik tsu im..." (*EbA* 11).
80. "Iz Got a khanuni, a kremer velkher zitst bay zikh in kleytl, shraybt in panks unzere khovot un tsolt mitn groshn zayne liblinge..." (*EbA* 12).

ception of God is the root of Kafka's ironic portrait of the Castle authorities, who almost certainly also symbolize some form of the Absolute. The mysterious figure of Klamm, an official of the Castle, seems to be a play on Elishe's statement made in response to the charge that he is deifying the poet Homer: "Better to make a god of a man, than to make a man of a god."[81] Whatever the Castle is intended to symbolize, on one level at least, it and all of its representatives seem to be the fruit of just such an irreverent "making human of the Absolute" against which Elishe warns.[82] Another of Elishe's ideas which seems to be reflected ironically in *The Castle* is his belief that so long as man searches for salvation "up above" he will never find it on earth.[83] By his single-minded efforts to reach the Castle, K. misses the opportunities offered to him in the village or beyond.

In yet other scattered details *The Castle* reflects the Yiddish plays. The assistants, described as dark-skinned young men, seem duplicates of Tsingitang, the wild, dark youth who serves the hero of *Shulamit*. Like the assistants, Tsingitang's intelligence appears limited (attributable to his being a "native"), but like them, he is good-natured, childlike, and always ready to serve his master. Tsingitang and the assistants weep easily, dance, jump about, gesticulate with exaggeration, and laugh at their master's lovemaking, which they openly envy. It has been suggested that the assistants derive from a pair of characters who appear in Latayner's play *The Apostate*, described by Kafka in detail in the *Diaries* (D1 79–81; T 79–82).[84] The text of *The Apostate* appears to be lost, but even if the suggestion is correct, as is likely, this connection in no way precludes the possibility of other models for the two assistants. As we have

81. "Beser a mentsh vergetern, eyder a got vermentshlikhn" (*EbA* 15).

82. A similar humanizing of the divine informs Kafka's irreverent portrait of the god Poseidon (*B* 100).

83. "Der mentsh zukht zayn glik. . . . Zolang er vet es zukhn dort in di himlen, vet er es nit gefinen do oyf der erdl" (*EbA* 6–7).

84. See Hildegard Platzer Collins, "Kafka's 'Double-Figure' as a Literary Device," and Brod's notes to the *Diaries* (D1 328; T 698).

seen, Kafka frequently fused elements from several works of the Yiddish theater to create a single image of his own.

An important boast made by K. during his interview with the child Hans—"Many a case that the doctors had given up he had been able to cure" (*C* 190)[85]—corresponds to a ruse employed by Avsholom in the play *Shulamit*. Avsholom poses as a doctor in order to be allowed to see his ailing fiancée, whom no one has been able to cure. Similarly, K. tries to persuade Hans to let him visit his mother, who is also suffering from a seemingly incurable disease. Whereas Avsholom succeeds in "curing" Shulamit (since he has made her ill, only he has the power to cure), K. is never given the opportunity to try.

The festival in *The Castle*—described by Amalia's sister Olga as one of the few occasions when village and Castle come together (and at which, it is predicted, Amalia will find a husband)—resembles the final scene in *Shulamit,* in which the high priests and the ordinary folk gather at the Temple to celebrate the festival of the harvest and the marriage of Avsholom and Shulamit.[86] The central symbol of Kafka's festival, the fire engine (*Feuerspritze*) which squirts or sprays water (interpreted as a phallic symbol by Politzer), parallels the central position of the *kiur* (ritual washstand in a synagogue or temple), which in *Shulamit* is described as "spraying [water] like a fountain."[87] Possibly the visual representation of this symbolic water spray was a model for the *Feuerspritze*. The music of the priests and the blowing of the shofar during the ceremony at the temple fill the same function as the loud trumpet blasts governing the festivities described in *The Castle*.[88] The elevated position of the Castle upon the hill corresponds to the

85. "Was Ärzten nicht gelungen sei, sei ihm geglückt" (S 172).

86. A similar festival with music and dancing, also culminating in a marriage, occurs earlier in the play.

87. "In der mit, sphritst der kiur, vi a fontan" (Su 103).

88. The herbs used in the temple ceremony bring to mind K.'s calling himself "the bitter herb" (*das bittere Kraut*). Here Kafka may also be playing on the German idiom "Muss ist ein bitter Kraut" (compulsion is unpleasant or painful).

physical as well as the symbolic situation of Jerusalem, the
Holy City, site of the Holy Temple; and K.'s journey resembles
the journey of the pilgrims who appear in *Shulamit*, stick in
hand, sack upon the back, preparing to climb the road which
leads up to Jerusalem.[89]

The search for and the struggle against the "powers" which
informs *The Castle* is also central to the themes of the Yiddish
theater. Shulamit and Avsholom bow to God's will, but Bar
Kokhba and Elishe, among other characters portrayed in the
plays, take up the challenge, and like K., fail. The dubious
peace which (according to Brod) was to be awarded to K. at
the end of his life, when the Castle was to grant him permission to remain in the village,[90] can hardly be called a victory.
Like Jehovah, the powers of the Castle remain essentially inscrutable.

While K. is often assumed to represent Everyman or the
wandering Jew, Kakfa's "A Hunger Artist" is most often taken
to be a symbol or allegory of the suffering artist in society.[91] In
a long article which challenges this interpretation, Meno
Spann suggests that "A Hunger Artist" must be understood in
biographical terms as an "intimate revelation of Kafka's *Le-
bensgefühl* [spiritual sense]" of frustration and *Körpergefühl*
(physical sense) of a suffering vegetarian.[92] According to
Spann, the granting of the hunger artist's lifelong dream—that
there be no restriction placed on the duration of his fast—ironically brings to the artist the realization that his life was built

89. Jerusalem is significant in *Bar Kokhba* and *Shulamit*. The towers
of Jerusalem, as portrayed on the Yiddish stage, may have reinforced
the image of the Castle. It has also been suggested that Kafka had the
Prague Hradschin Castle in mind when he created the image of the
Castle.

90. See Max Brod, ed., "Nachwort zur ersten Ausgabe," in S 415.
The epilogues to the first, second, and third editions are not included
in the English text of *The Castle*.

91. See, for example, Politzer, *Parable and Paradox*, pp. 302–8; and
especially William C. Rubinstein, "Franz Kafka: A Hunger Artist,"
Monatshefte 44 (1952): 13–19.

92. Meno Spann, "Franz Kafka's Leopard," *GR* 34 (1959): 85–104.
Spann includes a bibliography for this story to 1959.

on "illusion and error," and that his fame rested on what was only "a weakness, an essential lack." From this perspective, the hunger artist is no martyr, but a "sick freak"; the leopard not crass, but simply a healthy being. Spann's argument is quite convincing, although, as Politzer has demonstrated in *Parable and Paradox,* one reading by no means excludes others. Especially if the hunger artist is viewed as a symbol for the author's feelings, there is every reason to suppose that this creature, like Kafka himself, represents a suffering artist as well as an unfortunate being, ill-adjusted to ordinary life.

Kafka's choice of fasting as a central symbol relates "A Hunger Artist" to "A Report to an Academy" in which the performing ape—like the hunger artist, a caged being who performs for the public—confesses that he thinks with his belly. In "Franz Kafka's Leopard," Meno Spann documents the extensive food imagery in Kafka's work and concludes that for Kafka, physical deprivation or hunger represents spiritual hunger and is associated with the "unknown nourishment" (*unbekannte Nahrung*) so many of Kafka's characters seek. Thus, when Kafka tells us that the ape "thinks with his belly," he is ironically suggesting that the ape suffers no spiritual anguish. As it happens, food holds a dominant position in the Jewish household, even among assimilated Jews like Kafka's family, and serves as an important symbol of group cohesion. Jewish holidays are associated with special foods, and many Jewish idioms are based on food images. This emphasis on food must have been strongly impressed upon Kafka both in his home and through the Yiddish plays, which reflected Jewish culture.[93] It may well

93. According to Orthodox Law, Jews may not eat unclean foods (e.g., pork, shrimp, lobster) and may not take milk and meat together; meat must be slaughtered according to the Laws of *Shekhite.* Jews celebrate communally through the sharing of food, while the holiest day of all, Yom Kippur, is a day of fasting. The Jewish mother is renowned for pushing food on her children, while visitors insult a Jewish hostess if they do not stuff themselves with the abundant food she offers.

The Yiddish plays include many examples of Jewish idioms based on food. For example, a character describes his situation, "Ikh bin oyf gehakte tsures" ("I am in chopped trouble"). The idiom is a play on favorite Jewish foods like chopped herring and chopped liver. Another

be that the loss of appetite associated with Kafka's characters (Georg, Gregor, the hunger artist, the dog) represents a deliberate turning away, close to revulsion, from this Jewish emphasis on food. While the hunger artist's ability or need to fast is symbolic of his isolation from the community of men, one can also see in his "art" a grotesque distortion of the fasting associated with Yom Kippur, which, ironically, is intended to have the opposite effect of bringing Jews together before God.

Spann analyzes the structure of "A Hunger Artist" in terms which suggest a dramatic structure. He observes that the passing of narrated time slows considerably the closer the story approaches its denouement, the hunger artist's surprise confession that he is not to be admired, for he could not help fasting: "Because I could not find the food [nourishment] I liked. If I had found it, believe me, I would have ... eaten my fill like you and all the others."[94] In its use of stage whispers and surprise revelations, this scene creates the effects of melodrama. Spann views the epilogue of "A Hunger Artist" (in which a virile leopard replaces the sickly hunger artist) as a necessary contrast to the hunger artist's "unauthentic existence," but one must agree instead with Politzer, who rejects this epilogue because it simplifies the situation and removes the paradox inherent in the hunger artist's dilemma.[95]

While the stories that follow "A Hunger Artist" (Spring 1922) are animal fables, the themes of these late stories are

describes the chaos in his home: "Ir zolt zen vos far a mishkenine bay unz in shtub iz, azoy vi ir zet kashe mit borsht mit lokshn in aynem" ("You should know the mess we're in here, as you see, groats and soup and noodles in one [pot]"). A husband refers to his wife, who is behaving peculiarly, as "treyfe brihe mayn" ("my unclean food"). Familiar insults are "farfresn" and "ungeshtopt"; both refer to overeating.

In the "Letter to His Father" (*DF* 147–48; *H* 172), Kafka describes the fuss his father made at the dinner table and recounts the father's eating habits, which were obviously repugnant to Kafka.

94. "Weil ich nicht die Speise finden konnte, die mir schmeckt. Hätte ich sie gefunden, glaube mir, ich hätte ... mich vollgegessen wie du und alle" (*E* 267).

95. Politzer, *Parable and Paradox*, p. 308. A similar attempt to clarify an essentially ambiguous situation mars "The Metamorphosis."

nevertheless related to those of the earlier work. Politzer accurately observes that "Investigations of a Dog" (Summer 1922) "unites the themes of nourishment (material and spiritual), individual versus community, and art, the latter represented by the mysterious 'soaring dogs' or *Lufthunde*.... [which] are linguistically patterned after the Yiddish expression *Luftmensch*."[96] Kafka's awareness of the great tradition of Jewish learning, brought home to him vividly in the fabric of the Yiddish plays, informs this story. The entire thrust of the dog's inquiries resembles the argumentation associated with Talmudic dispute, a leitmotif in *The Slaughtering*. It has been suggested that the satiric portrait of the dog-narrator in "Investigations of a Dog" constitutes an ironic portrait of Kafka as he saw himself in his late thirties.[97] Yet, in spite of these connections, the symbolism of "Investigations of a Dog" remains obscure. One must once again agree with Politzer when he concludes that the story "never crystallize[s] into one cogent image and ... dissolves in imperfection."[98]

Music, as a symbol of the Absolute, plays a central role in the dog's experiences (as also in the life of Gregor and Josefine the Singer). The significance given to music in "Investigations of a Dog" and "Josefine the Singer, or the Mouse Folk" reminds us that music was an essential component of the Yiddish plays. Kafka himself was moved by the power of this music (*Di* 80–81; *T* 81–82), although he considered himself generally unmusical. A critic present at a New York performance of *Bar Kokhba* in 1885 describes the impact that the music of the Yiddish plays could have, even on the outsider unfamiliar with this musical idiom: "But underlying the whole narration, and vivifying even the dullest portions is the music—a melodious monody

96. Ibid., p. 319. *Luftmensch* does not refer to a swindler or braggart, as Politzer suggests, but to an impractical person, often an artist, scholar, or dreamer.

97. Binder, "Kafkas Hebräischstudien," p. 531. Binder identifies the seven dancing dogs with the artists of the Yiddish theater troupe, and suggests that "musicology" (*Musikwissenschaft*) refers to Kafka's Hebrew studies.

98. Politzer, *Parable and Paradox*, p. 319.

which swells sometimes into a chorus of tearful and tender lamentation. It is quaint, eloquent, and touching, full of heart and feeling, but never angry. So idealized is it, in fact, that it lifts up both play and players, and creates an illusion stronger than would be possible by the most deft arrangement of ordinary dramatic materials."[99] Not only the music which accompanied the performances, but also the theme of music as symbol of the Divine or Absolute within the plays can be related to Kafka's work. In Gordin's *God, Man, and Devil* Hershele plays the violin only on the Sabbath or other holy days. Hershele's niece, who greatly admires this playing would, it is said, gladly give up food, drink, and sleep if only Hershele would play. She confesses that the music of the violin, which she describes as "something that comes from another world," transforms the house and makes it brighter (*GMT* 19–20). In *David's Violin* the music of the violin is identified with healing powers which restore harmony and which prove, as the subtitle of the play indicates, "the magic power of music"; in *The Savage One* Lemekh is soothed by music, as is Esterke in *The Slaughtering*. This "holy music" which "comes from another sphere" and takes the place of "earthly sustenance" has direct relevance to Kafka's work. In the Yiddish plays, as in Kafka's narratives, music which can replace earthly food is associated with the bright light of the Absolute.

In "Josephine the Singer, or the Mouse Folk," Carl R. Woodring views Josefine, on one level, as a portrait of Mrs. Tshisik, the Yiddish actress Kafka loved and admired, and on another, as a symbol of the "universal artist," possibly Kafka himself.[100] In "Kafka's Views of Institutions and Traditions," Hildegard Platzer Collins rejects not only Woodring's interpretation, but Tauber's more purely religious reading as well. She suggests instead that the basic theme of the story is the relationship of Josefine to the community. According to her view, Josefine represents "the whole body of cultural beliefs and traditions ... [while] the community itself is not simply the Jews, but man-

99. *New York Sun*, February 22, 1885. Quoted by Zohn, "A Survey of the Yiddish Theater," p. 32.
100. *Franz Kafka Today*, ed. Flores and Swander, pp. 71–76.

kind as it is related to the forces of the universe."[101] More recently, Hartmut Binder has identified Josefine with a Palestinian girl Kafka befriended in his last years, who, like Josefine, mysteriously disappeared.[102] In this connection, B. B. Kurzweil argues effectively that the root situation from which Kafka's themes stem is the dilemma of "Jewish existence without faith": "What is said about the hunter Gracchus, about Odradek, about Josefine, and the 'Crossbred,' can serve as the classical model of Jewish existence outside of the sphere of belief."[103]

Whatever the symbolic significance of Josefine, it is difficult to overlook the similarities between Josefine's community and the Jewish people. Like the Jews, Josefine's people live in dispersion, always on the run, and yet remain close to laughter in spite of the terrors they know await them. And like the Jews, Josefine's community is said to be childlike, although they have no proper time of youth and only the briefest childhood.[104] Josefine's music, "only a piping" with power to unite people by evoking strong emotion, brings to mind the traditional melodies of Jewish song and prayer, which became familiar to Kafka chiefly through his experience of the Yiddish theater and through concerts of Jewish folk songs. Kafka described the effect created by Mrs. Klug, one of the singers at the Savoy, "who, on the stage, because she is a Jew, draws us listeners to her because we are Jews ... made my cheeks tremble" (*D1* 80).[105]

But Mrs. Klug's singing is not the only possible model for Josefine's song. The performances of the Jewish actor Yitskhok Levi and the Jewish folksinger Leo Gollanin bear striking re-

101. *GQ* 35 (1962): 493.

102. Binder writes: "In his conception of the girlish, delicate singer ... Kafka must have had the small, childlike Puah Bentorim in mind; she was the only one in Prague who mastered Hebrew completely" ("Kafkas Hebräischstudien," p. 552).

103. Kurzweil, "Jüdische Existenz ohne Glauben," p. 428.

104. Kafka once remarked to Janouch: "But we Jews are born old" (*CwK* 33; J 24).

105. "Die auf dem Podium, weil sie Jüdin ist, uns Zuhörer, weil wir Juden sind, an sich zieht ... ging mir ein Zittern über die Wangen" (*T* 81).

semblance to the concert described in "Josefine"—particularly
in the effect upon the audience—and we know that Kafka attended recitals given by both men (*Di* 223–24, 232–33; *T* 243,
249–50). Like Josefine's song, the art of these entertainers was
not of the first rank and was clearly intended to evoke strong
emotional response—that is, to unite the people and to
strengthen their sense of community. It is interesting to compare the reviews of Levi's and Gollanin's performances with
the assertions made by the narrator in Kafka's story. Levi's reviewer writes: "What was lacking in artistry was gained by a
degree of historical, documentary value. . . . The audience, at
first a little strangely moved by the unaccustomed language
[Yiddish], nonetheless got into the right mood, reached the desired understanding, and received the performance . . . with
rich applause."[106] Gollanin's reviewer emphasizes the purpose
of the concert (to give Prague Jews insight into the psychology
of Eastern European Jews) and expresses the hope "that
among our allegedly completely assimilated Western Jews, kindred chords would stir, . . . [that] there would also grow a permanent strengthening and revival of our own inner Judaism."[107]
In a close parallel, Kafka's narrator asserts of Josefine's concert: "It is not so much a performance of songs as an assembly
of the people. . . . yet something . . . irresistibly makes its way
into us from Josefine's piping. This piping . . . comes almost like
a message from the whole people to each individual" (*PC*
265).[108] Levi's lack of artistry, compensated for by his authen-
ticity, is analogous to Josefine's piping, which, we are told, is
nothing out of the ordinary, is perhaps not even singing at all.
It must have been obvious to Kafka, as it clearly was to the
reviewers from *Selbstwehr*, that these Eastern European Jews

106. "Ostjüdischer Rezitationsabend," *Selbstwehr*, February 23, 1912,
p. 3.
107. "Der jüdische Volksliederabend," *Selbstwehr*, January 26, 1912,
pp. 4–5. It is extremely likely that Kafka read both of these reviews.
The reviews in full are included in Appendix 4.
108. "Es ist nicht so sehr eine Gesangsvorführung als vielmehr eine
Volksversammlung. . . . dringt doch . . . etwas von ihrem Pfeifen unwei-
gerlich auch zu uns. Dieses Pfeifen . . . kommt fast wie eine Botschaft des
Volkes zu dem Einzelnen" (*E* 277–78).

were not welcomed to Prague so much for their talent as for
what they symbolized. It is extremely likely that in creating
the portrait of Josefine, Kafka was drawing on his memory of
these somewhat inartistic performers who brought fragments
of an authentic Jewish tradition to the assimilated Jews of
Prague.

Though closely related to the themes of the Yiddish plays,
Kafka's last stories are more expository than dramatic.[109] Both
"Josefine the Singer" and "Investigations of a Dog" are monologues in which the history of an individual is recounted. Josefine's story is told through the eyes of a narrator who is one of
the "many"; the dog speaks for himself. Although this kind of
introspection would seem to be completely nondramatic, both
stories contain sections in which the techniques of the drama
are visibly and effectively adapted—as, for example, the description of Josefine's singing and her tantrums on stage, the
encounter of the dog with the seven dancing dogs, and especially the dog's tense confrontation with the hunter-dog.

Apart from its representation of a people who closely resemble the Jewish community attending the Yiddish theater at the
Savoy, "Josefine" also relates to the Yiddish plays by the nature
of its title, "Josefine the Singer, or the Mouse Folk." In a note
to Max Brod, written when Kafka was no longer able to speak,
Kafka wrote of this story: "The story is going to have a new
title, 'Josephine the Songstress—or the Mice-Nation.' Sub-titles
like this are not very pretty, it is true, but in this case it has
perhaps a special meaning. It has a kind of balance" (FK 205–
6; Bg 251). This kind of double title was almost certainly familiar to Kafka from the Yiddish plays, which were often billed
in this form; he himself cites Blimele, or the Pearl of Warsaw
(D1 198; T 213). Others include Bar Kokhba, or the Last Days
of Jerusalem; Shulamit, or Daughter of Jerusalem; David's Violin, or the Magic Power of Music; The Vice-King, or A Night
in the Garden of Eden; Mr. Harry the Aristocrat, or Yekele the
Wagoner; Kol Nidre, or the Secret Jews of Spain. The function

109. Woodring observes that in "Josefine," "action comes late and no
scene ever develops" ("Josephine the Singer," in Franz Kafka Today,
ed. Flores and Swander, p. 75).

of this titling in the theater was clearly didactic; while the first part carried the name of the hero or heroine, the subtitle revealed the essence of the play. In giving to "Josefine the Singer" the subtitle "The Mouse Folk," Kafka seems to be (most uncharacteristically, although possibly ironically) underlining the fact that the true focus of the story is not the individual, but the community. It is difficult to say why Kafka chose to use this device at this time. Possibly the experience of the Yiddish theater preceding his literary breakthrough in 1912 was recalled to him forcefully, and with a degree of nostalgia, in what he must have sensed were to be the last months of his life.[110]

Finally, though they fall in the middle years of Kafka's writing (chiefly 1917/18), Kafka's parables are best discussed by themselves, apart from his narrative fiction. Kafka's portraits of Prometheus, Poseidon, Abraham, Sancho Panza, and Ulysses differ from his other works in that they use familiar figures of legend instead of stripped ciphers such as Josef K. or K. Parables are one of the earliest forms of Jewish expression, and although Kafka's parables must be considered as part of this Biblical and Hasidic tradition, they do not seem to be related to the plays of the Yiddish theater, either in theme or form. One exception is the parable "On Parables," which centers on the meaning of the words of the sage, "Go over" (*GWC* 258; *B* 95) and recalls the advice given to Elishe ben Avuya, "Turn back" (*EbA* 26). This advice is intended to recall Elishe to his people and his God, but is met with irony: "One cannot turn back

110. In the Argentine-Jewish newspaper *Di Yidishe Tsaytung* (August 24, 1966, p. 5), Dorfson reports that when, in the summer of 1922, a Yiddish troupe came to Prague from Vienna, Kafka attended their performances daily, and often went backstage to talk to the actors and to ask about his old friend, the actor Yitskhok Levi. Although this report is extremely suggestive, it sharply contradicts the facts: in the summer of 1922 Kafka was not living in Prague, but in Planá, in southeastern Bohemia, where he was recuperating at his sister Ottla's home. Brod writes that Kafka "used to come to Prague, at this time, only temporarily and for short periods" (*FK* 185; *Bg* 226). Possibly Dorfson is mistaken in the year, or is confusing Kafka with Brod.

without bringing oneself along."[111] Elishe here asserts the fact that the Jews do not want him back *as he is*, and establishes that he, on his part, is unwilling to change. This wordplay also brings to mind Kafka's aphorism "Beyond a certain point there is no return. This point has to be reached" (*DF* 35).[112] Elishe ben Avuya had clearly reached such a point of no return. Another of Kafka's aphorisms, "A cage went in search of a bird" (*DF* 36),[113] may be seen as an ironic inversion of Elishe's parable of the bird, the cage, and the king.

If we consider Kafka's writing from his earliest efforts in 1904 to his last story, "Josefine the Singer," twenty years later, it becomes clear that 1912 was the crucial year in Kafka's literary development. From 1904 to August 1912, Kafka's writing was diffuse, slow-moving, overly detailed, and generally unsuccessful. In 1912, following a two-year period of intense involvement with the Yiddish theater, Kafka produced his first successful story: "The Judgment" is dramatic in style and shows the impact of the Yiddish theater on Kafka's narrative prose most directly. The narratives that follow "The Judgment"—"The Metamorphosis," "In the Penal Colony," and sections of *The Trial* (1912–14)—are histrionic in style and continue to show the influence of the Yiddish plays in theme, character, and structure. From 1916 to 1920 we find echoes of the Yiddish theater in the fabric of Kafka's work (in, for example, "A Country Doctor," "A Fratricide," "A Report to an Academy," "The Problem of Our Laws"), although the relationship in technique is less immediate and Kafka shows a greater tendency to fabulize and to elaborate the details of the Yiddish plays. In *The Castle* (January–September 1922) we find many isolated details and a few thematic parallels, but in general, the influence of the Yiddish theater is somewhat diminished and less central to the

111. "Men ken zikh nit umkern un zikh aleyn nit bringn mit zikh" (*EbA* 27).

112. "Von einem gewissen Punkt an gibt es keine Rückkehr mehr. Dieser Punkt ist zu erreichen" (*H* 39).

113. "Ein Käfig ging einen Vogel suchen" (*H* 41).

work. Kafka's last stories, "A Hunger Artist" (Spring 1922), "Investigations of a Dog" (Summer 1922), and "Josefine the Singer" (March 1924), are more personal than the earlier works, and not surprisingly, less dramatic. Even so, these stories are closely related to the symbols and aggregate themes of Jewish tradition, to which Kafka was exposed most often and with the greatest intensity during the years of his involvement with the actors and the plays of the Yiddish theater in Prague.

It is impossible to guess how Kafka's writing might have developed had he not become familiar with the Yiddish theater, and it is equally difficult to know what other factors helped to produce Kafka's literary breakthrough in 1912. Nonetheless, beginning with "The Judgment," the thematic and stylistic parallels between Kafka's work and the Yiddish plays are fairly insistent. Kafka's abiding concern with the themes of Justice, Authority, and Law, and his exploration of the relationship between the individual and the Absolute and between the individual and the community may be seen as abstract formulations of the specifically Jewish problems raised by the Yiddish plays. The central symbols of Kafka's work—the Court, the Castle, the "machine"—the "cleanliness" his characters crave, the knowledge they seek, and the "hunger" they cannot sate may be seen as extensions or adaptations of cultural symbols used in the Yiddish plays. In addition, the dramatic structure of individual scenes within the larger works, the staged qualities of the actions described, the emphasis on gesture, tableau, timing, lighting, exaggeration, and surprise effects typical of melodrama link Kafka's methods to the Yiddish plays.

The enclosed quality of the world created by Kafka's narratives and the apparent necessity and immediacy of even the most bizarre events recall the self-contained nature of the performed play. In some cases, entire scenes from the Yiddish plays correspond to parts of Kafka's work, in the rhetoric as well as in the actions portrayed. On the evidence, one must conclude that by reinforcing his personal concerns, the plays of the Yiddish theater exercised a lasting influence on Kafka's style and helped to give shape to the problems that tormented Kafka the man.

Reference
matter

appendix one
Table of equivalent spellings

Kafka's spelling   *YIVO transliteration*

THE PLAYS

Bar-Kochba	Bar Kokhba
Blümale oder die Perle von Warschau	Blimele oder di Perle fun Varshe
Davids Geige	Davids Gayge [Fidele]
Elieser ben Schevia	Elishe ben Avuya
Gott, Mensch, Teufel	Got, Mentsh, un Tayvel
Herzele Mejiches	Hertsele Miyukhes
Der Meschumed	Der Meshumed
Die Sejdernacht	Di Seydernakht
Schhite	Di Shekhite
Der Schneider als Gemeinderat	[Moyshe Khayit] als Gemaynderat
Sulamith	Shulamit
Der Wilde Mensch	Der Vilder Mentsh
Vicekönig	Der Vitse-Kenig

THE AUTHORS

Feimann	Faynman
Lateiner	Latayner
Richter	Rikhter
Scharkansky	Sharkanski

THE ACTORS

Jizchak Löwy	Yitskhok Levi
Tschissik	Tshisik

THE CHARACTERS

Schmul Leiblich	Shmul Layblikh
Selde	Zelde
Lemech	Lemekh
Lise	Liza
Wladimir Worobeitschik	Vladimir Vorobaytshik

appendix two

Plays and operettas
seen or read by Kafka

The following list is based on Kafka's letters and diaries; unless otherwise indicated, dates refer to when Kafka mentions the plays, rather than to dates of performances. Yiddish plays, including recitations, are indicated by a dagger (†).

	1908
	Vizeadmiral, Karl Millöker
	1910
May [4]	† First brief encounter with Yiddish theater (Spiewakow Troupe); mentioned by Kafka in 1911
Nov 15	*Iphigenie auf Tauris* (Iphigenia in Tauris), Goethe
Dec 4	*Anatol,* Arthur Schnitzler; mentioned again on February 14/15, 1913
Dec 16	*Die Jungfern vom Bischofsberg* (The Maids of Bischofsberg), Gerhart Hauptmann
	1911
Jan 4	*Glaube und Heimat* (Faith and Country), Karl Schönherr
Jan 17	*Abschied von der Jugend* (Farewell to Youth), Max Brod
Feb	*Des Meeres und der Liebe Wellen* (The Waves of the Sea and of Love), Franz Grillparzer
Feb	*Miss Dudelsack* (Miss Bagpipes), Fritz Grünbaum and Heinz Reichert
Sept	*Phaedra,* Racine
Oct 5	† *Der Meshumed* (The Apostate), Yosef Latayner
Oct 10	† *Di Seydernakht* (The First Evening of Passover), Zigmund Faynman
Oct 14	† *Shulamit* (a girl's name), Avraham Goldfaden; mentioned again on January 24, 1912

Oct 20	*Dubrovnicka Trilogjia* (Trilogy from Dubrovnik), Graf Ivo Vojnović
Oct 22	† *Kol Nidre* (the opening prayer of the Yom Kippur service), Avraham Sharkanski
Oct 24	† *Der Vilder Mentsh* (The Savage One), Yakov Gordin
Oct 26	† *Got, Mentsh, un Tayvel* (God, Man, and Devil), Yakov Gordin
Oct 28	† *Elishe ben Avuya* (Elishe, son of Avuya), Yakov Gordin
Oct 30	*Konkurrenz* (Rivalry), Oskar Baum
Nov 5	† *Bar Kokhba* (Son of the Star), Avraham Goldfaden
Nov 19	*Das Weite Land* (The Distant Land), Arthur Schnitzler
Nov 24	† *Di Shekhite* (The Slaughtering), Yakov Gordin
Dec 13	*Der Biberpelz* (The Beaver Coat), Gerhart Hauptmann
Dec 13	† *Moyshe Khayit als Gemaynderat* (Moyshe the Tailor as Councillor), Moyshe Rikhter
Dec 18	*Hippodamie*, Jaroslav Vrchlicky
Dec 19	† *Davids Fidele* (David's Violin), Yosef Latayner
	1912
Jan 3	*Gabriel Schillings Flucht* (Gabriel Schilling's Flight), Gerhart Hauptmann
Jan 6	† *Der Vitse-Kenig* (The Vice-King), Zigmund Faynman
Jan 24	† *Reb Hertsele Miyukhes* (Mr. Harry the Aristocrat), Moyshe Rikhter
Jan 24	*Der Graf von Gleichen* (The Count Gleichen), Wilhelm Schmidtbonn
Jan 26	† Yiddish folksongs, Leo Gollanin
Feb 4	*Erdgeist* (Earth-Spirit), Frank Wedekind
Feb 4	*Orpheus in the Underworld*, Jacques Offenbach
Feb 25	† Recital of Yiddish poetry and prose, Yitskhok Levi
Mar 3	Recital by [Alexander] Moissi
Mar 6	*Die Journalisten* (The Journalists), Gustav Freytag
Mar 16	Cabaret Lucerna
Mar 17	*Mam'zelle Nitouche*, Henri Meilhac and A. Millaud
Mar 24	*Die Sternenbraut* (The Star Bride), Christian von Ehrenfels
May 6	*Die Ratten* (The Rats), Gerhart Hauptmann

May 22   *Madame la mort,* Rachilde
May 22   *Dream of a Spring Morning,* Gabriele D'Annunzio
              1913
Jan 16   *Jedermann* (Everyman), Hugo von Hofmannsthal
Feb 14/15   *Hidalla,* Frank Wedekind
Feb 14/15   *Zwischenspiel* (Intermezzo), *Der Ruf des Lebens*
              (The Call of Life), *Der junge Medardus* (Young
              Medardus), *Der Reigen* (Hands Around, or La
              Ronde), *Professor Bernhardi,* all by Arthur Schnitz-
              ler[1]
May 2   † An unidentified Yiddish performer, the "gigantic Me-
              nasse"
June   † Recital by Levi
              1914
Jan 8   *Tête d'or* (The Golden Head), Paul Claudel
June 30   *Narciss,* Carry Brachvogel
Dec 2   *Esther, Kaiserin von Persien* (Esther, Queen of
              Persia), Franz Werfel
Dec 2   *Kabale und Liebe* (Intrigue and Love), Friedrich
              Schiller
              1915
Nov 3   *Er und seine Schwester* (He and His Sister), Bern-
              hard Buchbinder
              1916
May 24/25   *Die Troerinnen des Euripedes* (adaptation of Euri-
              pides' *Trojan Women*), Franz Werfel
Sept 29   *Minna von Barnhelm,* Gotthold Ephraim Lessing
Oct 28   *Ritualmord in Ungarn* (Ritual Murder in Hungary),
              Arnold Zweig
              1917
Oct   *Ziehtochter* (Jenufa), Janáček
n.d.   *Eine Königin Esther* (A Queen Esther), Max Brod
              1919
n.d.   *Das Wunder* (The Miracle), Oskar Baum
              1921
June   *Literatur, oder Man wird doch da sehn* (Literature,
              or Well, We'll See), Karl Kraus
Oct 30   *The Miser,* Molière
Nov 1   *Bocksgesang* (Goat-Song), Franz Werfel

1. Kafka disliked Schnitzler's works intensely. See *Fe* 299.

	1922	
Mar 1		*Richard III,* Shakespeare
Dec		*Schweiger,* Franz Werfel
	1923	
Oct		*Die letzten Tage der Menschheit* (Last Days of Mankind), Karl Kraus
Oct 31		*Klarissas halbes Herz* (Clarissa's Half Heart), Max Brod

The following plays are mentioned in Janouch's *Conversations with Kafka.* This memoir includes the years 1920–23.

Der Gott der Rache (God of Vengeance), Sholom Asch; a Yiddish play performed in German

Der Sohn (The Son), Walter Hasenclever

The Playboy of the Western World, John Synge

Der Fälscher (The Forger), Max Brod

Tanja, Ernst Weiss; also mentioned in *Letters to Milena*

Hamlet, Shakespeare

Saul, Gustav Janouch

Der Spiegelmensch (Mirror-Man), Franz Werfel; also mentioned in *Letters to Milena*

appendix three
Djak Levi

Short biography of Levi[1]

Levi was born in Warsaw on September 10, 1887, to poor Hasidic parents. As a child, he was extraordinarily attracted to the theater, in spite of the fact that the professional stage was considered "unclean" by his extremely Orthodox parents. Nevertheless, custom, even among Orthodox Jews, permitted plays and skits as part of the traditional Purim festivities, and Levi took part in these with great enthusiasm. As a young man, he attended the Yiddish theater in Warsaw without his parents' knowledge or consent.[2]

Levi left Warsaw in 1904 for Paris, where he took a job in a factory. In 1905 he made his debut in an amateur production of Chekov's *The Bear* and in 1906 began his acting career on the professional Yiddish stage. At the age of twenty, in 1907, he joined a travelling theater troupe and played in Basel, Zurich, and Vienna. In 1911, with a similar troupe, Levi came to Prague, and it was there that he came to know Kafka. In addition to performing in the Yiddish plays in Prague, Levi presented a program of solo

1. This biography is based on information provided by Zilbertsvayg, *Leksikon fun Yidishn Teater*, 2:1139–40, 5:4135–58; and Yonas Turkov, *Farloshene Shtern* (Buenos Aires, 1953), 1:92–99. In addition, Kafka's letters, diaries, and other writings, and Brod's biography were used. In one instance, Kafka's statements seem to be inaccurate: compare *D*1 109 (*T* 114) with the opening sentence of this appendix.

Further information about Levi may be found in Yonas Turkov, "Frants Kafka un Djak Levi," *Di Goldene Keyt* (1967), pp. 147–54; and Jiřina Hlaváčová, "Franz Kafkas Beziehungen zu Jicchak Löwy," *Judaica Bohemiae* 1 (1965): 75–78. A photograph of Levi as Lemekh in *Der Vilder Mentsh* can be found in Klaus Wagenbach, *Franz Kafka, 1883– 1924: Manuskripte, Erstdrücke, Dokumente, Photographien* (Berlin, 1966), p. 58 (hereafter cited as *Manuskripte*); a facsimile of the play-bill for *Der Vilder Mentsh* can be found in idem, *Biographie*, p. 178.

2. See *DF* 129–34; *H* 154–59.

recitations (at Kafka's suggestion);[3] this mode of entertainment later became his specialty. Sometime in 1912 he left Prague for Berlin and Leipzig, though he returned to Prague on several occasions to give guest recitations.[4]

In Berlin, Levi became dissatisfied with his troupe and left it in order to form his own company. The enterprise ended badly, however; Levi became ill and lost much of his money. The outbreak of World War I found him in Budapest, where he remained until 1919.[5] According to Levi's friend, Yonas Turkov, Levi was extremely well-received in Hungary: he was lauded by the press and compared to great actors such as Alexander Moissi. In 1920 Levi returned to Warsaw and for a time performed there. In 1921 he toured the Polish provinces and in 1924 founded a Hebrew theater in Warsaw. A year later he formed a travelling company with Yonas Turkov and toured again. Gradually, however, Levi gave up acting in troupes and devoted himself solely to recitations and writing for newspapers.[6]

When World War II began, Levi was in Warsaw and found himself without work and with no real means of support. Although an "honorary" position with the Jewish Police was offered to him, Levi found the idea distasteful and declined the offer; from then on he lived a hand-to-mouth existence in the Warsaw Ghetto. During this period, whenever artistic entertainments were arranged in the ghetto, Levi once again gave his famous "word-concerts." Sometime in 1942, when the "transfer of population" began, Levi was arrested by the Nazis and sent to Treblinka, where he was killed.

3. Kafka gave the opening address for Levi's first recitation.

4. Zilbertsvayg seems to be confused on Levi's movements during these years. He lists 1909 as the year Levi played in Prague and 1911 as the year he returned to Warsaw. Yet the evidence of Kafka's and Brod's diaries and of the playbills, announcements, advertisements, and reviews for the theater plays and for Levi's recitations conclusively show that Levi was in Prague in 1911, 1912, and again in 1913.

5. It was here that Kafka met Levi again, in July 1917.

6. He had a weekly column in the Polish-Jewish paper *Undzer Ekspres*. Judging from the few articles of his still in existence, Levi does not seem to have been an especially talented writer. The translation that follows in the second section of this appendix captures the inelegant, repetitious, sentimental nature of Levi's prose style.

An article by Levi on Brod and Kafka[7]

The world of culture has now celebrated the fiftieth birthday of the German-Jewish writer Max Brod. Not long ago it was ten years since the strange writer Franz Kafka died. Both from Prague, both my friends. Both played a significant role in my life. With both I remained in contact for years, particularly with the deceased Franz Kafka. And now Brod is fifty years old, and it is ten years since Kafka's death. I would like to tell about them both, first about the writer Max Brod. And then about the prematurely departed Franz Kafka...

It was about twenty-three or twenty-four years ago. With a Yiddish theater troupe I was engaged to play in Prague. The "temple of culture" was hidden in a faraway corner of old Prague. We performed in a restaurant with set tables. The stage was in a corner. We, the actors, had a [place] underground and on the right side. And the audience we had on two sides: opposite us and to the left of the stage. The curtain fell in front, and at the same time, on the left. We played only "classics": Latayner, Hurwits, and company...

We also played Goldfaden. And we also smuggled in Yakov Gordin. We needed no decorations. Furniture on the stage: a table, several chairs and that's all. In this way we played theater in Maharal's Prague for the Bohemian Jews.[8] We also had an orchestra, which consisted of... one pianist. Our troupe called itself: "Polish-Yiddish-musical-drama-company."

The "theater" was full every evening. The people ran to see us as if to an amazing sight; they came to see the "Eastern-Jewish artists."

One day there appeared a review in the *Prager Tagblatt* by Dr. Max Brod. He writes about Goldfaden and Gordin. Of the actors, he mentions only me. This is the first review about me, a young man, and such a splendid review, by the then already famous

7. "Tsvey Prager Dikhter" [Two Prague writers], *Literarishe Bleter* 34 (1934): 557–58.

8. *Maharal* is an acronym for the words *Moraynu Harav Lev* [Löw], which means "our teacher, the Rabbi Lev." Sixteenth-century legend ascribes to Rabbi Yehuda Lev the creation of a *golem,* a clay figure that comes to life. From the viewpoint of the Jewish community, the Maharal was the single most important man of his time, and the phrase "Maharal's Prague" was similar to speaking of "De Gaulle's France."

writer Max Brod. My Bohemian director is pleased, shakes my hand: a review by Max Brod means a great deal. They tell me I must go and present myself to Max Brod. I become red with shame.

That same evening after the performance, the director runs to me behind the wings excitedly: I should hurry, Max Brod is waiting for me, he wants to meet me. I took off my makeup and with Max Brod went to a simple restaurant. There I also met Franz Kafka, Hugo Bergmann, Franz Werfel, Otto Pick, and the blind writer Oskar [Baum][9] and others.

Max Brod was at that time twenty-six years old. A small man with somewhat high shoulders, a long, charming face with intelligent eyes. Moses Mendelsohn must have had such a face when he was a young man. From the first meeting it became clear that one had to do with a person of stature. Already at that time Max Brod played a significant role in Prague. One reckoned with him, and all the young poets and writers—such as Werfel, Kafka, Hugo Bergmann, Weltsch, Otto Pick, Oskar [Baum], among others—were under his influence. Brod was the one who set the tone, although almost all the aforementioned writers were of the same age. Of Jewishness, the entire Pleiad of Prague writers—with the exception of Weltsch and Bergmann—knew almost nothing. Our Yiddish theater was exotic for them, tidings from a foreign world...

I used to meet often with Max Brod,[10] and indulge in long conversations with him about Gemara, Zohar,[11] Kabala, and Hasidism, up to the modern Yiddish and Hebrew literature.

9. Levi writes "Oskar Koym," but this is either a misprint or an error of Levi's memory. There is no trace of any Oskar Koym, but the blind writer Oskar Baum was part of the Prague group.

10. Although Kafka was Levi's close friend, Levi's memoir favors Brod, sometimes to the extent of confusing the two. In part, the passage of time (twenty-three years) explains the discrepancy, in part, the fact that in the early thirties it was Brod who was by far the more famous of the two in Polish-Jewish cultural circles. A comparison of Kafka's diaries and letters with Brod's autobiography, *Streitbares Leben* (Munich, 1960), and his memoirs for that period, *Der Prager Kreis* (Stuttgart, 1966), makes it almost certain that it was Kafka, not Brod, with whom Levi discussed these theological questions.

11. "Gemara" is another name for the Talmud, the central text of traditional Jewish study, and refers particularly to the part that comments on the Mishna. The Zohar is the holiest mystical book of the Kabala.

Max Brod was the first to encourage me to appear in public with excerpts, songs, and scenes from Yiddish literature. Max Brod opened the "evening," to which the elite of Prague came.[12] I recited Bialik, Frishman, Peretz, Rosenfeld, Reisin, Sholom Aleichem. When Max Brod gave me the honorarium for my recitation, I became bright red and didn't want to take the money. But Max Brod pushed the money into my pocket, saying that he too accepted money for a lecture.

I then remained in Prague the entire winter. Max Brod did not miss a single one of our theater performances. We frequently met at his place, or at someone else's for literary conversations and readings. He was already then famous as a masterful storyteller and essayist, and at the same time as a lyric poet and dramatist. At twenty-six he had already succeeded in writing three works: *Death to the Dead, Jewesses,* and *Arnold Beer.* The essence of his artistic creation at that time was love of life. Brod was full of the joy of life, and extraordinarily creative. He used to complain to me that he did not have enough time to write. At that time he worked in the post office. Even so, he wrote a great deal. From time to time he read to the previously mentioned poets from his manuscripts, chapters, and fragments from his new works. Afterwards there would follow interesting exchanges of opinion.

The exotic and religious qualities of Eastern Jewry[13] excited and attracted the Prague writers. I remember my agitation when, in one of his conversations with me, Max Brod spoke of the beauty of the fur hat and silken, long coat, truly Rembrandt-like. I answered him heatedly, "The fanatic Eastern Jewry can impress you modern, cultivated Jews, but we are happy that we pulled ourselves out and freed ourselves from that world." Max Brod only smiled good-naturedly.

For years I was in contact with Max Brod; we wrote to one another.[14] He was very interested in me, wanted to know what I was

12. Here we can say with certainty that Levi means Kafka. We know that Kafka introduced Levi at the only recital evening of which a record remains. See Kafka's diaries for February 13 and 25, 1912 (*D1* 232–35; *T* 249–52), his "Talk on the Yiddish Language" (*DF* 381–86; *H* 421–25), and Hlaváčová, "Franz Kafkas Beziehungen zu Jicchak Löwy."

13. Eastern European Jewry.

14. Levi probably is again confusing Brod with Kafka. There is no evidence to suggest that Brod and Levi corresponded or that they became close friends. We do know that Levi and Kafka corresponded for many

doing, and in what circumstances I was living. With time Max Brod grew in stature. It is enough to recall his works: *Paganism, Christianity, Jewry; Socialism in Zionism; The Redemption of Tycho Brahe;* and especially his *Reubeni, Prince of the Jews.*

Now there is a new Max Brod. He is proficient in Kabala, writes about the world of action and the world of creation and original sin, Lilith and the ten degrees...[15] From where so much erudition? From where so much Jewish knowledge? Whoever knows Max Brod's early work sees that during the war years a great crisis occurred...

Now Max Brod has turned fifty. It is hardly believable. Just recently he was so young!

---

years, although only one of Kafka's letters to Levi has been preserved. See *Br* 129–30.

15. The ten degrees are part of the Kabala. Their names are Inscrutable Height, Wisdom, Intellect, Grace, Power, Beauty, Firmness, Splendor, Foundation, and Authority.

appendix four

Reviews and announcements
of Yiddish performances
in Prague, 1910–1912

The following reviews and announcements are taken
from the Jewish weekly *Selbstwehr*. They constitute the
only surviving contemporary accounts of the Yiddish performances
that Kafka saw and recorded in his diaries. Paid advertisements for
these performances were rare, as the Yiddish actors were con-
tinually short of funds. Full citations for these articles are given in
the bibliography.

A Yiddish theater troupe in Prague

The Yiddish theater troupe which played in Vienna during last
year's and this year's winter season offered a dozen evenings at
the Café Restaurant Savoy. ... The company had to make do with
the most modest, most circumscribed stage sets: a small podium,
behind it, a green curtain—that was the whole stage. Naturally, the
plays had to be tailored to the [cramped] space conditions, the
actor's freedom of motion (here one can really say:) became illusory. For this reason, the whole effect could only stem almost
entirely from the spoken word. And in this respect the players really
excelled. ... (May 13, 1910)

A guest performance by the Yiddish theater

A visiting Yiddish theater troupe whose performance yesterday
was greeted with great enthusiasm by a rather large audience is
currently playing at the Hotel Zentral.[1] During the first part of the
performance, which took almost four hours, Mr. Treisin sang Jewish

1. Either the Café Savoy was located in the Hotel Zentral or the
troupe opened at the Zentral and later moved to the Savoy.

folksongs, whose melancholy-ironical characteristics are already familiar to us. Then Mrs. Klug, the male impersonator, a vivacious lady, appeared. Although her art tended towards a not-too-tasteful cabaret, she visibly amused the audience.[2] The second part [of the program] consisted of a four-act Yiddish play, *Kol Nidre,* which takes place in Spain at the time of the Inquisition and concerns the subject of the Marranos. The actors, with the exception of those who portrayed the comic servants, didn't show too much skill, and their efforts to speak High German were not especially favorable to the tragic effect of the play. Nonetheless, they were often greeted with much spontaneous applause in the middle of the performance, especially after the execution of "Kol Nidre," which wasn't badly sung. (H[ans] K[ohn], September 29, 1911)

Yiddish theater

For several weeks a Yiddish theater troupe from Lemberg [Lvov] has been presenting both familiar and unfamiliar works of Yiddish literature at the Café Savoy. During the last few years the reputation of the Yiddish theater, particularly in America and England, has made the whole world aware of the remarkable development of this dramatic curiosity. A great deal of well-deserved interest in the art of the Jewish players has been shown also in Prague; a frequently changing program which will surely prove worthwhile has been arranged for the next few days. (December 22, 1911)

Yiddish theater[3]

A Yiddish theater troupe which just completed a four-month visit in Prague and is now playing in Pilsen would like to give a few guest performances in the Bohemian provinces. As the troupe possesses considerable talents and presents most interesting plays, the arrangement of one or two theater evenings (for which a special

2. A photograph of Mrs. Klug as male impersonator appears in Wagenbach, *Manuskripte,* p. 58.

3. It is quite likely that this advertisement was written by Kafka. On January 24, 1912, Kafka noted in his diary: "Finally I spent a lot of time with the Jewish actors, wrote letters for them, prevailed on the Zionist society to inquire of the Zionist societies of Bohemia whether they would like to have guest appearances of the troupe; I wrote the circular that was required and had it reproduced" (*Di* 223; *T* 242–43).

stage is not necessary) is most warmly urged upon the Jewish societies in those cities which have a larger Jewish population. A guest
performance offers a truly valuable portrait of Eastern Jewish[4] life
in extremely entertaining form. In order not to protract negotiations,
the editors of *Selbstwehr* are prepared to take over the arrangements. (January 26, 1912)

An evening of Yiddish folksongs[5]

. . . The purpose of the folksong evening was to allow our Prague
Jewry to gain an enjoyable insight into the popular psychology of
the Eastern Jews; and to this purpose was joined the hope that
among our allegedly completely assimilated Western Jews, kindred
chords would stir, [that] their own Jewish feeling, usually buried by
the impressions of their environment, would respond to a sympathetic element, and that from the Eastern Jewish poetry, there
would also grow a permanent strengthening and revival of our
own inner Judaism. That this hope was fulfilled was admitted by
everyone who heard the gathering of Prague Jews exult as the songs
of Gollanin rang through the room; only he who finds himself again,
who recognizes in the voice from the outer world the ripening of his
own heart, rejoices in this way. . . . The Eastern Jews are not, as is
commonly held, people who always whine, who, oppressed and resigned, perceive their Jewishness as a terrible headache.[6] (January
26, 1912)

An eastern Jewish evening

Eastern Jewish literature has recently won many friends in
Prague. For this reason people will welcome the news that Mr.
J. Levi from Warsaw, the character actor now visiting Prague, will
present a recitation of Eastern Jewish poetry on Sunday, the eighteenth of this month, at 8 P.M. in the Jewish Town Hall. From his

4. In the articles quoted in this appendix, this phrase is used to refer
to Eastern European Jews.
5. Leo Gollanin's folksong evening took place on January 18, 1912,
at the Hotel Zentral. Kafka discusses it briefly in the *Diaries* on January
24 and 26, 1912 (*Di* 223–24; *T* 243).
6. The reviewer here uses the colorful expression "Katzenjammer,"
which literally means "the whining of cats" and is the German word
for a hangover; the reviewer's tone is somewhat contemptuous.

full and richly varied program we mention only the poetry of Rosenfeld, Frischman, Reisin, Nomberg, Dranow, Bialik, Frug, Sholom Aleichem, and Hasidic songs. An introductory lecture will precede the recitations.[7] The evening merits special attention because it promises us an excellent insight into the characteristics of this original literature which is so close to us. The appearance of Mr. Levi guarantees us a sympathetic interpretation. . . . (February 16, 1912)

An eastern Jewish recitation evening

On Sunday, the eighteenth of this month [February 1912], the announced recitation evening of the Warsaw actor Mr. J. Loewy [sic] took place in the banquet hall of the Jewish Town Hall. After a lovely, charming speech given by Dr. Kafka, Mr. Loewy opened his program with several recitations and presented, in gay profusion, serious and comic recitations, dramatic scenes, and songs. It was extremely interesting to hear these Eastern Jewish poems and songs (some of which were already known in Prague), not only from an Eastern Jew, but also [from one who was] without Western schooling. What was lacking in artistry was gained by a degree of historical, documentary value. Mr. Schneller explained the texts in a fine, discreet manner in a speech with which he untiringly opened every part of the program. The audience, at first a little strangely moved by the unaccustomed language [Yiddish], nonetheless got into 'the right mood, reached the desired understanding, and received the performance of Mr. Loewy with rich applause. The evening certainly added a great deal to our closer understanding of the Eastern Jewish spirit, and Mr. Loewy, who showed himself to be a powerful and effective performer, can be satisfied with the impression he produced. (February 23, 1912)

7. This was given by Kafka.

Bibliography

Primary sources

Kafka's works, both in the original German and in standard English translation, are now available from a number of publishers. To aid the reader in finding the passages quoted from Kafka, I have provided the name of the publisher, the series in which the work appears, and the date of publication for the volume I used; wherever possible these are paperback editions.

ENGLISH TRANSLATIONS OF KAFKA'S WORKS

Kafka, Franz. *Amerika*. Translated by Willa and Edwin Muir. New York: New Directions, 1946.

———. *The Castle*. Translated by Willa and Edwin Muir; additional translation by Eithne Wilkins and Ernst Kaiser. Definitive edition. New York: Random House, Modern Library, 1958.

———. *Dearest Father: Stories and Other Writings*. Translated by Ernst Kaiser and Eithne Wilkins. New York: Schocken Books, 1954.

———. *Description of a Struggle*. Translated by Tania and James Stern. New York: Schocken Books, 1958.

———. *The Diaries of Franz Kafka: 1910–1913*. Edited by Max Brod; translated by Joseph Kresh. New York: Schocken Paperback, 1948.

———. *The Diaries of Franz Kafka: 1914–1923*. Edited by Max Brod; translated by Martin Greenberg and Hannah Arendt. New York: Schocken Paperback, 1949.

———. *The Great Wall of China: Stories and Reflections*. Translated by Willa and Edwin Muir. New York: Schocken Books, 1946.

———. *Letters to Milena*. Edited by Willy Haas; translated by Tania and James Stern. New York: Schocken Paperback, 1953.

———. *The Penal Colony: Stories and Short Pieces*. Translated by Willa and Edwin Muir. New York: Schocken Paperback, 1948.

————. *The Trial*. Translated by Willa and Edwin Muir; revision and additional translation by E. M. Butler. Definitive edition. New York: Random House, Modern Library, 1956.

ORIGINAL GERMAN TEXTS OF KAFKA'S WORKS

Kafka, Franz. *Gesammelte Schriften*. Edited by Max Brod. New York: Schocken Books.
Vol. 2, *Amerika: Roman*, 3rd ed. 1946.
Vol. 4, *Das Schloss: Roman*. 3rd ed. 1946.
Vol. 5, *Beschreibung eines Kampfes: Novellen, Skizzen, Aphorismen aus dem Nachlass*. 2nd ed. 1946.
————. *Gesammelte Werke*. Edited by Max Brod. New York: Schocken Books. [Unless otherwise noted.]
Briefe: 1902–1924. 1958.
Briefe an Felice und andere Korrespondenz aus der Verlobungszeit. Edited by Erich Heller and Jürgen Born. Frankfurt am Main: S. Fischer Verlag, 1967.
Briefe an Milena. Edited by Willy Haas. 1952.
Erzählungen. 3rd ed. 1946.
Hochzeitsvorbereitungen auf dem Lande und andere Prosa aus dem Nachlass. 1953.
Der Prozess: Roman. 5th ed. 1946.
Tagebücher: 1910–1923. 1949.

PLAYS OF THE YIDDISH THEATER

Faynman, Asher Zelig [Feinmann, Zigmund]. *Der Vitse-Kenig, oder a Nakht in Gan Eydn*. Lvov, 1909.
Goldfaden, Avraham [Abraham]. "Bar Kokhba, oder di letste Teg fun Yerushalayim." In *Oysgeklibene Shriftn*, pp. 105–201. Buenos Aires, 1963.
————. "Shulamit, oder Bat Yerushalayim." In *Oysgeklibene Shriftn*, pp. 33–104. Buenos Aires, 1963.
Gordin, Jakov [Jacob]. *Elishe ben Avuya*. New York, 1907.
————. *Got, Mentsh, un Tayvel*. New York, 1903.
————. *Di Shekhite*. New York, 1899.
————. *Der Vilder Mentsh*. Warsaw, 1907.
Latayner, Yosef [Lateiner, Joseph]. *Blimele, oder Di Perle fun Varshe*. Cracow, 1903.
————. *Davids Fidele, oder Di Tsauberkraft fun Muzik*. Cracow, 1910.

Rikhter, Moyshe [Richter, Moses]. *Moyshe Khayit als Gemaynderat.* Lvov, 1907.
——. *Reb Hertsele Miyukhes, oder Yekele Bal Agola.* Lvov, 1907.
Sharkanski, Avraham Mikhel [Scharkansky, Abraham Michael]. *Kol Nidre, oder Di Geheyme Yudn in Shpanien.* Warsaw, 1907.

Kafka bibliographies

Ackermann, Paul Kurt. "A History of Critical Writing on Franz Kafka." *German Quarterly* 23 (March 1950): 104–13.
Beebe, Maurice, and Christensen, Naomi. "Criticism of Franz Kafka: A Selected Checklist." *Modern Fiction Studies* 8 (1962): 80–100.
Benson, Ann T[hornton]. "Franz Kafka: An American Bibliography." *Bulletin of Bibliography* 22 (1958): 112–14.
Flores, Angel. "Biography and Criticism: A Bibliography." In *Franz Kafka Today,* edited by Angel Flores and Homer Swander, pp. 259–85. Madison, Wis., 1964.
——. *Franz Kafka: A Chronology and Bibliography.* Houlton, Me., 1944.
Hemmerle, Rudolph. *Franz Kafka: Eine Bibliographie.* Munich, 1958.
Järv, Harry. *Die Kafka-Literatur: Eine Bibliographie.* Malmö and Lund, Sweden, 1961.
Jonas, Klaus. "Franz Kafka: An American Bibliography." *Bulletin of Bibliography* 20 (September–December 1952): 212–16.
——. "Franz Kafka: An American Bibliography." *Bulletin of Bibliography* 20 (January–April 1953): 231–33.

Secondary works

Ausubel, Nathan. *A Treasury of Jewish Folklore.* New York, 1948.
Beissner, Friedrich. *Der Erzähler Franz Kafka.* 2nd ed. Stuttgart, 1958.
Benjamin, Walter. *Illuminations.* Translated by Harry Zohn. New York, 1968.
Binder, Hartmut. "Franz Kafka und die Wochenschrift *Selbstwehr.*" *Deutsche Vierteljahrsschrift für Literaturwissenschaft und Geistesgeschichte* 41 (1967): 283–304. (Also published, in a shorter form, as "Franz Kafka and the Weekly Paper *Selbstwehr.*" *Publications of the Leo Baeck Institute: Yearbook* 12 [1967]: 134–48.)

———. "Kafkas Hebräischstudien: Ein biographisch-interpretatorischer Versuch." *Jahrbuch der deutschen Schillergesellschaft* (November 1967): 527–56.

———. *Motiv und Gestaltung bei Franz Kafka.* Bonn, 1966.

Blech-Merwin, Thekla. "Jüdisches Theater." *Der Merker* (1915), pp. 401–3.

Booth, Wayne. *The Rhetoric of Fiction.* Chicago, 1961.

Born, Jürgen. "Vom 'Urteil' zum *Prozess:* Zu Kafkas Leben und Schaffen in den Jahren 1912–1914." *Zeitschrift für deutsche Philologie* 86 (1967): 186–96.

Born, Jürgen, et al. *Kafka Symposion.* Berlin, 1965.

Bowman, Walter Parker, and Ball, Robert Hamilton. *Theater Language: A Dictionary of Terms in English of the Drama and Stage from Medieval to Modern Times.* New York, 1961.

Brod, Max. *Franz Kafka: Eine Biographie.* 3rd enl. ed. Berlin, 1954. (In English as *Franz Kafka: A Biography.* Translated by G. Humphreys Roberts and Richard Winston. 2nd enl. ed. New York, 1960.)

———. *Franz Kafkas Glauben und Lehre.* Munich, 1948.

———. "The Jewishness of Franz Kafka." *Jewish Frontier* 13 (1964): 27–29.

———. Letter to the author. May 10, 1967.

———. *Der Prager Kreis.* Stuttgart, 1966.

———. *Streitbares Leben.* Munich, 1960.

———. *Verzweiflung und Erlösung im Werk Franz Kafkas.* Frankfurt am Main, 1959.

Brooks, Cleanth, and Warren, Robert Penn. *Understanding Fiction.* 2nd ed. New York, 1959.

Carrouges, Michel. *Kafka versus Kafka.* Translated by Emmett Parker. University, Ala., 1968.

Clark, Barrett H., and Freedley, George, eds. *A History of Modern Drama.* New York, 1947.

Collignon, Jean. "Kafka's Humor." *Yale French Studies,* no. 16 (1955/56), pp. 53–62.

Collins, Hildegard Platzer. "Kafka's 'Double-Figure' as a Literary Device." *Monatshefte* 55 (1963): 7–12.

———. "Kafka's Views of Institutions and Traditions." *German Quarterly* 35 (November 1962): 492–503.

Dentan, Michel. *Humor et création littéraire dans l'oeuvre de Kafka.* Geneva and Paris, 1961.

Dorfson [or Horendorf], S. "Korespondents." *Di Yidishe Tsaytung* (Buenos Aires), August 21 and 24, 1966.

Edel, Edmund. "Franz Kafka: 'Das Urteil.'" *Wirkendes Wort* 9 (1959): 216–25.

Eisner, Pavel. *Franz Kafka and Prague.* Translated by Lowry Nelson and René Wellek. New York, 1950.

Emrich, Wilhelm. *Franz Kafka: A Critical Study of his Writings.* Translated by Sheema Zeben Buehne. New York, 1968.

Engerth, Ruediger, et al. *"Ein Flug um die Lampe herum:* Ein unbekanntes Werk von Kafka?" *Literatur und Kritik* 1, no. 6 (1966): 48–55.

Falke, Rita. "Biographisch-Literarische Hintergründe von Kafkas 'Urteil.'" *Germanisch-romanische Monatsschrift* 10 (1960): 164–80.

F[elheim], M[arvin]. "The Judgment." In *Study Aids for Teachers for Modern Stories,* edited by M. Felheim, F. B. Newman, and W. R. Steinhoff, pp. 36–39. New York, 1951.

Fergusson, Francis, ed. *Aristotle's Poetics.* New York, 1961.

Flores, Angel, ed. *The Kafka Problem.* New York, 1946.

Flores, Angel, and Swander, Homer, eds. *Franz Kafka Today.* Madison, Wis., 1964.

Goido, Isaak [pseud. Gorin, Bernard]. *Geshikhte fun Yidishn Teater biz 1920.* 3rd ed. 2 vols. New York, 1923.

Goldberg, Isaac. *The Drama of Transition.* Cincinnati, 1922.

Goldschmidt, Hermann L. "The Key to Kafka." *Commentary* (August 1949), pp. 129–38.

Goldstein, Bluma. "A Study of the Wound in Stories by Franz Kafka." *Germanic Review* 41 (1966): 202–17.

Gray, Ronald, ed. *Kafka: A Collection of Critical Essays.* Twentieth Century Views. Englewood Cliffs, N. J., 1962.

Greenberg, Martin. "The Literature of Truth: Kafka's 'Judgment.'" *Salmagundi* 1 (Fall 1965): 4–22.

Hapgood, Hutchins. *The Spirit of the Ghetto.* New York, 1965.

Hartnoll, Phyllis, ed. *The Oxford Companion to the Theater.* 3rd ed. London, 1967.

Hasselblatt, Dieter. "Echtheitsgefechte in der Nachhut Kafkas: Ein 'neues' und umstrittenes Schauspiel von... Kafka?" *Frankfurter Allgemeine Zeitung,* September 8, 1966.

Heselhaus, Clemens. "Kafkas Erzählformen." *Deutsche Vierteljahrsschrift für Literaturwissenschaft und Geistesgeschichte* 26 (1952): 353–76.

Hlaváčová Jiřina. "Franz Kafkas Beziehungen zu Jicchak Löwy." *Judaica Bohemiae* 1 (1965): 75–78.

Howe, Irving, and Greenberg, Eliezer, eds. *A Treasury of Yiddish Stories*. New York, 1954.

Jahn, Wolfgang. *Kafkas Roman "Der Verschollene" (Amerika)*. Stuttgart, 1965.

———. "Kafka und die Anfänge des Kinos." *Jahrbuch der deutschen Schillergesellschaft* 6 (1962): 353–68.

Janouch, Gustav. *Gespräche mit Kafka: Erinnerungen und Aufzeichnungen*. Frankfurt am Main, 1951. (Translated as *Conversations with Kafka: Notes and Reminiscences*. Translated by Goronwy Rees. London, 1953.)

The Jews of Czechoslovakia: Historical Studies and Surveys. Philadelphia, 1968.

"Eine jüdisch-deutsche Theatergesellschaft in Prag" [A Yiddish theater troupe in Prague]. *Selbstwehr*, May 13, 1910, p. 4.

"Jüdisches Theater" [Yiddish theater]. *Selbstwehr*, December 22, 1911, p. 7.

"Jüdisches Theater" [Yiddish theater]. *Selbstwehr*, January 26, 1912, p. 6.

"Der jüdische Volksliederabend" [An evening of Yiddish folksongs]. *Selbstwehr*, January 26, 1912, pp. 4–5.

"Kafka and the Yiddish Theater." *Drama Critique* 10 (Winter 1967): 6–12.

Karpeles, Gustav. *Geshikhte der Yidishn Literatur*. 4th ed. Graz, Austria, 1963

Kauf, Robert. "Once Again: Kafka's 'A Report to an Academy.' " *Modern Language Quarterly* 15 (December 1954): 359–65.

Kaufmann, M. "Die Entwicklung des 'Jiddischen' Jargon Theaters." *Der Merker* (1915), pp. 404–6.

"Kein Kafka-Stück: Goldstücker äussert sich zu *Flug um die Lampe*." *Frankfurter Allgemeine Zeitung*, September 23,1966.

Klatzkin, Jacob, et al., eds. *Encyclopaedia Judaica*. 10 vols. Berlin, 1928–32.

K[ohn], H[ans]. "Gastspiel des deutsch-Jüdischen Theaters" [A guest performance by the Yiddish theater]. *Selbstwehr*, September 29, 1911, p. 9.

Kurzweil, Baruch Benedikt. "Franz Kafka: Jüdische Existenz ohne Glauben." *Die Neue Rundschau* (1966), pp. 418–36.

Landman, Isaac, et al., eds. *Universal Jewish Encyclopedia*. 10 vols. New York, 1943.

Levi, Djak. "Tsvey Prager Dikhter." *Literarishe Bleter* 34 (1934): 557–58.

Levi, Margot P. "K.: An Exploration of the Names of Kafka's Central Characters." *Names* 14 (1966): 1–10.

Lifson, David S. *The Yiddish Theater in America.* New York and London, 1965.

Liptzin, Solomon. *The Flowering of Yiddish Literature.* New York and London, 1963.

Madison, Charles. "The Yiddish Theater." *Poet Lore* 32 (Winter 1921): 497–519.

Marson, E. L. "Franz Kafka's 'Das Urteil.' " *AUMLA: Journal of the Australasian Universities Language and Literature Association,* no. 16 (1961), pp. 167–78.

Mestel, Yakov. *Literatur un Teater.* New York, 1962.

——. *Unzer Teater.* New York, 1943.

——. *70 Yor Teater Repetuar: Tsu der Geshikhte fun Yidishn Teater in Amerika.* New York, 1954.

Miller, James Albert. *The Detroit Yiddish Theater.* Detroit, 1967.

Miller, Norbert. "Erlebte und verschleierte Rede: Der Held des Romans und die Erzählform." *Akzente* 5 (1958): 213–26.

Neider, Charles. *The Frozen Sea: A Study of Franz Kafka.* New York, 1948.

Nemeth, André. *Kafka ou le mystère juif.* Translated by Victor Hintz. Paris, 1947.

Niger, Shmul [pseud. Charney, Samuel], et al., eds. *Leksikon fun der Nayer Yidisher Literatur.* 6 vols. New York, 1956–.

"Ostjüdischer Abend" [An eastern Jewish evening]. *Selbstwehr,* February 16, 1912, p. 4.

"Ostjüdischer Rezitationsabend" [An eastern Jewish recitation evening]. *Selbstwehr,* February 23, 1912, p. 3.

Pasley, Malcolm. "Two Literary Sources of Kafka's *Der Prozess.*" *Forum for Modern Language Studies* 3 (April 1967): 142–47.

Pinski [Pinsky], David. *Di Yidishe Drame.* New York, 1909.

Politzer, Heinz. *Franz Kafka: Parable and Paradox.* Rev. ed. Ithaca, N. Y., 1966.

——. "Prague and the Origins of Rainer Maria Rilke, Franz Kafka, and Franz Werfel." *Modern Language Quarterly* 16 (March 1955): 49–62.

Pondrom, Cyrena Norman. "The Coherence in Kafka's 'Das Urteil': Georg's View of the World." *Studies in Short Fiction,* in press.

Rabi, Wladimir. "Kafka et la néo-Kabbale." *La Table Ronde* (1958), pp. 116–28.

Reiss, Hans S. *Franz Kafka: Eine Betrachtung seines Werkes.* Heidelberg, 1952.

———. "Franz Kafka's Conception of Humour." *Modern Language Review* 44 (1949): 534–42.

Review of Avraham Goldfaden's *Bar Kokhba. New York Sun,* February 22, 1885.

Robert, Marthe. "L'Humor de Franz Kafka." *Revue de la Pensée Juive* 6 (1951): 61–72.

Rubinstein, William C. "Franz Kafka: A Hunger Artist." *Monatshefte* 44 (1952): 13–19.

———. "Kafka's 'Jackals and Arabs,'" *Monatshefte* 59 (1967): 13–18.

Ruhleder, Karl H. "Franz Kafka's 'Das Urteil': An Interpretation." *Monatshefte* 55 (1963): 13–22.

Scholes, Robert, and Kellogg, Robert. *The Nature of Narrative.* New York, 1966.

Schultze, Ernst. "Das jiddische Theater." *Die Neue Rundschau* 27 (July 1916): 939–54.

Schulz-Behrend, G. "Kafka's 'Ein Bericht für eine Akademie': An Interpretation." *Monatshefte* 55 (1963): 1–6.

Seifert, M. "Di Geshikhte fun Yidishn Teater in Dray Zayt Periodn." In *Yidishe Bihne.* New York, 1897.

Shatski, Yakov [Schatsky, Jacob]. *Arkhiv far der Geshikhte fun Yidishn Teater un Drame.* Warsaw, 1930.

Shipley, Joseph T., ed. *Encyclopedia of Literature.* New York, 1946.

Shiper [Schipper], Ignats. *Geshikhte fun Yidishn Teater, Kunst, un Drame fun di eltere Tsaytn biz 1750.* 4 vols. Warsaw, 1923–28.

Singer, Isaac Bashevis. "A Friend of Kafka." *The New Yorker,* November 23, 1968, pp. 59–63. (Reprinted in Isaac Bashevis Singer, *A Friend of Kafka and Other Stories* [New York, 1970], pp. 3–16.)

———. Private interview. Madison, Wis., February 7, 1968.

Sokel, Walter H. *Franz Kafka: Tragik und Ironie—Zur Struktur seiner Kunst.* Munich and Vienna, 1964.

———. "Kafka's 'Metamorphosis': Rebellion and Punishment." *Monatshefte* 48 (1956): 203–14.

Spann, Meno. "Franz Kafka's Leopard." *Germanic Review* 34 (1959): 85–104.

———. "The Minor Kafka Problem." *Germanic Review* 32 (1957): 163–77.

Spilka, Mark. *Dickens and Kafka: A Mutual Interpretation.* Bloomington, Ind., 1963.

Standaert, Eric. "Gibs Auf: Ein Kommentar zu dem Methodologischen Ausgangspunkt in Heinz Politzers Kafka-Buch." *Studia Germanica Gandensia* 6 (1964): 249–72.

Steinberg, Erwin R. "The Judgment in Kafka's 'The Judgment.'" *Modern Fiction Studies* 8 (1962): 23–30.

———. "Kafka and the God of Israel." *Judaism* 12 (1963): 142–49.

Strich, Fritz. *Kunst und Leben.* Bern and Munich, 1960.

Styan, J. L. *The Elements of Drama.* Cambridge, Eng., 1963.

Tauber, Herbert. *Franz Kafka: An Interpretation of His Works.* Translated by G. Humphreys Roberts and Roger Senhouse. New Haven, 1948.

Tramer, Hans. "Prague: City of Three Peoples." *Publications of the Leo Baeck Institute: Yearbook* 9 (1964): 305–39.

Turkov, Mark. "Frants Kafkas Prag." *Der Veg* (Mexico City), January 24, 1967.

Turkov, Yonas. *Farloshene Shtern.* 2 vols. Buenos Aires, 1953.

———. "Frants Kafka un Djak Levi." *Di Goldene Keyt* (1967), pp. 147–54.

Uyttersprot, H. *Eine neue Ordnung der Werke Kafkas? Zur Struktur von "Der Prozess" und "Amerika."* Antwerp, 1957.

Wagenbach, Klaus. *Franz Kafka: Eine Biographie seiner Jugend, 1883–1912.* Bern, 1958.

———. *Franz Kafka, 1883–1924: Manuskripte, Erstdrücke, Dokumente, Photographien.* Berlin, 1966.

Waxman, Meyer. *A History of Jewish Literature.* 2nd ed. 5 vols. New York, 1960.

Weichert, Michael. "Zur Entwicklungsgeschichte des Jüddischen Theaters." *Der Jude* 8 (1917): 548–59.

Weinberg, Kurt. *Kafkas Dichtung: Die Travestien des Mythos.* Bern, 1963.

Weinstein, Leo. "Kafka's Ape: Heel or Hero?" *Modern Fiction Studies* 8 (1962): 75–79.

Weltsch, Felix. "Franz Kafkas Humor." *Der Monat* 6 (1954): 520–26.

———. *Religion und Humor im Leben und Werk Franz Kafkas.* Berlin-Grünewald, 1957.

———. "The Rise and Fall of the Jewish-German Symbiosis: The

Case of Franz Kafka." *Publications of the Leo Baeck Institute: Yearbook* 1 (1956): 255–76.

White, John J. " 'Das Urteil': An Interpretation." *Deutsche Vierteljahrsschrift für Literaturwissenschaft und Geistesgeschichte* 38 (1964): 208–29.

Wiener, Leo. *The History of Yiddish Literature in the Nineteenth Century.* New York, 1899.

YIVO [Yidisher Visenshaftlicher Institut] Institute for Jewish Research. "Transcription Key for Yiddish into Latin Letters." New York, n.d. Mimeographed.

Zilbertsvayg [Zylbercweig], Zalmen. "Frants Kafka un dos Yidishe Teater." *Yidishe Kultur* 30 (January 1968): 38–43, 56.

———. *Leksikon fun Yidishn Teater.* Vols. 1–2, Warsaw, 1931–34; vols. 3–4, New York, 1959–63; vol. 5, Mexico [City], 1967.

———. Letter to the author. March 18, 1967.

———. Letter to the author. April 24, 1967.

Zohn, Harry. "The Jewishness of Franz Kafka." *Jewish Heritage* (Summer 1964), pp. 44–50.

Zohn, Hershel. "A Survey of the Yiddish Theater." M.A. thesis, University of Denver, 1949.

Index

Kafka's works are listed individually by their English titles; all other works are to be found under their author's name.

Abraham: Kafka's portrait of, 208

"Absent-minded Window-Gazing," 55*n*, 56

"Aeroplanes at Brescia, The," 49*n*

Aleichem, Sholom, 227

America: as symbol, 127–28

Amerika. See Verschollene, Der

Amkhorets (*am ha'arets*): Josef K. as, 29, 168–69

Anti-Semitism: Kafka's awareness of, xii, 89*n;* as theme in Yiddish theater, 154, 166

Aphorisms (by Kafka), 208–9

Apostasy, from Judaism: reflected in "A Report to an Academy," 181–82, 186; as theme in *Blimele,* 182–83; reported in *Selbstwehr,* 188*n*

Apostate, The. See Latayner, Yosef

Aristotle: definition of dramatic plot, 4; recognition and reversal, 10*n,* 45, 117; his *Poetics,* 40*n;* mentioned, 107

"Bachelor's Ill Luck," 56

Bar Kokhba. See Goldfaden, Avraham

Bauer, Felice: and Kafka's breakthrough, 6; Kafka's engagements to, 6*n;* and Kafka's relationship to Yiddish theater, 17–19; and "The Judgment," 70, 121; mentioned, 15, 47, 121, 146

Baum, Oskar, xi, 221

Beautiful New Akhashverosh Play, A, 20

"Before the Law," 29, 190*n,* 167–68

Beissner, Friedrich: on dramatization of Kafka's works, 106*n*

Benjamin, Walter: on dramatic aspects of Kafka's works, 4, 41*n*

Bentorim, Puah: as model for Josefine, 205

Bergmann, Hugo, xi, 221

Berliner Tageblatt, 18

Bialik, Hayim Nahman (Hebrew poet), 227

Biblical allusions: in *Der Verschollene,* 128–30, 131

Binder, Hartmut: on "Investigations of a Dog," 7; on the number of Yiddish theater troupes in Prague, 14*n;* on "The Hunter Gracchus," 179*n;* on *Selbstwehr,* 190*n;* on "Josefine the Singer," 205

Blimele. See Latayner, Yosef

Booth, Wayne: on the dramatic in prose narrative, 9; on the rhetoric of titles, 32*n*

Brecht, Bertolt: his epic theater, 11*n*

Brod, Elsa (wife of Max Brod), 28*n*

Brod, Max: discusses Kafka's breakthrough, 5; his works, 5, 6, 221*n,* 222, 223; on Kafka's interest in

Yiddish theater, 6, 7, 13; his friendship with Kafka, 16; his omissions from the *Diaries,* 21*n;* describes the Café Savoy, 26; his titling of Kafka's works, 32, 122*n,* 146*n;* connects Levi to "the friend in Russia," 87; his epilogue to *The Castle,* 200*n;* described by Levi, 220–23; mentioned, xi, xii, 49*n,* 126*n*
"Burrow, The," 146*n*

"Cares of a Family Man, The," 189–90
Carrouges, Michel: Kafka's work as dramatic, 4; number of Yiddish theater troupes in Prague, 14*n*
Castle, The: the assistants in, 7, 46*n;* comic irony in, 30; related to the Yiddish plays, 194–200; Hebrew puns in, 195; compared to *The Trial,* 195–96; mentioned, 23, 34*n,* 209
Chekov, Anton: *The Bear,* 218
"Children on a Country Road," 56, 58
Chinese, the: compared to Jews, 192*n*
Choruses: in Yiddish plays, 126–27, 174; in "A Country Doctor," 174
"Clothes," 55*n,* 56, 58
Collins, Hildegard Platzer: relates the assistants to Yiddish theater, 7; on "The Great Wall of China," 191; on "Josefine," 204–5
"Commentary, A": dramatic qualities of, 4–5, 31–48 *passim;* turning point in, 39*n;* exposition in, 40; open ending of, 45
"Country Doctor, A": related to Latayner's *Blimele,* 172–75; the image of the wound in, 173; structure of, 174; dramatic devices in, 174–75; interpretations of, 175; mentioned, 209

"Conversation with the Drunken Man," 55*n*
"Conversation with the Praying Man," 55*n*
Costume: Kafka's use of, 62, 107, 158–59; in *The Vice-King,* 158–59
"Crossbreed, A," 188–89, 193*n,* 205
Czech drama: Kafka's attitude toward, 30

David's Violin. See Latayner, Yosef
"Description of a Struggle," 31–32, 49–55, 56
Diamant, Dora, 6*n*
Diaries: Kafka's interest in Yiddish theater recorded in, 12–17 *passim,* 135–36, 198; omissions from German edition of, 21*n;* Yiddish expressions used in, 43*n;* early prose pieces in, 70*n;* Russia connected with Eastern European Jewry in, 88*n;* Kafka discusses significance of names in, 96; mentioned, 46, 49, 56, 59
Dorfson, S. (or Horendorf): on Kafka's interest in Yiddish theater, 208*n*
Dostoievski, Fyodor: *Crime and Punishment,* 112
Drama: methods of, as compared to those of prose, 10–11, 107–8; immediacy of, 11*n;* notation in, 40
Dramatic: as applied to Kafka, 38*n*
Dramatic elements: in Kafka's work, discussed by other critics, 4–5, 9, 11, 39–41, 117, 142–43; use of, in narrative literature, 9–11
Dramatic structure, 10*n*
Dranow (Yiddish poet), 227

Eastern European Jews: Kafka's interest in, xii; folk humor of, in Yiddish theater, 42; mannerisms of, 43; connected with Russia, 88n, 118n; in Prague, 206–7; strange to Western Jews, 226

Eden, Garden of: as symbol in *God, Man, and Devil*, 125

Elishe ben Avuya. See Gordin, Yakov

Emrich, Wilhelm: on style of "Wedding Preparations in the Country," 37; on "Cares of a Family Man," 189–90

Everyman: and "A Commentary," 42; K. as, 200

"Excursion into the Mountains," 56

Expressionism, 154, 178

Faynman, Zigmund: *The First Evening of Passover*, 12, 24; *The Vice-King*, 24, 71, 100, 106n, 146n, 155–60 *passim*, 174n, 191

Fergusson, Francis: discusses Aristotle's definition of action, 40n

First Evening of Passover, The. See Faynman, Zigmund

"First Long Train Ride, The" (by Max Brod and Franz Kafka), 49n

Flores, Kate: on Kafka's breakthrough, 6

Flug um die Lampe herum, Ein: attributed to Kafka, 7n

Food, as symbol: in Kafka's work, 185, 193n, 201–2; in Jewish culture, 185, 201–2

Fragments (by Kafka): "In our synagogue there lives an animal about the size of a marten," xiin; "When I think about it, I must say that my education has done me great harm in some respects," 70n; " 'You,' I said and

gave him a little shove with my knee," 70n

"Fratricide, A," 4, 41n, 175–78, 209

Frischman, David (Yiddish poet), 227

Frug, S. (Yiddish poet), 227

Gesture: Kafka's use of, 4–5, 8, 27, 41, 43n, 62, 69, 107, 116, 154, 174–76 *passim*, 210; in drama, 10; on the Yiddish stage, 43

"Giant Mole, The," 146n

"Give It Up!" *See* "Commentary, A"

God, Man, and Devil. See Gordin, Yakov

Goethe: *Faust*, 72n

Goldfaden, Avraham, 20–21, 220

—*Bar Kokhba:* kneeling in, 27; related to works by Kafka, 150, 161–66, 192, 193, 195, 196; attitude toward Orthodox Jews in, 181; Jewish people portrayed as childlike in, 190

—*Shulamit:* 12, 13, 14, 21, 22–23, 154, 174n, 198, 199–200, 207

Gollanin, Leo (Yiddish folk singer), 205–6, 226

Gordin, Yakov: *The Jewish King Lear*, 24; *Mirele Efros*, 24; Kafka's view of, 71; as critic of Orthodox Judaism, 191–92; mentioned, xxi, 22, 220

—*Elishe ben Avuya:* tradition vs. enlightenment, as theme in, 147; analogues to "In the Penal Colony," 147–54 *passim;* analogues to *The Trial*, 166–70 *passim;* attitude toward Orthodox Jews in, 181; related to "An Old Manuscript," 192; related to *The Castle*, 194, 196–98; mentioned, 23, 146*n*, 155, 191, 193, 194, 208–9

—*God, Man, and Devil:* related to "The Judgment," 71–74, 74–121 *passim;* productions of, 72*n;* water as symbol in, 90–91; significance of names in, 96–97; prologue to, 126–27; relationship to *Der Verschollene,* 125–27; music in, 204; mentioned, 23, 106*n*, 108*n*, 109*n*, 119, 120, 146*n*, 148, 174*n*, 176*n*

—*The Savage One:* analogues to "The Judgment," 118–20; analogues to *Der Verschollene,* 133–35; analogues to "The Metamorphosis," 135–46; Oedipal conflict in, 139–40; ending of, compared to "The Metamorphosis," 144; related to "A Fratricide," 176–78; music in, 204; mentioned, 21, 23, 71, 88*n*, 113, 136, 146*n*

—*The Slaughtering:* ritual slaughter in, 176–77; related to "A Fratricide," 176–78; related to "Investigations of a Dog," 203; music in, 204; mentioned, 23, 88*n*, 146*n*, 147

"Great Wall of China, The," 190–92

Greenberg, Clement: on "The Great Wall of China," 191

Haas, Willy, xi

Hasidism, xii, 97, 182–84 *passim,* 221

Hebrew language: Kafka's interest in, xii; distinguished from Yiddish, xii*n;* elements of, in Yiddish, 28–29; Kafka's knowledge of, 180; puns in, used by Kafka, 195

Heller, Erich: on *The Castle,* 195*n*

Heselhaus, Clemens: connects Kafka's stories to Yiddish theater, 7

Hoffmann, E. T. A., 8*n*

Hradschin Castle, 200*n*

Humor: in Yiddish plays, 26–29 *passim,* 43; in Kafka's works, 28, 42, 43

"Hunger Artist, A," 193*n*, 200–202, 210

"Hunter Gracchus, The," 179, 205

Hurvits, M. (Yiddish dramatist), 220

Ibsen, Henrik: *A Doll's House,* 45*n; Ghosts,* 105*n; Rosmersholm,* 105*n*

"Imperial Message, An," 190*n*

Inquisition, the: as theme in Yiddish theater, 25, 98, 225; mentioned, 150, 155–56, 159

Interior monologue: as dramatic element in prose, 9; in *The Trial,* 170

"In the Penal Colony," 146–54; conflict between tradition and enlightenment, 147; the Law in, 147–48; water as symbol in, 148–49; ritual cleanliness in, 149; parabolic nature of, 152, 167; staged quality of, 154; murder as ritual in, 176; mentioned, 146, 166, 209

"Introductory Talk on the Yiddish Language, An," 28*n*, 43, 222*n*

"Investigations of a Dog," 7, 203, 207, 210

Irony: in Jewish humor, 29; comic, in Yiddish theater, 46; Kafka's use of, 29, 117, 142–43, 193

"Jackals and Arabs," 7, 179–81, 193*n*

Jahn, Wolfgang: on dramatic elements in Kafka's work, 8; on the

dramatic structure of *Der Verschollene*, 123n; relates the style of *Der Verschollene* to the cinema, 124
James, Henry, 10
Janouch, Gustav, 22n, 97n, 112, 205n
Jargontheater. See Yiddish theater in Prague
Jerusalem: in Yiddish plays, 200n
Jesenská, Milena, 189
Jewish attributes: reflected in "A Commentary," 44
Jewish humor: in Yiddish plays, 28–29
Jewish tradition: related to "The Judgment," 85n, 92, 120; compared to Chinese, 192n; ritual slaughter in, 192; food in, 201–2
Jews: hidden, as theme of Yiddish plays, 25, 98, 150–51; portrayed in *Bar Kokhba*, 190; reflected in "Josefine," 205
—in Prague: position of, x–xi; participation in German literature, xi; attitude toward Yiddish, 16n; response to Eastern European Jews, 226
"Josefine the Singer": music in, 203, 204–7; mentioned, 208, 209, 210
Judaism: Kafka's attitude toward, ix–xiii, 6, 189; references to, in Kafka's work, xii
"Judgment, The," 70–121 *passim;* style of, 3–4; dramatic elements in, 5, 104–21 *passim;* and Felice Bauer, 6; gesture in, 27; compared with "The Urban World," 59–69 *passim;* ambiguity in, 67; as Kafka's first mature prose work, 70; related to Yiddish plays, 70–71; interpretations of, 75; theatrical scenes in, 76–78;

Oedipal elements in, 79n; comic elements in, 80–81; word play in, 81–82, 94–95; the verdict in, 83; the "friend in Russia" in, 84n, 105n, 110, 118n; water as symbol in, 90–91; and Yom Kippur, 91–92; Yiddish idioms relevant to, 90, 93; symbols in, 95–96; setting in, 95, 106; lighting in, 95, 108; names in, 96; letter writing in, 99–100; analogies to Sharkanski's *Kol Nidre*, 99–104 *passim;* title of, 100, 101n; modes of narration in, 104; structure of, 104–7; exposition in, 105; nonverbal communication in, 106–7; description of characters in, 107; dialogue in, 109–11; the father's defect of vision in, 110; turning point in, 111–12; reader as spectator in, 113; definition of characters in, 114; denoument in, 114–17; dramatic irony in, 117; dramatic visions in, 118–19; linked to Jewish culture, 120; and Kafka's father, 120; mentioned, ix, 5, 8, 19n, 49, 55n, 57, 122, 135, 148, 154, 155, 170, 209, 210
Jüngste Tag, Der, 124

Kabala, 221, 223n
Kafka, Franz: attitude toward Judaism, ix, xi–xii, 6, 189; interest in German theater, x; his literary breakthrough, x, 5, 69, 208; interest in Czech theater, x, 30; and his Jewish contemporaries in Prague, xi; his parents' attitude toward Judaism, xi; fragments by, xii, 70n; and the Hebrew language, xii, 180–81, 195; his Bar Mitsvah, xii, 181n; and Zionism, xiii; marriage en-

gagements, 6n; friendship with Max Brod, 16; and his father, 16n, 120; attitude toward clock time, 47–48; dating of his works, 49n; his bachelor hero, 57; approaches to his work, 74–75; awareness of anti-Semitism, 89n; attitude toward acting, 97n; his concept of truth, 112; preoccupation with cleanliness, 185; vegetarianism, 193n, 200; and music, 203
—his prose: incantatory quality of, 4n; described as dramatic, 4–5, 11; his juvenilia, 5; change in style, 8, 31–48 passim; characteristics of, before and after 1912, 8, 37–38; humor in, 28, 42, 43; subjectivity in the early work, 56; use of dramatic method before 1912, 64; transition in style, 68–69. See also titles of individual works; Aphorisms; Fragments; Parables; Reviews; Yiddish language; Yiddish literature; Yiddish theater in Prague
Kafka, Hermann, xi, 16n, 120
Kafka, Ottla, 208n
Kashrut, Laws of, 149
Kellogg, Robert: on dramatic prose, 9
Kisch, Egon Erwin, xi
Kisch, Paul, xi
Kleist, Heinrich von, 8n
Klug, Mr. (Yiddish actor), 15n, 136
Klug, Mrs. (Yiddish actress), 13, 15, 205, 225
Kohn, Hans, 225
Kol Nidre. See Sharkanski, Avraham
Kraft, Werner: on "A Fratricide," 41n

Kurzweil, Baruch Benedikt: on "A Crossbreed," 188–89; on Kafka's themes, 205

Latayner, Yosef: David's Violin, 7n, 21, 23, 144n, 146n, 204, 207; The Apostate, 21, 23, 198; Blimele, 23, 100, 146n, 172–75, 182–188 passim, 207; mentioned, 24, 71, 220
"Letter to His Father," xi–xii, 189n, 202n
Letters, 17, 223
Letters to Felice, 12, 17–19, 70n
Letters to Milena, 189
Letter writing: in the Yiddish plays, 98, 100; in "The Judgment," 99–100
Levi, Djak. See Levi, Yitskhok
Levi, Yitskhok: his "Two Prague Writers," xxi, 16, 17n, 26, 220–23; friendship with Kafka, 16n, 17–19, 208n, 218–19; recitations and readings, 19, 28n, 71, 219, 226, 227; as model for the "friend in Russia," 19n, 87–89; describes Yiddish stage in Prague, 26; and Jewish humor, 30; as model for Rotpeter, 187–88; on yeshivas in Eastern Europe, 194; related to "Josefine," 205–6; biography of, 218–23; compared to Alexander Moissi, 219; confuses Kafka and Brod, 222n; mentioned, 12n, 15n, 118n, 136
Liebgold couple (Yiddish actors), 12
Lifson, David: on Yiddish theater, 25–26
Löwy, (Kafka's mother's maiden name), 189n
Löwy, Jizchak (Isak). See Levi, Yitskhok

Maeterlinck, Maurice: *The Intruder*, 105n
Maharal (Our Teacher, Rabbi [Yehuda] Lev), 220
Mandaus, Ludek, 7n
Marranos, 225
Meditation, 49, 55–58
Melodrama: in Kafka's work, 5, 178, 202; in Yiddish theater, 23, 27
"Metamorphosis, The": setting in, 27, 141, 143; irony in, 29, 30, 142–43; central metaphor of, 31, 137–38, 144–46; analogues to *The Savage One*, 135–46; Oedipal conflict in, 139–40; sexuality in, 140; fainting as a theatrical device in, 141; structure of, 143–44; role of the family in, 144; ending of, 144; mentioned, 154, 155, 202n
Meyrink, Gustav, 8n
Milena Jesenská, 189
Mirele Efros, 24n
Mishna, 180
Mr. Harry the Aristocrat. See Rikhter, Moyshe
Moissi, Alexander: Levi compared to, 219
Morality plays, 42, 154
Moyshe the Tailor as Councillor. See Rikhter, Moyshe
Music: as symbol in Kafka's work, 203–4; in the Yiddish plays, 203–4

Narrative voice: in Kafka's work before 1912, 51
Naturalism: in Yiddish theater, 23
"Nature Theater of Oklahoma, The," 4, 124, 126
Nemeth, André: connects *The Castle* to Yiddish theater, 7
Nietsche, Friedrich, 118n
Nomberg, H. D. (Yiddish poet), 227

Oedipal conflict: in "The Judgment," 79n; in "The Metamorphosis," 139–40; in *The Savage One*, 139–40
"Old Manuscript, An," 190, 192–93
"On the Tram," 55n, 56

Parables (by Kafka), 208
"Passers-by," 55n, 56
Pick, Otto: describes Yiddish stage in Prague, 26; mentioned, xi, 221
Pines, M.: *A History of Yiddish Literature*, 20
Pipes, M. (Yiddish actor), 15n, 136
Podzamcze, S. (Yiddish actor), 15n
Politzer, Heinz: on the dramatic quality of Kafka's work, 4–5; on Kafka's early style, 5; relates "The Judgment" to Felice Bauer, 6; links "Jackals and Arabs" to Yiddish plays, 7; on "A Commentary," 32, 39, 41, 44; on *Der Verschollene*, 122n, 125n; on the titling of Kafka's works, 122n, 146; on "The Metamorphosis," 140, 145n; on "The Village Teacher," 146n; on "The Burrow," 146n; on the meaning of Josef K.'s death, 165; on the "man from the country" as *amkhorets*, 168; on "A Fratricide," 178; on *The Castle*, 195n; on "A Hunger Artist," 202; on "Investigations of a Dog," 203
Pollak, Oskar, xi
Pondrom, Cyrena Norman: on "The Judgment," 75, 86n
Poseidon: Kafka's portrait of, 208
Prager Tagblatt, 188n, 220
"Problem of Our Laws, The," 190, 193–94, 209
Prometheus: Kafka's portrait of, 208

"Reflections for Gentleman-Jockeys," 55n, 56
"Refusal, The," 191, 194
Reisin, A. (Yiddish poet), 227
"Rejection," 55n, 56
"Report to an Academy, A," 149n, 181–87, 201, 209
"Resolutions," 55n, 57
Reviews (by Kafka), 49n
Rikhter, Moyshe: *Moyshe the Tailor as Councillor*, 12, 24, 100, 127–33, 135, 146n; *Mr. Harry the Aristocrat*, 13, 24, 146n
Ritual slaughtering: as theme in Yiddish drama, 176–77; in Jewish tradition, 192
Rosenfeld, Morris (Yiddish poet), 227
Rubinstein, William A.: on "A Report to an Academy," 181, 186; on "Jackals and Arabs," 193n
Russia: significance of, for Kafka, 88; and "The Judgment," 88; pogroms in, 89n, 118n; and Eastern European Jewry, 118n; yeshivas in, 194

St. Therese: related to *Der Verschollene*, 131n
Sancho Panza: Kafka's portrait of, 208
Sanhedrin: in *Bar Kokhba*, 161
Satan: in *God, Man, and Devil*, 72, 126
Savage One, The. See Gordin, Yakov
Savoy, Café, 12, 13, 15, 20, 21, 22, 26, 60n, 180, 205, 224, 225
Schildkraut, Rudolph (German actor), 22n
Schneller, Mr.: explains Yiddish texts at Levi's recitations, 227
Scholes, Robert: on dramatic prose, 9

Schulz-Behrend, G.: discusses "A Report to an Academy," 181–82, 186
Selbstwehr, xii, 14, 15n, 89n, 118n, 149n, 157n, 188n, 190n, 192n, 206, 224, 226
Sexual allusions: in *Moyshe the Tailor as Councillor*, 133; in *Der Verschollene*, 133; in "The Metamorphosis," 140; in *The Savage One*, 140
Sharkanski, Avraham
—*Kol Nidre:* 97–104 *passim;* ambiguous language in, 98; compared to "The Judgment," 99–104; review of, 225; mentioned, 21, 24, 27, 71, 106n, 146n, 155, 174n, 176, 191, 207
Shtetl tradition, 85n
Shulamit. See Goldfaden, Avraham
Singer, Isaac Bashevis: "A Friend of Kafka," 17n
Sokel, Walter: on Kafka's style as dramatic, 4; on theater as symbol in *Der Verschollene*, 7; on "The Judgment," 82, 85n, 86n; on Russia in Kafka's work, 88n; on the "friend in Russia," 110n–11n; on "The Nature Theater of Oklahoma," 127; on "The Metamorphosis," 145n; on the meaning of Josef K.'s death, 165; on "A Report to an Academy," 181-82
Soliloquies: in the Yiddish theater, 170
Spann, Meno: compares Kafka's attitude to Yiddish and Czech theater, 30; on "A Hunger Artist," 200–202 *passim*
Spiewakow, Fr. (director of 1910 Yiddish theater troupe), 14n
Standaert, Eric: on Politzer's methodology, 32; on "A Commentary," 39

Star of David, 190
Steinberg, Erwin R.: on "The Judgment," 91–92
"Stoker, The," 123–24
"Street Window, The," 56
Strindberg, August: *Miss Julie*, 105
"Sudden Walk, The," 55n, 57
Swander, Homer: on *The Castle*, 195n

Talmudic debate: related to Jewish humor, 42
Ten Commandments, the, 148
Ten Degrees (of Kabala), the, 223
"Tradesman, The," 55n, 56
"Trees, The," 55n, 56
Treisin, Mr. (Yiddish folk singer), 224–25
Trial, The, 154–71; comic irony in, 30; scene of arrest in, 155–59; as parody of *The Vice-King*, 156–59; costume in, 158–59; related to Gordin's *Bar Kokhba*, 161–66; parody of stage devices in, 162–63; Josef K. as anti-hero, 165; on Josef K.'s death, 165, 169–70; theatricality of its ending, 165–66; related to *Elishe ben Avuya*, 166–70; parabolic nature of, 167; Josef K. as *amkhorets*, 168–69; theatrical elements in, 170; interior monologue in, 170; murder as ritual in, 176; mentioned, 5, 11, 146, 196, 209
Tshisik, Mrs. (Yiddish actress): Kafka's attachment to, 19–20; as model for Josefine, 204; mentioned, 12, 136
Turkov, Yonas: on Kafka's knowledge of Yiddish, 43; as friend of Yitskhok Levi, 219
"Two Prague Writers." *See* Levi, Yitskhok

Ulysses: Kafka's portrait of, 208
"Unhappiness," 56
"Unmasking a Confidence Trickster," 55n, 57
"Urban World, The," 59–65; in relation to Yiddish theater, 59–60; dramatic elements in, 61–65; relationship to "The Judgment," 59, 65–69; use of gesture in, 62–63; nondramatic elements in, 63–64
Urzidil, Johannes, xi
Utitz, Emil, xi

Verschollene, Der, 122–35; development of, 49n, staged sequences in, 122–23; gesture in, 122–23; related to cinema, 124; Kafka's difficulties with 124; controversy over ending of, 124, 126n; relationship to *God, Man, and Devil*, 125–27; Biblical allusions in, 128–30, 131; names in, 132; election motif in, 132–33; sexual allusions in, 133; analogues to *The Savage One*, 133–35; mentioned, 7
Vice-King, The. See Faynman, Zigmund
"Village Teacher, The," 146n

Wagenbach, Klaus: on Kafka's breakthrough, 5; on number of Yiddish troupes, 14; on the dating of Kafka's works, 32n; on Kafka's knowledge of Yiddish, 43n
Wandering Jew, the: the Hunter Gracchus as, 179n; K. as, 200
"Warden of the Tomb, The," 106n
Warren, Robert Penn: on dramatic prose, 9
"Way Home, The," 55n, 56
"Wedding Preparations in the

Country," 31–39, 41, 46–49
passim, 55n, 58–59, 60, 61, 135n
Weinberg, Moritz (Yiddish actor),
15n
Weinberg, Pepi (Yiddish actress),
15
Weinberg, Salcia (Yiddish folk-
singer), 15n
Weinstein, Leo: on "A Report to
An Academy," 181
Weiss, Ernst, xi
Weltsch, Felix, xi, 221
Werfel, Franz, xi, 221
White, John J.: on "The Judg-
ment," 75, 88n, 93, 95n
Winder, Ludwig, xin
"Wish to be a Red Indian, The,"
56
Wohryzek, Julie: Kafka's engage-
ment to, 6n
Woodring, Carl R.: on "Josefine,"
204
Wordplay: on the Yiddish stage, 43;
in "The Judgment," 81–82, 94;
in "Jackals and Arabs," 180; in
The Castle, 195
Wound, image of the: in "A Coun-
try Doctor," 173

Yiddish language: distinguished
from Hebrew, xiin; Kafka's com-
prehension of, xiin, 28–29, 43;
transliteration into English from,
xxi; Kafka's attitude toward,
15n–16n; attitude of Prague Jews
toward, 16n; characteristics of,
28–29, 43–44, 194; proverbs and
idioms, 29, 42, 89n, 90n, 93,
201n–2n; form of, in Yiddish
theater, 101n
Yiddish literature (nondramatic):
Kafka's interest in, xii, 20–21
Yiddish theater in Prague: problem of texts, xxi; troupe of 1910,

14, 15; controversy over number
of troupes, 14–15; troupe of
1911, 15n, 57n, 62, 69; description of, 22, 25–27; repertoire of,
22–25, 71; sensationalism in, 23;
difficulty of identifying plays, 24;
stagecraft, 25–26; acting style of,
26–28; comic elements in, 26–29
passim, 42, 43, 46, 133; as expression of Yiddish culture, 29,
30; gesture in, 43; wordplay in,
43, 94–95; attitudes reflected in,
44; in relation to "The Urban
World," 59–60; beards in, 62,
89n; letter writing as a device in,
99–100; form of Yiddish spoken
in, 101n; related to "The Nature
Theater of Oklahoma," 127; Hasidism in, 182–84; titling of the
plays, 207–8; music in, 203–4;
reviews and announcements of,
224–27. *See also* Klug, Mrs.;
Levi, Yitskhok; Tshisik, Mrs.;
Weinberg, Pepi
—and Kafka: his interest in, ix, xii,
12–22; as factor in his literary
development, x, 5, 6, 210; related to his diction, 5; related to
his change in style, 6, 8; equated
with his interest in his Jewish
heritage, 6; discussed in Yiddish
newspapers and journals, 6n;
number of times attended, 13,
15–16; his first encounter with,
13, 55n; relationship with Yiddish actors, 16–20, 71, 218–19,
220–23 *passim*, 222n, 225–26;
performances seen, 21; his view
of its function, 21n–22n; elements that impressed him, 21, 71;
his attitude toward, compared to
Czech theater, 30; playbill, his
comments on, 113–14
—themes: Biblical and Talmudic,

22, 128–30; apostasy, 25, 182–83; hidden Jews, 25, 98, 150–51, 155; the Inquisition, 25, 98, 150, 155–56, 159, 225; the Jew as "little man," 44; judgment, 100–101, 169; father-son relationship, 120; America, 127–28; community, 131, 205–6; obedience, 146–47; general, related to *The Trial*, 154–56; man against the powers, 155; enemies of the Jewish people, 158; anti-Semitism, 166; ritual slaughter, 176–77

—conventions: asides, 108; visions, 118; choruses, 126–27, 174; soliloquies, 170
Yom Kippur: related to "The Judgment," 91–92; related to "In the Penal Colony," 150; significance of, in *Blimele*, 183

Zentral, Hotel, 224, 226
Zilbertsvayg, Zalmen: memoirs of Levi, 17n
Zionism: Kafka's interest in, xii
Zylbercweig, Zalmen, 17n